# Principled Ethics

Moral philosophy has long treated principles as indispensable for understanding its subject matter. However, the underlying assumption that this is the best approach has received almost no defence, and has been attacked by particularists, who argue that the traditional link between morality and principles is little more than an unwarranted prejudice.

In *Principled Ethics*, Sean McKeever and Michael Ridge meet the particularist challenge head on, and defend a distinctive view they call 'generalism as a regulative ideal'. After cataloguing the wide array of views that have gone under the heading 'particularism' they explain why the main particularist arguments fail to establish their conclusions. The authors' generalism incorporates what is most insightful in particularism (e.g. the possibility that reasons are context-sensitive—'holism' about reasons) while rejecting every major particularist doctrine. At the same time, they avoid the excesses of hyper-generalist views according to which moral thought is constituted by allegiance to a particular principle or set of principles. Instead, they argue that insofar as moral knowledge and practical wisdom are possible, we both can and should codify all of morality in a manageable set of principles even if we are not yet in possession of those principles. Moral theory is in this sense a work in progress. Nor is the availability of a principled codification of morality an idle curiosity. Ridge and McKeever also argue that principles have an important role to play in guiding the virtuous agent.

# Principled Ethics

*Generalism as a Regulative Ideal*

Sean McKeever and Michael Ridge

CLARENDON PRESS • OXFORD

# OXFORD
UNIVERSITY PRESS

Great Clarendon Street, Oxford OX2 6DP

Oxford University Press is a department of the University of Oxford.
It furthers the University's objective of excellence in research, scholarship,
and education by publishing worldwide in

Oxford New York

Auckland Cape Town Dar es Salaam Hong Kong Karachi
Kuala Lumpur Madrid Melbourne Mexico City Nairobi
New Delhi Shanghai Taipei Toronto

With offices in

Argentina Austria Brazil Chile Czech Republic France Greece
Guatemala Hungary Italy Japan Poland Portugal Singapore
South Korea Switzerland Thailand Turkey Ukraine Vietnam

Oxford is a registered trademark of Oxford University Press
in the UK and in certain other countries

Published in the United States
by Oxford University Press Inc., New York

© Sean McKeever and Michael Ridge 2006

British Library Cataloguing in Publication Data

Data available

Library of Congress Cataloging in Publication Data

Data available

Typeset by Laserwords Private Limited, Chennai, India
Printed in Great Britain
on acid-free paper by
Biddles Ltd., King's Lynn, Norfolk

ISBN 0–19–929065–2   978–0–19–929065–9
ISBN 0–19–929066–0 (Pbk.)   978–0–19–929066–6 (Pbk.)

10 9 8 7 6 5 4 3 2 1

For Benjamin and Lillian

# Acknowledgments

ONE of the many pleasures of collaborative work is a near doubling of the opportunities to share and discuss one's idea with other philosophers. For this pleasure, we have been gluttons.

Thanks first and foremost must go to Jonathan Dancy for posing the particularist challenge in such a bracing manner. It will be obvious how much our own work is inspired by that challenge. We have always learned a great deal from his work and from his generous feedback on our own even though we disagree on many of the fundamental questions.

The ideas that eventually led to this book began to take shape while we were still graduate students at the University of North Carolina at Chapel Hill. In this regard, we are grateful to Geoff Sayre-McCord and Simon Blackburn for bringing Dancy's work to our attention in the first place and for very useful discussions of particularism and the issues it raises. We are also grateful to Thomas Hill and Jay Rosenberg for helpful discussion on specific issues and arguments. Thanks also to those of our then fellow graduate students who read and discussed early versions of some of what are now chapters of the book (in particular, Lorraine Besser-Jones and Angela Coventry both provided useful feedback on what is now Chapter 1).

As our critique of particularism sharpened and our own version of generalism began to take shape, we benefited greatly from discussion with many generous audiences. James Dreier and Mark van Roojen provided useful discussion of one of our earliest attempts to argue for generalism at the APA meetings in New Orleans in 1999. We should also like to thank audiences at Florida State University and the University of Reading as well as the participants at the Moral Epistemology Conference held at the University of Edinburgh in 2003 for very helpful discussion of what is now roughly Chapter 6 of the present book. In addition to Jonathan Dancy (again), we should here extend special thanks to Brad Hooker, Alfred Mele, David McNaughton, Philip Stratton-Lake, and Piers Rawling. We are also grateful to participants at a session of the Central Division APA meetings in 2004, and especially to our commentator Pekka Väyrynen, for providing valuable feedback on an early presentation of our ideas about the role principles must play to count as guides. Thanks also to those who took part in the discussion of our "Turning on Default Reasons," at the Particularism Conference held at the University of Kent in Canterbury

(2004), as well as those who discussed our work on the contingent a priori at the Particularism Conference in Bled (2005). Both of these conferences also provided contexts in which some very useful discussions of particularism took place, so a hearty thanks is owed to the organizers of those conferences as well (Simon Kirichin and Vojko Strahovnik, respectively). Special thanks here are also owed to David Bakhurst, Roger Crisp, Terence Horgan, Mark Lance, Margaret Little, Christian Piller, Anthony Price, John Quilter, Sabine Roeser, Benedict Smith, and Rebecca Stangl. Mark Lance and Margaret Little deserve additional special thanks for giving us some comments at very short notice (just before the book went to press) on our discussion of their work. Thanks also to Andy Clark for some useful last minute comments and suggestions.

Numerous people have read versions of the whole book and given us some very helpful feedback. Here our debts are very great indeed. Special thanks go to the participants in a reading group on our manuscript at Dartmouth in the summer of 2004: Julia Driver, Heather Gert, Timothy Rosenkoetter, Roy Sorensen, and Kathleen Wallace. Very special thanks are owed to Walter Sinnott-Armstrong, who would often continue discussing the issues raised in the book for several hours after the reading group had finished. The result of all this is a book much changed and we are sure much improved.

Pekka Väyrynen also deserves special thanks. We learned a lot from his work, and in addition Pekka read and provided extensive written commentary on a draft of the whole book, and these comments helped us see where more work needed to be done. Jonathan Dancy also patiently read an earlier draft of the book and provided some very useful comments, for which we are extremely grateful. Brad Hooker, Simon Kirchin, and Brad Majors also read versions of the whole book and provided helpful and extensive commentary, and they too deserve very special thanks and recognition.

Thanks also go to the *Canadian Journal of Philosophy* and *Ratio* for allowing us to reproduce materials first published in their pages. Chapter 1 draws heavily on our *Canadian Journal of Philosophy* paper, "The Many Moral Particularisms." Chapter 2 draws heavily on our *Ratio* paper, "What Does Holism Have to Do with Particularism?"

*Michael Ridge*: I should like to express my thanks to a number of individuals and institutions for making possible my work on particularism. Thanks to Geoff Sayre-McCord, Simon Blackburn, and Thomas Hill for encouragement, advice, and countless philosophical conversations. Thanks also to the Philosophy Program at the Research School of Social Sciences, Australian National University. My time as a postdoctoral fellow there helped me 'find my feet' as a philosopher, and it is hard to imagine a better context in which to do this.

I spent considerable time at the ANU working on the ideas developed in this book. I should specifically thank Michael Smith for some very illuminating discussions of particularism as well as for making the ANU such a wonderful place to do philosophy. Thanks also to Philip Pettit and Karen Jones, as well as those who discussed some of our early work on particularism at a meeting of the Australasian Association of Philosophy (in Melbourne, 1999).

I should also thank the Philosophy Program at the University of Edinburgh, who provided me with an extremely generous period of research leave, during which a great deal of the work on the book was done. Thanks also to the AHRB (Arts and Humanities Research Board) and the Philip Leverhulme Trust. A grant from the former and a prize from the latter subsidized my period of research leave from Edinburgh. Thanks also are owed to my colleagues (and former colleagues) at Edinburgh, with whom I had numerous useful discussions of the issues addressed here. Thanks in particular go to Richard Holton, whose own work on particularism has been enormously helpful for us (see especially Chapter 6 and the Appendix).

Finally, I should also like to extend warm thanks to Robin Flaig. She not only provided encouragement as I worked on the book and put up with the insanity associated with having a partner so submerged in an all-consuming passion. She also actually read and provided helpful comments and suggestions on the penultimate draft of the book. Since Robin is not a professional philosopher and her real academic interests are in medieval European history, it is hard to overstate the significance of this or how much it is appreciated.

*Sean McKeever.* I should like to thank a number of individuals for their support and guidance over the years. Stephen Crites, Victor Gourevitch, and Lydia Goehr introduced me to philosophy and showed me the work and pleasure of doing it well. I should like to thank especially Thomas Hill, Geoff Sayre-McCord, and Simon Blackburn for their encouragement and advice while I was at Chapel Hill as well as for countless philosophical conversations then and since. I should also like to thank Michael McKenna, Hans Muller, and Stephen Schwartz for valuable philosophical conversation, especially in the month of March when the winter in Ithaca seemed like it might never end. I am grateful to my family, and especially to Rebecca, for all of the patience and support that made my work on this book possible.

# Contents

# PART I
# The Particularist Challenge

# 1

# Many Moral Particularisms

Particulars are not to be examined before the whole has been surveyed.

(Dr Samuel Johnson)

## 1.1. Preliminaries

This book is a defense of moral principles, yet it is not a defense of any specific moral principle. Although we are as interested as anyone in determining the specific content of morality, we here address the prior question of whether morality is principled at all. Moral philosophy has long presupposed that it is, with Kantians, consequentialists, and others arguing about which principles are correct. Unfortunately, this presupposition rarely receives a defense independent of the defense of a particular moral theory. Naturally, if we start out assuming that morality is principled, then we are apt to find what we came looking for. We cannot take the fact that moral philosophy is dominated by principled approaches as evidence that morality really is principled if our theorizing has been shaped by an unjustified prejudice in favor of principles.

The need to reexamine the place of principles in morality and in moral philosophy is especially pressing in the wake of the work of moral particularists who have forcefully argued against giving moral principles the prominence they have long enjoyed. If particularists are right, then much of moral philosophy has labored under a false presupposition. This book takes up the challenge posed by particularism, and argues that the presuppositions of traditional moral philosophy are justified. Morality is principled, and our philosophical attempts to understand morality are right to invoke principles. As against particularism, we defend generalism.

The debate between moral generalists and moral particularists is a debate about the extent to which morality can and should be understood in terms of moral principles. This characterization paints with an extremely broad brush.

Moral principles might play many roles, and the debate between generalists and particularists is thus a multi-faceted one. In this opening chapter we aim to sharpen the terms of the debate. Before laying out and explaining the different dimensions along which generalist and particularist positions can vary, we first (in this introductory section) explain why the debate is important. We then provide a map of the dialectical terrain that generalists and particularists inhabit. This map provides a useful point of reference throughout the rest of the book. Finally, we end this chapter by explaining where generalism as a regulative ideal, the positive position we defend in the second part of the book, fits into our proposed taxonomy.

Moral particularism poses a challenge to the generalist approach that has long dominated moral philosophy. For the history of moral philosophy is in large part a history of attempts to map the moral landscape with a set of principles. Socrates famously searched for 'true definitions' for moral predicates. Plato's attempt in *The Republic* to define justice in terms of the functional organization of the tripartite soul can be seen as the attempt to analyze an important moral concept in a principled fashion. Epicureans argued, in effect, that morality is best captured by a principle of enlightened self-interest. According to the Stoics, the ultimate moral principle recommends a kind of radical detachment from anything beyond the agent's control. Medieval philosophers argued for the generalist thesis that morality is best understood in terms of a set of 'natural laws.' Modern moral philosophy is often understood as a debate between utilitarians like John Stuart Mill and deontologists like Immanuel Kant. Crucially, both sides of this modern debate are committed to the generalist idea that morality can be reduced to a fundamental principle. Nor indeed is the idea that morality is best understood in terms of principles limited to moral philosophy. Influential religious traditions also implicitly endorse moral generalism, as witnessed in the Judeo-Christian tradition by the Ten Commandments and the Golden Rule.

Each of these different forms of generalism has its own virtues and vices, but the particularist urges us to take a step back and question the underlying assumption that morality can and should be understood in terms of principles at all. For in spite of the dominance of moral principles in our tradition, the basic presupposition that morality can and should (indeed, on some accounts, must) be captured by a set of principles has not so much been argued for as assumed. On reflection, though, this presupposition is not nearly so obvious as its historical dominance might suggest. Moreover, in spite of the dominance of principled approaches to moral philosophy, there have always been voices of dissent. Indeed, the issues posed by moral particularism have captured philosophical attention at least since Aristotle.

We venture to guess that were he able to comment on the contemporary debate over particularism Aristotle might say, "Particularism is said in many ways." The remark would be apt, as 'particularism' has come to have a wide variety of meanings. Nor is it always clear in discussions of particularism which of these meanings is intended. This is unfortunate; unless we are clear about particularism's content it will be difficult to assess its plausibility. Moreover, many of the arguments in favor of particularism are extremely interesting and deserve careful examination. They emerge from diverse areas of philosophical inquiry including metaphysics, epistemology, semantics, theories of practical reasoning, and first-order moral theory.[1] We therefore begin our discussion of particularism by distinguishing various species of the genus. The different species are united in that they all assert what intuitively is a negative thesis about moral principles. We then identify three dimensions along which particularist and generalist positions may vary. The first dimension is set by the conception of what a moral principle *is* (Section 1.2). Second, particularist positions can vary in their *content*, the thesis they advance about moral principles (Section 1.3). Third, particularist positions can vary in terms of the *scope* of their doctrine; that is, to which sorts of moral principles the doctrine is meant to apply (Section 1.4). Our taxonomy is couched in terms of different forms of particularism, but each form of particularism which falls out of our taxonomy corresponds neatly to a form of generalism which is the negation of that particularist thesis.

While we focus in this book on *moral* particularism, particularism has been advanced in a number of other domains. Those who defend particularism about morality typically defend particularism about practical reasoning more generally (Dancy 2004; Little 2000). This is unsurprising since particularists typically argue from premises about reasons quite generally. Following particularists, we shall here focus on the debate over moral particularism, but we think that if our arguments succeed then they could be extended to support similar conclusions about practical reasoning more generally. Whether at least some of our arguments would also carry over to other domains, such as aesthetics, is a question which must await another day.

## 1.2. What is a Moral Principle?

On any plausible account, not just any generalization, employing a moral concept counts as a moral principle. For instance, 'Any action is either morally required or it is not' is a true generalization employing a moral concept which

---

[1] For arguments from virtue theory, see Hursthouse 1995 and Little 1997. For discussion of anti-theory, see Baier 1985, Clarke 1987.

even the most hardened moral particularist need not deny. To distinguish those moral generalizations which qualify as principles from those which do not, we should look to the functions historically associated with moral principles. On the one hand, moral principles are often understood as providing the truth-conditions for moral judgments by referring to those features of the world which explain why those judgments are true. Picking up on this strand of generalist tradition, one criterion for a generalization's counting as a moral principle might be that the generalization articulates true application conditions for a given moral concept by referring to those features of the world which explain why the concept applies when it does. The notion of explanation in play here simply requires that the generalization in question articulates features which are of direct moral relevance—reasons for action, so-called 'defeaters' and 'enablers' of those reasons, and the like (see Chapter 2 for an explanation of the latter notions).

To be clear, to count as a moral principle on this criterion a generalization need not explain why those considerations which are of direct moral relevance themselves count as having such relevance. For example, if some form of Ideal Adviser theory provides the correct analysis of our concept of 'ought' then a moral principle in our sense would not refer to ideal advisers but rather to those features in virtue of which ideal advisers would recommend actions. This is really just to say that the notion of explanation in play here is at the level of normative ethics rather than at the level of metaethics, as that distinction is typically understood.[2] Principles understood as explanatory in this way are in our terminology *standards* for the application of those predicates.

Principles qua standards can play an important role in moral theory, but moral principles are often thought to be of more than purely theoretical interest. Moral principles have historically been thought to play an important role in guiding action. Picking up on this strand of generalist tradition, our criterion for a generalization's counting as a moral principle might emphasize its suitability for guiding action. In our terminology, such principles are *guides*. These two conceptions of a moral principle are logically independent. A guiding principle might be a useful fiction and hence no standard. A moral standard might be useless in actual practice (too complicated to apply in real time, say) and hence no guide.

Of course, we could combine both of the preceding strands of generalist tradition and insist that to count as a principle a generalization must both provide explanatory truth conditions *and* be well suited to guiding action. Principles in this sense are *action-guiding standards*.

---

[2]  Thanks to Walter Sinnott-Armstrong and Roy Sorensen for helpful discussion on this score.

Principles qua standards and principles qua action–guiding standards can be well suited for guidance while requiring some insight or imagination to apply. A much more demanding criterion would insist that a moral principle must provide an algorithm which could be followed perfectly without any imagination, insight, or judgment. Principles in this sense could be modeled by computer programs. Although we doubt that principles in this sense have played much of a role in the history of moral philosophy, it is worth including them in our taxonomy at least because some particularist critiques seem to apply only to generalism in this very strong form. We call principles in this sense *algorithmic decision-procedures*.

Moreover, moral principles might represent not simply standards for the correct application of moral concepts, but conceptual truths. On this view, anyone who deploys moral concepts must accept (perhaps implicitly) a moral principle. In this sense, moral principles are *preconditions of conceptual competence*.

Finally, one might insist that to count as a moral principle a generalization must be a *truth-maker* for particular moral truths rather than vice versa. That is, the generalization itself must in some sense explain why each of the particular moral truths is true rather than vice versa. Note that this is distinct from the explanatory conception of principles as standards. Principles qua standards must refer to features which explain why a given moral concept applies when it does. Principles qua truth-makers must themselves figure in the explanation of why a moral concept applies when it does. Each of these six criteria for what makes a generalization qualify as a moral principle requires further articulation.

### 1.2.1. *Standards*

Very roughly, to think of moral principles as standards is to take the criterion for being a moral principle to be the provision of sufficient conditions for the application of a given moral concept. Standards are understood as entirely exceptionless generalizations which in this sense provide the truth-conditions for the application of a moral concept. Standards in our sense should be understood as necessary truths; any merely contingent principle would leave open the possibility of a deeper standard which explains why the contingent principle holds true in our world but not in others. Moreover, paradigmatic moral standards like the principle of utility and the categorical imperative are most plausibly understood as supposed necessary truths.

However, this initial characterization of what it is to be a standard must be qualified in at least two respects. First, even particularists typically admit that the moral supervenes on the nonmoral. That is to say, particularists typically admit that there can be no moral difference between two objects of evaluation without some nonmoral difference. Supervenience alone entails that there are generalizations providing the application conditions for a moral concept in purely descriptive terms. For any given possible object of moral evaluation in a given world there corresponds a comprehensive characterization of the entire world in which that possible object exists. Given supervenience, that characterization of the entire world is guaranteed to provide a sufficient condition for the application of the moral concept in question. From this it follows that there are moral principles if we understand principles merely as generalizations which provide sufficient conditions in nonmoral terms for the application of a moral concept and if we allow that principles can be infinitely long. Indeed, the infinitely long disjunction of all the possible ways the world might be in which a given object of evaluation satisfies the moral concept in question will provide individually sufficient and jointly necessary conditions for the application of that concept in purely descriptive terms.

Particularists argue persuasively that such 'supervenience functions' are not moral principles in the relevant sense. At least two considerations are relevant here. First, infinitely long generalizations are of limited interest since they are forever beyond our ken. Any generalization worthy of the name 'moral principle' must be only finitely long. Secondly, a moral standard should do more than provide a nontrivial application condition for a moral concept; it should do so in a way that can help *explain* why that concept applies when it does. In other words, a moral standard should provide us with more than the extension of the moral concept in question, indeed more than its extension in all possible worlds. This is a second reason that supervenience functions are not moral standards. Supervenience functions include far too much irrelevant information to qualify as principles. The fact that Hitler exists in a world in which Alpha Centauri is the nearest star to our sun will figure in a complete description of the world in which Hitler exists, but is no part of the explanation of the wrongness of Hitler's actions.

### 1.2.2. Guides

Standards are good in theory but might be useless in practice. For if the moral truth is complex then moral standards might be cumbersome and difficult to apply. So being a moral standard is not sufficient for being a guide. Neither is being a standard necessary for counting as a guide. For unlike standards, guides need not provide entirely accurate application conditions for moral concepts. A guide might not cover all cases and might even have some false implications. Instead, guides must only provide useful direction to a conscientious moral agent. Very roughly, utility here should be understood in terms of reliably leading the agent to perform the right action for the right reason(s). On some versions of generalism, this rough idea will be cashed out in terms of rules which maximize expected utility, but this interpretation of the basic idea is not mandatory. Daniel Dennett draws a similar distinction and argues moral philosophers have been too focused on (in our terms) standards as opposed to guides:

For the most part, philosophers have been content to ignore the practical problems of real-time decision-making, regarding the brute fact that we are all finite and forgetful, and have to rush to judgment, as a real but irrelevant element of friction in the machinery whose blueprint they are describing. It is as if there might be two disciplines—ethics proper, which undertakes the task of calculating the principles determining what the ideal agent ought to do under all circumstances—and then the less interesting 'merely practical' discipline of Moral First Aid, or What to Do Until the Doctor of Philosophy Arrives, which tells, in rough and ready terms, how to make 'online' decisions under time pressure. (Dennett 1995: 496)

Of course, what is a useful heuristic for one moral agent might well be worthless for another. The principles that should guide a small child are likely to be very different from the principles that should guide an adult. So it would be unhelpful to conduct a debate as to whether there are guides *simpliciter*. We should instead consider whether there are guides for particular kinds of agents in particular kinds of contexts.

A good guide might be a useful oversimplification. The maxim 'buy low and sell high' might be the ultimate standard for success in playing the stock-market but 'diversify' and 'cost average' might be much better guides for most people. If a valid standard is especially complicated, it might leave an agent confused or stymied and hence unable to make a timely decision or worse yet might lead them to make poor decisions in virtue of their inability to apply the principle correctly. Guides also can allow for indeterminacy and leave room for judgment. For example, W. D. Ross's famous list of so-called "prima facie duties" (Ross 1930) could be construed as constituting a kind of guide, although we do not here claim that Ross intended his list in just this way. As Ross emphasized, his list clearly leaves considerable indeterminacy and room for judgment about what is one's duty, all things considered. Finally, different accounts of guides will differ in their accounts of what it takes for a principle to be well suited for guidance. We return to these issues in the development of our positive account of principled guidance in Chapter 9.

### 1.2.3. Action-guiding standards

Standards provide truth-conditions for moral claims by referring to explanatory features of the world without necessarily being of any use in guiding action. Guides are well suited to help with practical decision-making but need not provide truth-conditions for moral claims. We can combine these aspirations and insist that to count as a moral principle a generalization must both provide truth-conditions for moral claims which refer to explanatory features and be well suited to guiding action. Call such principles 'action-guiding standards.'

One could understand action-guiding standards simply as standards that are good guides for most people most of the time. However, there is another more interesting way of understanding action-guiding standards. For it may well be that a standard in our sense would only very rarely provide a useful guide for most people because the complexities involved in its application to a particular case might simply be overwhelming for finite creatures like ourselves. This is most clear in the case of a standard like utilitarianism, given the apparently overwhelming difficulty of estimating the consequences of all of one's available actions on the total amount of happiness in the world. Perhaps we should instead maintain that an action-guiding standard is a standard that necessarily figures in the moral psychology of any virtuous moral agent at some level. This is compatible with an action-guiding standard not providing much direct guidance. Two-level forms of utilitarianism, like R. M. Hare's famous account, provide a nice illustration of how a moral theory might make use of the idea of such an indirectly action-guiding standard (Hare 1981). The principle of utility on this account does not typically function by directly guiding our deliberations, since in most ordinary contexts we should rely on more familiar moral precepts like 'don't lie' and 'be kind.' Nonetheless the principle of utility is on this account still the ultimate standard of right and wrong.

Moreover, it is plausible to suppose that the virtuous moral agent necessarily will be disposed to employ the principle of utility in some kinds of contexts. For, as Hare argues, the virtuous moral agent presumably must be able "ascend" to a more critical level and assess the soundness of her more everyday moral rules. Anyone who lacks this capacity to ascend to a critical level is not ideally virtuous. For such an agent would be liable inappropriately to follow a rule which should be broken for the greater good. All of this is compatible with supposing that for utilitarian reasons a virtuous agent might need to abandon her virtue to maximize utility. The point is that we should describe this as a case of virtue precisely requiring that the agent sacrifice her own virtue for the greater good.

Action-guiding standards so understood helpfully bring the question of whether there are any interesting connections between so-called virtue ethical approaches to moral philosophy and particularism into sharp relief. For action-guiding standards are characterized in terms of features necessarily had by an ideally virtuous agent. At least some important strands of thought in virtue ethics imply that the ideally virtuous agent need not be understood as having internalized anything like a moral principle (see e.g. McDowell 1981). So a generalist about action-guiding standards must reject these forms of virtue ethics. Hence the suspicion that virtue ethics is incompatible with generalism is vindicated, albeit only on fairly specific conceptions both of generalism and virtue ethics that not all self-styled proponents of those doctrines would accept.

### 1.2.4. Algorithmic decision-procedures

The previous characterizations of principles are all consistent with the idea that applying those principles requires imagination, judgment, or insight. A much more ambitious conception of moral principles holds that an adequate set of moral principles must function as a kind of algorithm. Such principles would provide a purely mechanical moral decision-procedure. It is not clear that any of the major historical defenders of generalist accounts have understood principles in this way. Certainly, utilitarians must not hold such a view since there is no algorithm for determining all of the relevant consequences (or even rationally expected consequences) of a given action, character trait, or set of rules. Moreover, as John Stuart Mill rightly put it, "there is no difficulty in proving any ethical standard whatever to work ill if we suppose universal idiocy to be conjoined with it" (Mill 1979: 23 [1861, ch. 2]). Nonetheless, utilitarianism is a generalist position par excellence.

Kant's categorical imperative is perhaps a less obvious case. While some Kantians may have supposed that the categorical imperative provides an algorithm for moral decisions, Kant himself suggests that a proper application of the categorical imperative requires "a power of judgment shaped by experience partly in order to decide in which cases they apply, and partly to procure for them access to man's will and to provide an impetus to their action" (Kant 1990: 5 [1784: K 389]). Many of Kant's leading contemporary interpreters agree. Commentators (most notably, Barbara Herman) have emphasized passages like this one as revealing that Kant's conception of moral judgment is nonalgorithmic.

If particularists are skeptical of algorithmic decision-procedures, then we share their skepticism. Though perhaps some moral philosophers have sought to defend such principles, we do not share this ambition or think that it is an important one for moral theory. Such principles find a place in our taxonomy as an outer bound of what a generalist might claim, but are no part of what a sensible generalist should claim.

### 1.2.5. Preconditions of conceptual competence

On one important view, principles are constitutive of moral judgment itself. On this view, which we call *constitutive generalism*, the (perhaps implicit) acceptance of the fundamental standard of morality is necessary for competence with moral concepts. Constitutive generalism has a long history in Anglo-American moral philosophy, and has recently been offered as a refutation of particularism (Jackson, Pettit, and Smith, 2000). Constitutive generalism goes beyond the view that there are moral principles conceived as standards, and claims that the correct moral standards are conceptual truths. Constitutive generalism therefore represents another outer bound of generalism. In Chapter 5 we argue against constitutive generalism.

### 1.2.6. Moral truth-makers

Yet another conception of moral principles insists that for a generalization to count as a moral principle it must be the case that particular moral truths are 'made true' by the generalization rather than vice versa. Terence Irwin casts the debate in these terms, characterizing particularism as the thesis that moral principles are true "to the extent that they summarize the particular perceptual judgments of virtuous agents," and generalism as the thesis that particular judgments are "correct insofar as they conform to true general principles" (Irwin 2000: 103). The issue here is one, as Irwin puts it, of "normative priority." Perhaps some examples can clarify this potentially obscure idea. Consider the generalization, 'all the coins in my pocket are made of copper.' Intuitively, it is just an accident that this generalization is true, and its truth should be explained in terms of the truths about each of the individual coins in my pocket. By contrast, the generalization 'copper is electrically conductive' does not seem to be a mere summary of the accidental particular cases in which copper is conductive. Rather, it is a law of nature that copper is conductive and this is what explains why any particular bit of copper is electrically conductive. So in this case it seems like the generalization explains the particulars rather than vice versa. The analogy suggests that the defender of moral principles should perhaps understand moral principles as being in some rough way analogous to laws of nature. Irwin usefully points out that if we cast the debate in terms of normative priority then generalism and particularism are exclusive but not exhaustive. For someone might embrace a middle path, according to which neither particular moral truths nor moral principles have priority over the other. Indeed, Irwin makes heavy use of this middle path in his discussion of whether particularists are right to see Aristotle as the historical champion of their view.

While the question whether moral principles have what Irwin charac-terizes as "normative priority" is philosophically interesting, it is not a ques-tion we address in this book. This is not because we think the question is ill-formed, though the notion of a truth-maker is perhaps problematic. As defenders of truth-maker approaches to metaphysics have themselves allowed, it is difficult to see what the truth-makers might be for negative existentials like 'there are no unicorns' (for discussion, see http://encyclopedia.thefreedictionary.com/truthmaker). Rather, we avoid the question of whether principles are usefully conceived as truth-makers because the challenge we are interested in meeting is one which implies that the centuries-old tradition of moral theorizing is somehow defective. We take it that the metaphysical question of whether principles are truth-makers for particular moral truths is orthogonal to this question.

Suppose, for example, that the principle of utility was not only true but necessarily true and knowable a priori. This would surely be a major victory for generalism. Yet if we insist that to be worthy of the name 'principle' a generalization must be a truth-maker for particular moral truths then the necessary and a priori truth of the principle of utility is logically consistent with particularism. Perhaps even more shockingly, R. M. Hare presumably would come out as a particularist on this way of casting the debate. For as a prescriptivist, Hare presumably would deny that morality is usefully understood in terms of 'truth-makers' at all (see Hare 1981). This would be shocking because particularists have so often taken R. M. Hare's position as the generalist position par excellence. Indeed, Jonathan Dancy's development of particularism was in part a response to perceived problems with Hare's generalism. In our view, it should be a constraint on a plausible construal of this debate that Hare's position is properly classified as a form of generalism.

This is not to say that there is not an interesting debate to be had about whether there are moral principles qua truth-makers. Our point is simply that it is not the debate in which most particularists and generalists are engaging and in any event it is not the debate with which we are concerned here. For the record, we think that the idea of moral principles qua truth-makers requires a lot of work to be made both precise and tractable. Irwin himself allows that his notion of normative priority is "difficult to describe clearly" (Irwin 2000: 103). For a start, we would at least need a clear account of the metaphysics of principles themselves. For example, for generalism in this sense to have even a prayer of being true we had better not characterize principles as linguistic entities. The wrongness of Hitler's actions is not dependent on anyone having expressed in language a true principle which explains its wrongness. Presumably for this debate to be interesting we must conceive of principles as something like true propositions or perhaps general facts (assuming facts and true propositions are not identical types). This also seems to suggest that this way of construing the debate is unhelpful. For this construal now seems not only to have implausibly tied anti-realists like Hare to particularism, it also implausibly entails that Quineans whose ontology does not include propositions or facts are thereby automatically particularists.

For the record, our hunch is that insofar as the debate cast in these terms can be made precise and tractable, it collapses into the familiar in-house debate between moral realists who are reductionists and those who are anti-reductionists, with the reductionists coming out as generalists and the anti-reductionists coming out as particularists. However, we mention this hunch just to put our cards on the table, as we lack the space here to defend it with argument. The main point remains that, whatever its philosophical interest, the debate over principles as truth-makers is not one we shall engage here, nor is it the one we take most particularists and generalists in the literature to be engaging.

## 1.3. Content

Different forms of particularism are defined by the different negative claims they make about moral principles. Before exploring these different approaches, we must register two important caveats. First, the debate between particularists and generalists is most usefully understood as taking place against the background assumption that nontrivial moral knowledge is possible and indeed that we have quite a bit of it.[3] Of course, this is not to deny that an error theorist who argues that there are no nontrivial moral truths (Mackie 1977) is in one sense a particularist. For if there are no nontrivial moral truths then there will also be no nontrivial moral principles. Similarly, if moral skepticism is true then a form of particularism follows rather quickly, in that if we can have no nontrivial moral knowledge then we cannot know any nontrivial moral principles. However, if we classify the error theory and moral skepticism as forms of particularism then the debate over particularism will in part collapse into the old and well-worn debates over the error theory and moral skepticism. While these debates are indeed important, they are not our concern here. The question we address throughout is whether generalism is defensible against the background assumption that moral knowledge is not merely possible but commonplace. Moreover, this assumption is in no way controversial or question-begging in the dialectic over particularism. For all self-styled particularists in the literature take themselves to be firmly opposed to moral skepticism and the error theory and indeed sometimes suggest that their own account is especially well suited

---

[3] Thanks to Roy Sorensen and Walter Sinnott-Armstrong for helpful discussion here.

to avoiding these depressing doctrines (see e.g. Dancy 2004: 156). The second caveat we must register here is that our taxonomy maps the logical space of the debate over particularism but does not sort figures in the literature. Indeed, part of the problem with the existing literature is that the parties to the debate have not noticed some of the distinctions we draw here. However, we suspect that once these distinctions are drawn many particularists would want to inhabit large swaths of the logical space we carve out rather than only one quadrant of that space.

The first and arguably most ambitious form of particularism simply denies that there are any moral principles:

(1) **Principle Eliminativism:** There are no true moral principles.

Principle Eliminativism's denial that there are any true moral principles provides a stark challenge to the moral philosopher's traditional attempts to capture morality in a finite and manageable set of principles. Of course, the exact content of this doctrine depends on the conception of moral principles with which it is paired. At some points John McDowell seems to endorse a form of Principle Eliminativism. He expresses a hunch that particular moral cases may "stubbornly resist capture in any general net" (McDowell 1985 as reprinted in McDowell 1998: 149). Insofar as principles are understood as exceptionless generalizations, Margaret Little also endorses Principle Eliminativism, arguing that "we have reason to doubt that there are any moral principles, *even* very complicated ones, capable of codifying the moral landscape" (Little 2000: 277).[4]

(2) **Principle Skepticism Particularism:** There is no good reason to think there are any true moral principles.

On this view, the supposition that there are true moral principles is an unwarranted conceit. Principle skeptics may defend their position with elimination arguments, contending that none of the reasons given for thinking there are true moral principles is sound, and that the alternative is a coherent position which resists internal critiques.[5] Principle Skepticism is intuitively a weaker doctrine than Principle Eliminativism, leaving open the possibility that there may be some true moral principles. Nonetheless, it still poses a challenge to

---

[4] Little's position is more moderate than this might suggest since she goes on to argue that we should instead understand moral principles as tolerating exceptions and that so understood moral principles and theorizing remain important and worthy of our attention. For more detailed discussion, see Lance and Little forthcoming *a*. We discuss their views in more detail in Ch. 3.

[5] For example, the principle skeptics may wish to show that particularism is not committed to an implausible account of moral epistemology. See Little 2000.

traditional forms of moral theorizing. For if there is no reason to believe there are true moral principles then searching for them is unmotivated.

(3) **Principled Particularism**: Any finite set of moral principles will be insufficient to capture all moral truths.

Although seemingly oxymoronic, this version of particularism is actually very interesting. For principled particularism imposes an important limitation upon the possibility of codifying morality, a limitation that prominent first-order moral theories clearly exceed. Richard Holton has developed this view and suggested that it represents a plausible compromise position without actually endorsing it himself. Precisely because Holton's account represents a compromise, it is not entirely clear whether it should be classified as a form of particularism or generalism. In any event, Principled Particularism relies heavily on the idea of what Holton calls a *That's It* principle. On Holton's account, moral deliberation can reasonably lead us to endorse principles of the form "Any action that has such-and-such features and *That's It* is wrong" (Holton 2002). So, for example, I might reason that 'Any action that causes pain and *That's It* is wrong, this action causes pain and *That's It*, so this action is wrong.' The rough idea behind a *That's It* clause is that no other morally relevant features are present which would shift the verdict endorsed in the principle's consequent. The idea is made more precise in terms of no other true moral principle plus the relevant facts superseding (in roughly the sense of entailing an incompatible moral verdict) the original *That's It* principle in the case at hand. One consequence of the self-reference of a *That's It* clause is a *That's It* principle gets a truth value only in the context of the argument in which it appears. Holton gives a considerably more precise and technical account of *That's It* and the idea of supersession. For those interested, we discuss Holton's proposal in more detail in the Appendix. To anticipate, we think Holton's proposal is onto something deeply right and important but argue that his account of a *That's It* clause has implausible consequences which our own account can avoid.

So far we have explained the role principles can play in Principled Particularism, but one might reasonably wonder, 'Where is the particularism in this so-called Principled Particularism?' The answer to this question stems from the compatibility of holding that for each moral truth there is a corresponding *That's It* principle *and* supposing that no finite set of principles could ever cover all possible cases. Here Holton draws a nice analogy with Godel's Incompleteness Theorem in first-order arithmetic. For any truth of first-order arithmetic there is a set of axioms from which the truth follows. However, Godel showed that this does not mean that there is any consistent way of capturing all of first-order arithmetic in any single finite axiomitization. The model provides some inspiration for Principled Particularism, which holds that while each moral truth is backed by some principle, there nonetheless is no finite set of principles from which all moral truths follow. Principled Particularism is most usefully understood as embracing a conception of principles as standards as opposed to guides (or action-guiding standards). For the Principled Particularist insists that while we need not be guided in our decision-making by moral principles (the familiar particularist metaphor of 'moral vision' may instead be more germane here; see Chapter 4), still those principles figure in the proper justification of our action. So the idea is that while there may be a moral standard which figures in the justification of each particular action, no finite set of moral standards will be sufficient to codify all of morality.

Principled Particularism denies that morality could ever be completely codified by a finite and manageable set of moral principles, so the notion of codification is doing some real work here. A set of moral principles S codifies all of morality in our sense of 'codifies' just in case (a) the moral principles in question have purely descriptive antecedents and moral consequents (codification is understood here in terms of a purely descriptive coding) and (b) for any moral truth, there is a moral principle or set of principles in S such that the principle(s) in question together with the relevant descriptive facts entail the moral truth in question. The idea of codifying all of morality is therefore a very ambitious one. However, codification in this sense does *not* presuppose that the principles in S are algorithmic or constitutive of competence with moral concepts. These caveats are essential to a proper appreciation of the positive account of the codifiability of morality we develop in Part II of this book.

Our preceding three characterizations of the content of particularism (Principle Eliminativism, Principle Skepticism, and Principled Particularism) focus on whether and to what extent morality can be codified. These forms of particularism are therefore directed in the first instance at theory rather than practice. Other particularists emphasize the more directly practical question of whether everyday moral thought and decision-making should involve moral principles:

(4) *Principle Abstinence Particularism:* We ought not rely upon moral principles.[6]

---

[6] Incidentally, there seems to be nothing to distinguish Principle Eliminativism about guides and action-guiding standards from Principle Abstinence Particularism. We suspect that the distinction between these doctrines is a purely notational one that falls out of our taxonomic structure.

Proponents of principle abstinence particularism need not deny that there are moral principles. Instead, the Principle Abstinence Particularist's characteristic claim is that moral principles are "at best useless, and at worst a hindrance" (McNaughton 1988: 191).[7] Jonathan Dancy has argued that reliance on moral principles can easily distort our judgment, leading us to import moral salience for considerations which were important in one situation but not important in the case at hand. He argues that the virtuous moral agent "is not conceived as someone equipped with a full list of moral principles and an ability correctly to subsume each new case under the right one. There is nothing that one brings to the new situation other than a contentless ability to discern what matters where it matters" (Dancy 1993: 50). If correct, this position would have dramatic implications for moral philosophy. McNaughton makes the point quite crisply when he explains that this form of particularism "claims, in effect, that there is no such subject as moral theory, in this sense, and no such subject as practical ethics. Insofar as the teaching of practical ethics encourages both pupils and teachers to believe in the will o' the wisp of moral theory it is pernicious" (McNaughton 1988: 204).

Debates over consequentialism should make it clear just how important it is to heed the distinction between Principle Abstinence Particularism and other forms of particularism. A number of philosophers have argued that direct forms of act consequentialism are 'self-effacing' in the sense that given the empirical facts such theories recommend their own suppression. The idea here is that for a variety of reasons the best way of maximizing the good would involve having people reject the consequentialist principle itself. Typically, the idea has been that ordinary people would do better in terms of promoting the good by relying on principles other than consequentialism. The idea is that these principles are ones which are easier to apply and less likely to lead to self-serving rationalization than the consequentialist principle itself. Many defenders of consequentialism admit that their theory is self-effacing in this way but insist that this does not suggest that the theory is false (for a classic discussion see Parfit 1984). Such consequentialists are committed to rejecting Principle Eliminativism and Principle Skepticism about moral standards, as on their view the consequentialist principle is the ultimate moral standard and

---

[7] Some commentators suggest that the defining feature of particularism is its commitment to what we are calling principle abstinence plus the thesis that principles do not actually underwrite our moral practice. Walter Sinnott-Armstrong, for example, claims that "What unites particularists is their claim that such moral judgments should not be based on general principles or rules" (Sinnott-Armstrong 1999: 2). It should be clear from our discussion why we think this characterization is too narrow to capture every species of particularism, though it does capture one important strand of particularist thought.

can be known to be so. So such consequentialists are in an important sense generalists about standards. However, such consequentialists are at the same time Principle Abstinence Particularists about those very same standards. This is not to say that they are Principle Abstinence Particularists in all respects. For such consequentialists typically endorse other nonconsequentialist principles as the ones that ordinary people should deploy. They are what we might call 'Principled Guidance Generalists' about these nonconsequentialist heuristic principles. An interesting piece of logical space which has not been explored in this area (so far as we know) would be a form of self-effacing consequentialism which held that we would do best to promote the good if we abandoned principles altogether. Such a position would be robustly generalist in its theory but radically particularist in practice.[8]

Finally, some particularists advance the more modest and cautious thesis that moral thought and judgment at least do not presuppose moral principles:

(5) *Anti-Transcendental Particularism*: The possibility of moral thought and judgment do not depend on the provision of a suitable supply of moral principles.

In effect, this version of particularism simply denies the possibility of a Kantian transcendental deduction of moral principles from the necessary presuppositions of moral thought and judgment. This is arch-particularist Jonathan Dancy's considered characterization of particularism (see Dancy 2004: 7). We take Anti-Transcendental Particularism to be a thesis about what is presupposed by our ability to make moral judgments *successfully or correctly*, where this includes the ability to have moral knowledge.[9] Thus construed Anti-Transcendental Particularism is clearly a more modest doctrine than Principle Eliminativism and Principle Skepticism. Assuming that morality is not in some way deeply defective and that some of our actual moral thought and judgment is coherent and justifiable, Principle Eliminativism and Principle Skepticism each entail Anti-Transcendental Particularism but not vice versa. Anti-Transcendental Particularism, indeed, is compatible with the availability of a complete and finite axiomitization of morality and so in one sense is weaker even than Principled Particularism. Moreover, Anti-Transcendental Particularism seems ill-suited to provide the radical challenge to the possibility of moral theory

---

[8] Many thanks to Julia Driver for drawing us out on these important points.

[9] There is a weaker reading of Anti-Transcendental Particularism according to which it is a thesis about the presuppositions of our counting as competent with moral predicates (or as possessors of moral concepts). With this thesis, we would actually agree (as we argue in Ch. 5), but we take it that particularists mean more than this. If this weaker thesis were definitive of particularism, after all, anyone who rejected analytic moral principles would count as a particularist.

particularists sometimes envisage. Even a hardy act–utilitarian might agree that the principle of utility is not presupposed by the very possibility of moral thought. So long as it is admitted that the principle of utility is both true and in some interesting sense explanatory, most utilitarians will reasonably suppose that their view is vindicated. Indeed, Anti-Transcendental Particularism is compatible with the thesis that morality both can and should be codified. For the mere fact that moral thought and judgment do not presuppose the availability of a suitable stock of moral principles does not itself entail that such a stock of principles is unavailable nor does it entail that articulating such principles would not be desirable from both a practical and a theoretical point of view. Anti-Transcendental Particularism therefore poses a challenge not to principled morality as such, but merely to transcendental arguments for it. By itself, this need not render Anti-Transcendental Particularism uninteresting. It remains an important question in its own right whether the possibility of moral thought does presuppose moral principles. Generalism as a regulative ideal as we develop it in Part II of this book entails that in one important sense it does.

## 1.4. Scope

Particularists also differ over the scope of the principles about which they are particularists:

### 1.4.1. Moral, nonmoral, intra-moral

Some moral principles are meant to carry us from the nonmoral to the moral. For example, 'pain is morally bad' is such a principle since, intuitively at least, 'pain' is a nonmoral predicate while 'morally bad' is a moral one.[10] Other principles are intra-moral; they carry us from moral concepts to other moral concepts. For example, *courage is virtuous*, is such a principle since both 'courage' and 'virtue' are moral concepts. Some intra-moral principles order different values. For example, one might claim that it is better to be just than to be merciful if one must choose. One might be a particularist about either of these kinds of principles.[11] Of course, it is controversial just how to

[10] We prefer to put the point in terms of predicates and in terms of the moral and the nonmoral. Often the point is put in terms of properties, and often in terms of moral versus *naturalistic* properties. We hesitate to put the point this way since a naturalist may wish to say that moral properties are *identical* to natural properties. See Jackson, Pettit, and Smith 2000. Readers who prefer to draw this contrast differently may simply make the necessary modifications.

[11] This may not be an exclusive division of principles, since some principles seem obviously to employ both moral and nonmoral concepts.

demarcate the boundary between moral and nonmoral predicates. We strive throughout to present our arguments in ways that do not prejudge the best way to draw the distinction. We do, however, assume that a complex predicate that is formed by logically gathering several nonmoral predicates (for example a long disjunction of nonmoral predicates) is itself a nonmoral predicate. There arises here an epistemological issue of what justifies conjoining several nonmoral predicates in the first place. It might be that to justify conjoining several nonmoral predicates, one would need already to have a sensibility for the moral predicate that correctly applies whenever the complex predicate applies. Whatever the merits of this suggestion (and we shall have some things to say about it along the way) we do not think that we should let these epistemological issues settle whether some predicate is moral or nonmoral.

### 1.4.2. Hedged versus unhedged principles

Principles may also be sorted according to whether they include familiar qualifications such as 'ceteris paribus,' 'prima facie,' and 'pro tanto.' Someone impressed by particularism might admit that we have no reason to believe that all of morality could be captured algorithmically, but still insist that certain hedged moral principles are both possible and desirable. Margaret Little describes such a position nicely:

> Many who claim sympathy to particularist sentiments believe that those sentiments still leave room for some sort of codified law-like generalities linking moral and non-moral properties. After all, it is thought, we can at least still say of all cases that ceteris paribus (roughly 'all things equal'), or again pro tanto (roughly, 'in so far as this goes'), intentional falsehoods are breaches of fidelity and breaches of fidelity are wrong. Thus while it is true that arriving at moral answers requires judgment rather than mere application of algorithm, it is still judgment backed by an architecture of sorts—the generalities comprising that architecture are simply of a less ambitious sort than is sometimes supposed. (Little 2000: section 4)

The distinction between principles which are qualified in this way and those which are not cuts across distinctions in scope. Thus we may have principles linking the moral and the nonmoral as well as intra-moral principles which are qualified by *ceteris paribus* or *pro tanto* clauses, and we may have all things considered principles of either scope. Whether particularism applies to such qualified principles, or whether it is restricted to all things considered principles has emerged as an important question in the debate between particularists and generalists.

## 1.5. Going Forward

With our map of the particularist/generalist terrain in hand, we can now outline what is to come. In the remainder of Part I, we assess the most important argumentative strategies for resolving the debate between generalists and particularists. In Chapters 2, 3, and 4 we consider the most significant arguments for particularism. In Chapter 2 we take up arguments that seek to derive particularism from the thesis of holism about reasons, roughly the view that a consideration may count as a reason in one context but not in another. We conclude that while holism provides no positive and non-question-begging support for particularism, particularists are committed to holism. This raises the question of whether holism itself is defensible, and one worry here is that when combined with particularism that holism implausibly 'flattens the moral landscape,' so that we can draw no interesting and important distinction between suffering and shoelace color since either can, in the right circumstances, be of direct moral significance on a particularist version of holism. Particularists have tried to meet this problem by drawing a distinction between default reasons and nondefault reasons. In Chapter 3 we explore three different ways of drawing that distinction and argue that the more philosophically ambitious versions of the distinction (the ones defended by leading particularists) are problematic. Instead, we advocate an alternative and more deflationary version of the distinction. We doubt that the distinction so understood can do all the work the particularist requires. In Chapter 4 we explore the often invoked metaphor of 'moral vision' and argue that its dialectical importance to the debate over particularism is easily exaggerated if we are not extremely careful to heed the distinctions between different species of particularism and generalism drawn here. We close Part I of the book with a discussion of constitutive generalism in Chapter 5. Here we raise a familiar problem for constitutive generalism and then consider an interesting strategy for defending a sophisticated version of constitutive generalism which is supposed to evade that problem. We argue, however, that the strategy is not successful and that a suitably updated version of Moore's Open Question Argument shows why constitutive generalism is untenable. To this limited extent, we agree with particularists.

We thus reach the end of Part I in a dialectical standoff, with arguments on both sides of the divide having failed to settle matters. While some generalists might be willing to rest content in the thought that the burden of proof is on the particularist, we find this unsatisfying. If the practice of moral philosophy has simply presupposed prominent roles for principles, then these presuppositions need a critical examination and defense if we are to continue to endorse them. Generalists should wake from their dogmatic slumbers. If morality really can and should be understood in terms of principles, then there ought to be a convincing positive argument for that conclusion. While meeting the particularist's arguments against a principled approach to morality is an important task, completing this task is not sufficient to meet the particularist challenge. For the absence of a sound argument for particularism is not itself the presence of a sound argument for generalism. So our critical discussion of the arguments given in favor of particularism in Part I set the stage for our own positive view in Part II.

In Part II we present and defend a form of generalism we call "generalism as a regulative ideal." The argument comes in stages, but ultimately we reject virtually all of the forms of particularism we have identified. In Chapter 6 we defend a species of hedged moral principles that we call *default principles*. We argue that default principles represent moral standards and that the availability of default principles is presupposed by the possibility of moral knowledge. Chapter 6 leaves open two possibilities, though. First there might be infinitely many valid default principles (a result that would confirm Holton's Principled Particularism). Secondly it might be impossible to eliminate or even make fully explicit the hedges inherent to default principles (thus restricting generalism in scope to hedged principles). In Chapter 7 we argue against these possibilities. We argue that the best explanation of the possibility of practical wisdom is that there is a limited number of valid moral principles. Moreover, we argue that, whatever qualifications must be attached to them, they are qualifications that it is at least possible in principle to make fully explicit. In Chapter 8 we argue that moral principles (as we defend them) are not merely objects of curiosity. Rather, morality itself gives us reason to articulate moral principles. Though moral practice rightly incorporates a kind of division of labor, the effort to articulate moral principles is one in which all moral agents participate. In Chapter 9 we argue that moral principles have a proper place as guides and this provides us with another reason (in addition to those laid out in Chapter 8) to articulate them. Together these last two chapters refute Principle Abstinence Particularism, and vindicate the practical role given to principles in everyday practice.

Even though we will not defend any specific moral principles as ultimately valid, someone may ask whether we should have any hope that we really will succeed in articulating the moral principles that we know there are. Because constitutive generalism is untenable, we cannot assume that we have an implicit grasp of these principles already simply in virtue of our possession of moral concepts. Nevertheless, moral principles are in another sense presupposed by moral thought itself. At least if we take 'moral thought' to comprise not simply our possession of moral concepts but also the success we exhibit in deploying those concepts, then moral thought itself supports our confidence in a generalist approach to morality. Hence generalism as a regulative ideal entails that even anti-transcendental particularism is false. Will we ever fully succeed in articulating a moral theory which successfully codifies all of morality? Perhaps not. Generalism as a regulative ideal does not insist that the practice of moral theorizing is guaranteed ever to terminate in a moral theory we can know is absolutely complete. Nevertheless, we have ample reason to engage in precisely those forms of moral theorizing which would lead to a complete moral theory if such a thing is possible for us.

Moreover, we also have ample reason to believe that the ultimate limit to our ability to capture the moral landscape with a set of principles just is the limit on our ability to have moral knowledge at all. If there are unknowable moral truths, then these will also escape the net of even an ideal moral theory, but few generalists will lose sleep over this prospect. More interestingly, it may be that our moral knowledge will continue to grow without ever fully terminating, in which case our moral theorizing might continue to grow and indeed flourish without ever terminating in a final complete moral theory. Just as scientific progress understood in terms of articulating laws of nature might well continue without ever terminating in a 'grand theory of everything,' moral progress understood in terms of articulating and being guided by sound moral principles might also continue without ever terminating in a final and complete moral theory. Even if we can never actually succeed in fully articulating a moral theory which covers all possible scenarios, generalism remains a regulative ideal.

# 2

# Holism about Reasons

The character of every act depends upon the circumstances in which it is done.

(Oliver Wendell Holmes, Jr.)

Moral verdicts uncontroversially depend upon context, but the precise nature of this context-dependence is controversial. One strategy for supporting particularism depends on identifying and defending specific forms of context-dependence and arguing that they should undermine our confidence that morality is principled. Indeed, particularists have with near unanimity claimed that the most powerful support for their view comes from a doctrine about context-dependence they call "holism about reasons." For example, Jonathan Dancy claims that holism about reasons is "the leading thought behind particularism" and goes on to claim that "if there is a holism of reasons ... the prospects for substantial moral principles look bleak" (Dancy 1993: 60 and 66). In later work, Dancy contends that "A principle-based approach to ethics is inconsistent with the holism of reasons" (Dancy 2000: 135). Margaret Little maintains that "if reason-giving considerations function holistically in the moral realm then we simply shouldn't expect to find rules that mark out in nonmoral terms the sufficiency conditions for applying moral concepts" (Little 2000: 284). Moreover, Little suggests that this line of argument is considerably more fruitful than the alternative strategy of arguing that any proposed moral principle is vulnerable to counter-examples:

Obviously, to defend particularism, it is not enough to keep offering counterexamples to proposed principles. Even if they are accepted, just what they suffice to show is precisely what is in question—those attuned to the richness of morality but loyal to the existence of principles will see counterexamples as evidence of complexity, not irreducible complexity.... But the particularist's doubt does not stem from philosophical obsession with counterexamples or lazy extrapolation from them; it is not brute pessimism floating free of any other philosophical commitment. The particularist doubt is born of reflection about the nature of the moral domain. (Little 2000: 279)

It is clear from the context that the further philosophical commitment to which Little refers here is holism about reasons. Even opponents of particularism typically concede that holism about reasons would provide substantial support for particularism and accept the burden of arguing against holism about reasons. Philip Stratton-Lake, for example, rejects particularism but maintains that holism about reasons entails that "there cannot be a principled relation between certain natural and moral properties; or, at least, if there is, it can only be by some sort of world historical chance" (Stratton-Lake 2000: 129; see also 128–30).[1]

In fact, holism provides no positive support for particularism in any of its guises. There are two ways of understanding holism about reasons. On the first interpretation, holism is an interesting account of the context sensitivity of reasons but does not provide any support for particularism. On the second interpretation, holism is the combination of two theses—an interesting thesis about the context sensitivity of reasons and the thesis that this context sensitivity transcends finite codification. Holism in this latter sense entails particularism only because the second of these two theses simply *is* a form of particularism; specifically, it is a form of Principled Particularism (see Chapter 1). So any argument from holism in this second sense to particularism begs the question. Moreover, defining holism in this second way has the unfortunate consequence of eclipsing the important question of whether the context sensitivity of morality might itself be codifiable.

So there is no sound and non-question-begging argument from holism to particularism. However, there may still be a plausible argument in the other direction—from particularism to holism. This would suggest a more indirect way in which holism about reasons supports particularism—by blocking otherwise damning objection(s). This, however, is a far cry from holism providing positive support for particularism, much less its being 'inconsistent' with a principle-based approach to morality. Finally, we must mention a possible terminological source of confusion. Sometimes discussions of particularism actually use 'particularism' or 'particularism about reasons' simply to *mean* what is usually referred to as holism (see e.g. Cullity 2002). If the arguments developed in this chapter are correct, then this terminological move implausibly severs any essential connection between moral particularism and opposition to

---

[1] Stratton-Lake traces holism to G. E. Moore's doctrine of organic wholes, and claims that to give a satisfactory reply to particularists, "One must attack the doctrine that is doing the real damage, namely, the doctrine of organic wholes." Whether Moore's doctrine is a form of holism or even presupposes holism as the particularists understand that doctrine is a difficult question that would require careful Moore exegesis. Here we simply set that issue to one side. We do note, however, that Dancy explicitly rejects Moore's doctrine. See Dancy 2000: 139–40.

moral principles. It would be best to avoid confusing the issue by confining the use of 'particularism' to refer to the sorts of explicitly anti-principle views laid out in Chapter 1.

## 2.1. Holism and Codifiable Context-Dependence

Holism about reasons usually is characterized as the thesis that what functions as a reason in one case may not be a reason at all or may even be a reason with the opposite valence in another case. Here is Jonathan Dancy's canonical statement of the doctrine and its opposite atomism:

*Holism* in the theory of reasons: a feature that is a reason in one case may be no reason at all, or an opposite reason, in another.

*Atomism* in the theory of reasons: a feature that is a reason in one case must remain a reason, and retain the same polarity, in an other. (Dancy 2004: 73–4; see also Dancy 2000: 130; Dancy 1993: 60)

Holism so understood is easy to motivate with examples. Suppose my seeing a movie would give me pleasure. Plausibly, the fact that seeing a movie would give me pleasure is a reason for me to see it. However, in another case that very same consideration might be no reason at all to perform the action. If, for example, I would take pleasure in seeing someone tortured in the movie (suppose it is a documentary on human rights abuses) then the fact that I would take pleasure in the film plausibly is no reason whatsoever to see it.[2] There is some temptation in light of the case of sadistic pleasure to maintain that the original description of the agent's reason was mistaken. This is the temptation to be an atomist about reasons. On an atomistic interpretation, my reason to see the movie in the first case was not simply that it would give me pleasure but that it would give me nonsadistic pleasure. The main point of holism about reasons is to resist this temptation. The holist argues that we can instead understand the reason to see the movie in the first case as simply being the fact that it would give me pleasure even though that very same consideration might be no reason at all in another context.

Thinking about cases which motivate a holistic conception of reasons suggests some further potentially useful distinctions. The fact that someone's pleasure would be sadistic seems to undermine the putative status of the fact that my action would give her pleasure as a reason. Facts which function to undermine candidate reasons in this way are sometimes referred to as

---

[2] Of course, there is room for the atomist to insist that even here the pleasure provides some room but just not sufficient reason to carry the day in most cases involving sadism. Our point here is that the holistic interpretation is prima facie plausible enough to support the idea that reasons can function holistically.

'defeaters.'[3] The idea of a reason being defeated in the intended sense must be sharply distinguished from its being overridden. A candidate reason is overridden when countervailing reasons are weightier and should carry the day. The idea of a reason being overridden is a familiar one, but the idea of a candidate reason being defeated in our sense is one which emerges only in the context of holism about reasons. The opposite of a defeater is a fact which makes a consideration which otherwise would not be a reason with a certain valence into a reason with that valence. Facts which function in this way are usually referred to as 'enablers.' On a holistic view, there are also facts which leave a consideration's status as a reason intact, but serve to increase or decrease its normative force. For example, the fact that my visiting your mother was something I knew you cared about very dearly might make the fact that I promised to visit her into a stronger reason. We call facts which function in these ways 'intensifiers' and 'diminishers.'

To those uninitiated in the literature, the preceding way of regimenting the atomism/holism terminology can be slightly confusing. 'Holism about reasons' might easily be taken to refer to the view that reasons themselves are constituted by the (perhaps large) whole made up by everything necessary for their instantiation. That would be putting the 'whole' into 'holism.' Clearly, the holists we have in mind are keen to reject this view of reasons and instead maintain that some of the features relevant to the instantiation of a reason need not be part of the reason itself (Dancy 2004: 95–9). The term 'holism' is apt only in the sense that an adequate understanding of when a consideration functions as a reason requires one to look at the larger whole of the context in which the candidate reason appears, and not in the sense that reasons themselves should be understood expansively as incorporating in their content everything relevant from the whole context. In any event, whatever its merits this terminological choice is by now well entrenched in the literature and we shall not here quarrel over the word.

Particularists do not have a monopoly on holism about reasons. Holism is compatible with the generalist view that morality can and should be codified. Moreover, there is no reason to suppose that the generalist could not reap just as many theoretical dividends from holism about reasons as the particularist. The basic point is simply that there are two distinct issues here. First, there is the question of whether reasons are context-dependent. Secondly, assuming that reasons are context-dependent there is the question of whether their

---

[3] The literature on epistemology often uses the idea of a defeater in a broader and more inclusive sense than the one we use in the text. Readers heavily stepped in the epistemological literature should be careful to note how our use differs from the standard epistemological use of this term of art.

context-dependence is codifiable. An affirmative answer to the first question in no way dictates a negative answer to the second. The clearest way to make this point is with a series of examples. Consider the following moral theory:

(U) The fact that an action would promote pleasure is a reason to perform the action if and only if the pleasure is nonsadistic. The fact that an action would promote pain is a reason not to perform the action. An action is morally right just in case it promotes at least as great a balance of reason-giving pleasures over pain as any of the available alternatives; otherwise it is wrong.

(U) is a utilitarian theory that differs from classical forms of utilitarianism only in that it gives no weight to sadistic pleasures. Clearly, (U) is incompatible with the particularist idea that morality cannot be codified. (U) is a comprehensive codification in purely descriptive terms of the morality of right and wrong. We could append theories of supererogation (roughly, actions 'above and beyond the call of duty') and virtue as well, but (U) already is just the sort of codification of morality that particularists would reject as either impossible, unnecessary, or undesirable. The crucial point is that holism cannot support a particularist critique of (U), for (U) *presupposes* holism about reasons.[4] According-ing to (U) whether the fact that an action would promote pleasure is a reason for performing the action depends on the context—in particular, it depends on whether the pleasure is sadistic. Nonetheless, on this theory it is the fact that an action would promote pleasure that is a reason when it is a reason and not the fact that it would promote nonsadistic pleasure. So (U) presupposes holism about reasons.

(U) does not maintain that the status of facts about pain as reasons is context sensitive, though it could easily be revised in this respect. However, such a modification is not necessary to make the point that holism about reasons is consistent with principles like (U) capturing all of morality. For the fact that pain might necessarily always function as a reason actually is compatible with holism about reasons. For holism about reasons maintains

---

[4] Frank Jackson, Philip Pettit, and Michael Smith argue at the end of their paper on particularism and patterns that holism is compatible with a form of "expected value" utilitarianism, but the version of utilitarianism they consider is unnecessarily technical and obscures the basic point. The theory they consider maintains that, "the moral value of A is a weighted sum of the value of each possible world at which A obtains: $V(A) = \sum w \, Pr(w/A).V(w)$, where $V(w)$ is a measure of total happiness at w. And R is a reason for A if and only if the value of A given R is greater than the value of A, i.e., $\sum wPr(w/A.R).V(w) > \sum wPr(w/A).V(w)$, which obtains if and only if $V(A.R) > V(A)$" (p. 97). Their explication of this form of utilitarianism and its presuppositions may succeed, but the basic point does not depend on the elaborate details of this particular version of expected value utilitarianism. See Jackson, Pettit, and Smith 2000: 79–99, esp. 96–9. For a similar point, see Holton 2002: n. 12.

only that a consideration's status as a reason *can* depend on other features of the context, not that it *must*. Dancy is clear on this point, emphasizing that holism about reasons is consistent with the existence of what he calls "invariant reasons"—considerations that function as reasons with the same valence in all circumstances:

I conclude, then, that particularism should accept the possibility of invariant reasons, so long as the invariance is not a matter of the logic of such reasons, but more the rather peculiar fact that some reasons happen to contribute in ways that are not affected by other features. (Dancy 2000: 136–7)

Actually, Dancy's discussion suggests that he would allow not only that some considerations might be *invariant reasons* in the sense that their valence and status as reasons is never undermined in our world, but also that some considerations might be *invariable reasons* in the sense that their valence and status is never undermined in any world. So long as this stronger context-invariability is due to the particular content of the reason in question and is not due to the mere fact that the fact in question can function as a reason, this too will be compatible with holism about reasons. For holism about reasons maintains only that there is nothing about being a reason which precludes the context-sensitivity of reasons. It is compatible with this that certain kinds of reasons are such that those particular reasons are not context-sensitive. As Dancy puts it when discussing invariance, such reasons will be invariant (and we would add, perhaps in some cases, invariable), "not because they are reasons but because of their specific content" (Dancy 2000: 136).[5] So holists about reasons should (as we think Dancy does) allow that reasons can be invariable as well as merely contingently invariant.[6] So long as this modal status is due to their specific content and not due to their merely being reasons, this will in no way be incompatible with holism about reasons. Indeed, strictly speaking, holism in Dancy's sense is logically compatible with the thesis that all reasons are invariable so long as in each case the reason's invariability stems from its specific content and not from the mere fact that it is a reason. So the fact that

[5] This quotation, incidentally, is the textual basis for supposing that Dancy would agree with us that holism is consistent with invariability. For if invariance can be due simply to the content of a reason then its invariance does not look contingent as its content will remain the same throughout all possible worlds in which it exists. Admittedly, this is a thin reed on which to base a philosophically important extrapolation, but considerations of charity also come into play here since we think holism is plainly compatible with invariability as well as invariance.

[6] Thanks to discussion with Pekka Väyrynen on this point. In Väyrynen 2004, he makes a good case for supposing that it is really invariability of reasons and not mere invariance that is philosophically interesting. As the text indicates, we entirely agree with Väyrynen on this point.

(U) leaves facts about pain as invariable reasons implies nothing incompatible with holism about reasons.

At this point a particularist might appeal to a much stronger version of holism about reasons, according to which all reasons not only can but *must* depend on their context for their status as reasons. This version of holism about reasons seems much less pre-theoretically attractive than holism about reasons as it is usually understood; Dancy seems right to allow that the status of certain considerations as reasons may well be invariant (and indeed invariable) in virtue of their specific content. However, even this stronger and less plausible version of holism is no threat to generalism. For example, this stronger doctrine is compatible with another form of utilitarianism:

(U★)  The fact that an action would promote pleasure is a reason to perform the action if and only if the pleasure is nonsadistic. The fact that an action would promote pain is a reason not to perform the action if and only if the person who will experience the pain has not autonomously consented to experiencing it. An action is morally right just in case it promotes at least as great a balance of reason-giving pleasure over reason-giving pain as any of the available alternatives; otherwise it is wrong.

(U★) maintains that the status of the fact that an action will cause someone pain as a reason depends on another feature of the context—whether the agent who will experience the pain has autonomously consented to experiencing it. On this theory all reasons—pleasure-based or pain-based—depend for their status as reasons on other features of the context. So (U★) is a codification of the categories of right and wrong in purely descriptive terms that is perfectly consistent with the very strong form of holism about reasons according to which all reasons' status as reasons *must* depend on other features of the context. Holism about reasons even on this very strong interpretation is compatible with codification in a strong sense.[7]

The preceding example is a utilitarian theory, but our point can be illustrated just as easily with holistic Kantian accounts of morality. Kant himself maintained that the good will and only the good will is unconditionally good, but allowed that other things are good in some circumstances but not others. The opening

---

[7] Notice that (U) and (U★) claim to provide necessary and sufficient conditions for there being a moral reason and for an action's being morally right or wrong; they do not simply claim to provide mere contingent statistical generalizations. Dancy at one point implies that holism would at most allow for codification only in the weak sense that it would allow for such mere contingent statistical generalizations; see Dancy 2000: 135. Our examples show that holism is compatible with a much more ambitious form of codification.

paragraph of the *Groundwork* is brimming with things Kant takes to have merely conditional value—intelligence, wit, judgment, courage, resoluteness, perseverance, power, riches, honor, health, and even happiness. Indeed among Kant's most central theses is that "the good will seems to constitute the indispensable condition even of worthiness to be happy" (K 393). Kantian views may thus accept that while the idea that an action would promote someone's happiness is sometimes a reason, sometimes it is not. On this view, the status of the consideration, "it would promote X's happiness" as a reason depends on another feature of the context—whether X has a good will. Kant's account thus presupposes holism. Nonetheless, Kant's account also aims to provide a very ambitious codification of morality. Once again we have a vivid illustration of the compatibility of holism with the codifiability of all of morality. Indeed, utilitarian and Kantian theories are perhaps the most influential and interesting systematic codifications of morality. So if plausible utilitarian and Kantian moral theories can both be understood in ways that presuppose holism about reasons, then it is hard to see how holism makes the prospects for substantial moral principles in any way 'bleak.'

So far we have seen that both Kantian and utilitarian moral theories can be formulated in ways that are not only compatible with holism but that presuppose it. However, even codifications of morality that do not presuppose holism are still compatible with it. For example, the classical utilitarian might maintain that the only moral reason to perform an action is that it would promote happiness. Once it is clear that holism about reasons is compatible with invariable reasons, it should be clear that this view is compatible with holism. Insofar as it is plausible, holism is a view about the way reasons *can* function just insofar as they are reasons, not a view about the way they *must* function. So long as the classical utilitarian admits it is possible for reasons qua reasons to function in a way that is context-dependent, her view is not incompatible with holism about reasons. There is no reason the classical utilitarian cannot consistently grant this thesis. Indeed, the classical utilitarian could even admit that many nonmoral reasons are in fact heavily context-dependent.

## 2.2. Holism and Cosmic Accidents

Faced with the evident consistency of holism and the codifiability of morality, particularists have more recently turned to a different version of the argument from holism. According to the revised version of the argument, if holism were true then it would be a 'cosmic accident' if morality were codifiable. Margaret Little argues in this vein: "The claim is not that such generalities are impossible, but that we have reason not to expect any: any we might come across would be, as it were, philosophically serendipitous" (Little 2000: 277). Even opponents of particularism who reject holism, such as Philip Stratton-Lake, concede that holism implies that any codifiability would depend upon "world historical chance" (Stratton Lake 2000: 129). Call the thesis that any substantive moral principle would be a cosmic accident the *cosmic accident thesis*. Given the cosmic accident thesis, holism might at least provide a good argument for Anti-Transcendental Particularism. For, given the cosmic accident thesis, holism would cast grave doubt on the idea that we could derive the existence of moral principles from what arguably is the most fundamental normative concept, the concept of a reason for action.

However, the cosmic accident thesis is itself far from obvious. Even allowing that moral principles are not entailed by the very concept of a reason for action, whether there are cosmic accidents afoot simply depends on one's background conception of moral properties and holism is neutral between many of these. So while there are indeed important and familiar worries in this neighborhood, holism about reasons is orthogonal to them.

Consider the different conceptions one might have of moral properties. Here we can leave aside those who deny that there are moral properties, among them nihilists, error theorists, and some noncognitivists. For those who agree that there are moral properties there are two main views one might hold about their relation to natural properties: (*a*) moral properties are reducible to natural properties (naturalism) or (*b*) moral properties are irreducible to natural properties (non-naturalism).[8] Perhaps the thought is that holism plus naturalism supports the cosmic accident thesis, but this inference is a non sequitur. Certainly naturalism itself provides no support for the cosmic accident thesis. Given the identity of moral properties with certain natural properties or the constitution of moral properties by natural properties (at the level of properties understood as types not tokens), the codifiability of the moral in terms of the natural is no mystery.[9]

Further, naturalism is compatible with holism. For a naturalist might maintain that for a fact to be a reason just *is* for it to be a natural fact of a certain kind *in a certain (naturalistically specified) context*. For example, so-called response-dependent forms of naturalism can be interpreted in a way that presupposes

---

[8] There are of course many ways of drawing the natural/non-natural distinction but this is not the place for a discussion of those nuances. Any of a number of plausible ways of drawing the distinction will be compatible with the points made here. Nor do particularists in general seem opposed to the distinction, as they typically deploy it or something very much like it to state their view.

[9] Morality might still be uncodifiable in finite terms given naturalism if the relevant natural properties are sufficiently complex but holism does not itself entail or even indirectly support the supposition that the moral terrain is complex in this way.

holism about reasons. Consider a naturalist ideal adviser theory according to which F's being a reason for an agent A to $\phi$ in circumstances C just is F's being a fact in virtue of which A's fully informed self would want A to $\phi$ in C.[10] On this theory it is always some particular fact F that is a reason for an agent to $\phi$, but F itself is a reason only in virtue of facts about A's idealized self which are not according to the account on offer themselves reasons for A to $\phi$. My idealized self might want me to have wine because I would enjoy it, in which case the fact that I would enjoy it is a reason for me to have wine. However, the fact that I would enjoy it is a reason only because of certain further facts about the context in virtue of which my idealized self would prefer my having wine in these circumstances. In other circumstances the fact that I would enjoy wine might well not move my idealized self at all—if, say, the wine was poisoned or the building was burning down. This form of naturalism could allow that in such circumstances the very same consideration would be no reason at all to drink the wine. So this form of naturalism is holistic.

This example of a form of naturalism that presupposes holism about reasons is purely illustrative; our aim is not to defend naturalism let alone a particular variety of it. The point is that there will be no metaphysical mystery about the relation of the moral to the natural nor will there be any mystery about the codifiability of moral reasons in naturalistic terms. Given naturalism, moral properties just are certain natural properties, so there need be no mystery about codifiability. Since naturalism is compatible with holism, holism about reasons as such gives us no reason to accept the cosmic accident thesis.

It might be replied that, if holism about reasons were true then it would be a mystery if naturalism were true, and that therefore naturalism cannot dispel the mysteriousness of the codifiability of morality. However, the inference from holism to "naturalism's truth is mysterious" is itself a non sequitur. There are interesting and powerful objections to naturalism but holism about reasons does not figure in any of them. Furthermore, those who accept such an argument presumably must turn to naturalism's alternative and combine holism about reasons with a non-naturalist conception of moral properties.[11] In this case, there will indeed be a mystery as to

---

[10] This sort of account has a long history. For a recent defense of a view along these lines, see Smith 1994.

[11] They might instead opt for sophisticated form of noncognitivism like Simon Blackburn's so-called "quasi-realism" (see Blackburn 1993) but this would fit very poorly with the particularist's more general dialectical aims. Dancy, for example, argues that one of particularism's major advantages is its ability to combine realism with internalism in the theory of reasons; see Dancy 1993, previously cited. Furthermore, noncognitivism is in any event equally available to the opponent of particularism, so the advocate of codifiability can avoid metaphysical mysteries in this way just as easily as the particularist can.

why moral properties track natural properties but here the mystery stems entirely from non-naturalism. A familiar and important objection to non-naturalism is that it is unable to explain why the moral even supervenes on the natural (roughly, why there can be no moral difference without some natural difference).[12] For if moral properties really are in Hume's terms "distinct existences," and in no way reducible to natural properties, then it does seem like it would be a 'cosmic accident' if the moral supervened on the natural. Since the codification of morality in useful and finite terms presupposes supervenience,[13] non-naturalism therefore also suggests that the codifiability of morality in finite terms would be a cosmic accident. Non-naturalism does all the work in this argument for the cosmic accident thesis.

Indeed, it is in this respect rather ironic that particularists charge their opponents with being committed to cosmic accidents or metaphysical mysteries. For the metaethical commitment most amenable to particularism (and most often accepted, at least implicitly, by particularists themselves) is some form of non-naturalism. The particularist's worries about cosmic accidents therefore seem slightly odd, insofar as non-naturalism itself makes the supervenience of the moral on the natural into a metaphysically mysterious cosmic accident. The main point for present purposes, though, is that holism about reasons does nothing to support the thought that the finite and useful codification of morality would be metaphysically mysterious.

In sum, whether there is a metaphysical mystery about the relationship between moral properties and natural properties depends entirely on one's metaphysical conception of those properties. If moral properties are reducible to natural properties, then there is no obvious mystery as to the finite codifiability of the moral in terms of the natural. Moreover, naturalism is itself perfectly compatible with holism about reasons and explicitly holistic versions of naturalism do not seem to create any new metaphysical mysteries. Finally, non-naturalism does leave us with metaphysical mysteries about the relation of the moral to the natural but holism about reasons has nothing to do with that mystery either. For quite independently of holism, non-naturalism itself threatens to make the relationship between moral and natural properties mysterious.

---

[12] See e.g. Mackie 1977.

[13] If morality is codifiable in finite naturalistic terms, then that codification will express a set of necessary truths about the co-variation of the moral with the natural that will itself entail the supervenience of the moral on the nonmoral. If necessarily all and only good actions are N actions where 'N' stands for some set of naturalistic predicates, then it is obvious that there can be no difference in goodness between two cases without some naturalistic difference.

So far we have understood the cosmic accident argument as an argument for Principle Eliminativism, which is indeed sometimes how it is presented. However, the argument is sometimes offered in support of the more modest doctrine of Anti-Transcendental Particularism. Here it is worth taking a careful look at Jonathan Dancy's statement of the argument in *Ethics without Principles*:

I think the best way to put the particularist conclusion is that, given the holism of reasons, it would be a sort of cosmic accident if it were to turn out that a morality could be captured in a set of holistic contributory principles of the sort that is here suggested. Most importantly, of course, it would be a cosmic accident if *our* morality could be expressed in this way, but the same would apply to any workable moral scheme. It would be an accident because, given the holism of reasons, there is no discernible need for a complete set of reasons to be like this. If our (or any other) morality turned out to be that way, there could be no possible explanation of that fact. It would be pure serendipity. There is no need for things to be so, and therefore there is nothing for the moral principles to do. (Dancy 2004: 82)

How should we understand Dancy's version of the cosmic accident argument? First, it seems safe for present purposes to put the thorny issue of relativism to one side, since Dancy claims that the argument extends to "any workable moral scheme." Having done that, we should be clear about the intended conclusion of Dancy's argument. The distinctions drawn in Chapter 1 are helpful. In *Ethics without Principles*, Dancy concedes that holism is at least logically consistent with the sorts of context-sensitive principles discussed above (in Section 2.1). So he no longer holds, as he once did, that holism is strictly 'inconsistent' with the thesis that morality is in fact principled. So Dancy should no longer be understood as arguing for Principle Eliminativism. Instead Dancy's canonical statement of the version of particularism he now wants to defend is a form of Anti-Transcendental Particularism. Specifically, he characterizes his version of particularism as the thesis that "the possibility of moral thought and judgement does not depend on the provision of a suitable supply of moral principles" (Dancy 2004: 7). Moreover, Dancy indicates that he characterizes particularism in just this way in order to shore up the connection between holism and particularism:

It was because of this issue that I characterized particularism as I did above, as the claim that the possibility of moral thought and judgement (and in general, one might say, of moral distinctions) in no way depends on the provision of a suitable stock of moral principles. So characterized, it seems to me that particularism does follow from holism. What does not follow is the straight denial of the possibility of a moral principle. (Dancy 2004: 82)

How, though, is the thesis that moral thought and judgment in no way depends on the provision of a suitable stock of moral principles supposed to follow from holism? Perhaps the idea is that if atomism were true then there would clearly be a need (or needs) for moral principles, but that given holism this need vanishes. In order to be logically valid, the argument would need to be understood as an elimination argument. Hence, the argument would require the further premise that the only needs we might have for moral principles (in order to engage in moral thought and judgment) would be needs we would have in virtue of atomism about reasons. In Dancy's presentation of the argument this premiss is suppressed, but it does seem essential to its logical validity. Admittedly, this reconstruction of the argument will not strictly vindicate Dancy's claim that holism itself *entails* particularism even when we understand particularism in its Anti-Transcendentalist guise. However, the elimination argument from holism and the further premiss that atomism is the only plausible candidate source of a need for principles is interesting in its own right.

Dancy certainly seems right that atomism would provide a need for moral principles. If atomism were true, then whatever is a reason in one context must always be a reason in any context. In that case there will be an exceptionless generalization associated with each reason. For example, if the fact that an action would produce nonsadistic pleasure is sometimes a reason in its favor, then that fact plus atomism entails that that fact is always a reason in an action's favor. If reasons were sufficiently complex, then these principles might not be available to us simply because the antecedents would be too complex for human comprehension. This, however, would entail that our reasons for action would be forever beyond our ken and for present purposes we simply share the particularist's optimistic assumption that we can sometimes know our reasons for action. So atomism appears to entail the following need for moral principles: insofar as we can know our moral reasons for action, a moral principle corresponding to each moral reason for action must be available to us. So the first stage of Dancy's argument is sound; atomism does indeed entail one kind of need for moral principles of a certain sort.

However, the second stage of Dancy's argument, according to which the *only* plausible candidate need for moral principles stems from atomism, looks much less promising. First, even if holism is true, we may still need moral principles about reasons for epistemic purposes. Even if moral reasons are context-dependent, it might well be possible for us to track those reasons only if we had access to a moral principle which articulated exactly how those reasons vary from one context to the next. Indeed, we shall argue in Chapters 6 and 7 that knowledge about moral reasons for action does indeed presuppose the availability of a suitable stock of moral principles, and our argument is entirely consistent with holism about reasons.

Secondly, Dancy's argument cannot possibly do justice to the generalist tradition he means to oppose. A plausible elimination argument against generalism would need to survey those considerations which have actually led philosophers to embrace generalism and then show that these considerations do not really support generalism after all. The crucial point to bear in mind here is that the need associated with atomism about reasons is at most a need for moral principles *about reasons*. Atomism may entail that we could know our reasons only insofar as a moral principle corresponding to each reason is available to us. However, these principles will be of the form, 'The fact that an action would be F is always a reason to perform it.' Clearly, though, our more than two thousand-year-old tradition of generalist moral philosophy has been interested not only in principles about reasons, but also principles about what ought to be done, all things considered.

Indeed, as Dancy himself rightly notes, the generalist tradition sometimes seems so obsessed with the all things considered 'ought' that it either ignores entirely or arrives at a distorted understanding of reasons for action. Presumably, defenders of the principle of utility and the categorical imperative and other principles about the all-things-considered would insist that there is a need of some kind for their own cherished principles. Whatever that candidate need is supposed to be, it should be clear that it will not be a need which follows from or presupposes atomism about reasons. As we have seen, atomism about reasons itself entails only a need for principles about reasons, and does not entail any need whatsoever for principles about what ought to be done, all things considered. Nor should this be at all surprising. Atomism and holism are, after all, doctrines about what is (or is not) necessary for a consideration to count as a reason and as such are entirely silent on how those reasons might weigh against one another to determine what should be done, all things considered.

A fair and non-question-begging elimination argument for particularism must carefully consider all prima facie (roughly on the face of it) plausible motivations for generalism. Methodologically, one way to be sure all prima facie plausible motivations have been considered is to try to determine which motivations actually animated those reasonable philosophers with whom one disagrees. Instead, Dancy's elimination argument seems to begin and end with the assertion that apart from atomism there is "nothing for the moral principles to do" (Dancy 2004: 82). So we should be swayed by the argument from holism understood as an elimination argument only if we are convinced either that generalism has held sway over countless generations of moral philosophers only because of an uncritical and unfounded commitment to atomism or that whatever other considerations have made generalism seem attractive are not worthy of consideration. However, neither of these hypotheses has much to recommend itself as a non-question-begging and persuasive argument against generalism.

We have already seen that it is extremely unlikely that most historical proponents of generalism have been committed to generalism because of a prior commitment to atomism. Indeed, the particularists' own reasonable complaint that so many moral philosophers have developed theories which entirely ignore reasons for action suggests that the argument from holism does not explain what has driven their opponents to embrace generalism. At least some of the moral philosophers who have historically championed moral generalism have themselves accepted holism in one form or another. For example, Kant's discussion of the merely conditional value of everything other than a good will suggests that he was at least a holist about value. Nonetheless, Kant held that the commitment to the moral law (in the form of the categorical imperative) is constitutive of moral agency. It is hard to imagine a more robust form of generalism, and whatever drove Kant to this robust form of generalism, it seems unlikely to have been a commitment to atomism given his highly holistic remarks about the value of anything other than a good will being context-dependent (the key contextual feature being the presence of a good will). Kant's interesting view instead seems to have been that autonomy presupposes a commitment to moral principle. This motivation for generalism seems to have nothing to do with atomism, and indeed Kant himself seems to have been a holist about value.

We do not mean to endorse Kant's account. Rather, Kant's views simply serve here as an especially vivid illustration of the implausibility of Dancy's diagnosis of what might have led philosophers like Kant to find generalism so attractive. Our own positive argument (in Part II) shall be that moral knowledge presupposes the availability of moral principles. However, we do here want to suggest that Kant's view is sufficiently interesting that it cannot reasonably be dismissed out of hand by anyone who wants to do justice to the generalist tradition in moral philosophy. An elimination argument for particularism therefore must say something about such Kantian autonomy-based accounts of why moral judgment needs principles. This is just an illustration of a much more general point. Our main suggestion is that moral philosophy's two thousand-plus-year love affair with moral principles has little or nothing to do with a prior infatuation with atomism about reasons. Particularists who want to do justice to the philosophically interesting and important historical roots of generalism must dig deeper than the level of a putative prior commitment to atomism.

So atomism about reasons cannot explain why historical proponents of generalism have felt a need for principles about what should be done all things considered. Moreover, it is very hard to see how holism might figure in any further argument that we have no need for principles about the all things considered. The supposed dialectical point of holism here is, after all, supposed to be its provision of a debunking explanation of the allure of moral principles. Once we see that the rejection of holism (atomism) at most entails a need for principles about reasons for action and not about the all things considered ought, it should be clear that the debunking explanation on offer fails to work against generalists about the all things considered ought as well. The particularist can, of course, assert that we have no need for all things considered moral principles either. However, this would simply be an assertion of particularism rather than an argument for it.

So far we have seen two fatal flaws with Dancy's elimination argument from holism. First, it does not canvass all the plausible candidate needs for principles about reasons for action (autonomy and moral knowledge are left out, for example). So the argument is not effective even as an argument for particularism about reasons for action. Secondly, it does not canvass all of the plausible candidate needs for principles about the all things considered since atomism is not a prima facie plausible source of such a need in the first place. This second point sets the stage for a third. Until we have some plausible argument that there is no need for all things considered principles we cannot have any confidence that there is no need for principles about *pro tanto* reasons either. For if it were to turn out that we did have some need for all things considered principles then that need might simply carry directly over to principles about reasons for action as well. For example, if Kant was right that a plausible view of autonomy presupposes the availability of moral principles about the all things considered, then the same argument might work for principles about *pro tanto* moral reasons (though Kant himself had very little to say about the latter). Until we see what the genuinely plausible prima facie needs for principles about the all things considered ought really are, we have no way of knowing in advance whether those needs might not also ground principles about moral reasons for action.

To be clear, Dancy's elimination argument does sharpen the particularist challenge even if it does not provide any direct support for particularism. For the preceding dialectic does help make it clear that generalists should do more to explain why we need moral principles. Indeed, this challenge is in our view a pressing one, and the need to meet it on several fronts is what inspires the second half of the present book. As we put the point in Chapter 1, the particularist challenge should awaken generalists from their dogmatic slumbers. Moreover,

Dancy does suggest that the argument from holism is best understood as an 'indirect' one and that it presents "a challenge to the opposition to come up with a picture of moral thought which, though it respects the truth of reasons-holism, still *requires* (rather than merely makes possible) a provision of principles that cover the ground" (Dancy 2004: 82). The challenge is an excellent one. Our point here is simply that, contra Dancy, holism really does nothing whatsoever to suggest that the challenge cannot be met.[14]

We are now in position to conclude that holism in itself does not support the claim that the codification of morality would amount to a cosmic accident, much less that it is impossible. Again, this is most clear when we bear in mind that some possible codifications of morality actually *presuppose* holism about reasons. Nor does holism support the thesis that the codification of morality is unnecessary for moral thought and judgment, and so holism in itself does nothing to support Dancy's Anti-Transcendental version of particularism. So far as holism goes, we might still need to codify morality in order to figure out what reasons there are in a given case or what morality demands all things considered in such a case. Holism is simply orthogonal to the issue of whether we have such epistemic needs. Even more obviously, holism does not imply that codifying the moral landscape is undesirable. Indeed, so far as holism about reasons goes, the decision-making of virtuous moral agents could just be the subsumption of particular cases under appropriate generalizations. The principles must not entail atomism about reasons, but the preceding examples illustrate the possibility of such principles. Insofar as it might be useful to get a clear picture of the principles guiding the virtuous moral agent (perhaps to help the less virtuous internalize them), it might be very useful to codify morality. Once again, holism about reasons is simply beside the point.

## 2.3. Radical Holism and Begging the Question

So holism about reasons as usually characterized does not provide any support for particularism. However, particularists sometimes characterize holism about reasons as the much stronger thesis that whether a consideration counts as

---

[14] Actually, Dancy seems now to agree that *by itself* holism is not enough to provide sufficient support for his brand of particularism (though this is hard to square with his continued assertion that holism does entail particularism in the Anti-Transcendental sense). For he goes on to consider other reasons one might reasonably suppose we need moral principles, at least some of which have nothing to do with the debate over holism. For example, he considers and then rejects an argument from the need for moral principles to function as a system of social constraints to generalism (see Dancy 2004: 83 and section 7.5). We would simply add that these further candidate needs for moral principles raise all the important issues; holism ultimately is just a red herring in this debate.

a reason depends *in a way that transcends codification* on its context. Here is Little:

> Natural features do not always ground the same moral import ... the moral contribution they make on each occasion is holistically determined: it is *itself* dependent, in a way that escapes useful or finite articulation, on what other nonmoral features are present or absent. It isn't just that we haven't bothered to fill in the background considerations because they are so complex—holism is not complicated atomism. The claim, rather, is that there is no cashing out in finite or helpful propositional form the context on which the moral meaning depends. (Little 2000: 280)

Jackson, Pettit, and Smith briefly discuss this form of holism:

> What is true, though, is that patterned connections are incompatible with what we might call unrestricted holism about moral reasons. Unrestricted holism maintains that, no matter the quantity and nature of the descriptive information you have that provides a reason for some moral conclusion, say, that X is right, more may come to hand that leaves the previous information undisturbed and yet, when combined with it, provides a reason against X being right. (Jackson, Pettit, and Smith 2000: 99)

This radical (or 'unrestricted') holism about reasons really amounts to two distinct theses. The first thesis is holism about reasons in the sense already discussed—the thesis that the status of a consideration as a reason with a given valence depends on other features of its context, so that shifts in context can make a consideration which is a reason with one valence into no reason at all or a reason with the opposite valence in another context. The second thesis is that the context dependence of reasons cannot be specified in finite or helpful propositional form. Radical holism about reasons certainly does entail particularism, but this is simply because the second clause just *is* the statement of a strong form of particularism. For the second thesis simply states that whether a consideration counts as a reason cannot be codified in finite terms. So radical holism about reasons cannot figure in an argument for particularism without gratuitously begging the question. Furthermore, it is unhelpful to define holism about reasons in this way, since it renders important questions invisible by implicitly suggesting that these two theses are some sort of 'package deal,' and that anyone who accepts the context-dependence of reasons must also accept their uncodifiability. This limits the logical space prematurely and without argument. A sensible advocate of the codification of morality can accept the first of these two theses but reject the second.[15]

---

[15] To be fair, Little does not appeal to holism as a premise in an explicit argument for particularism but seems more interested in characterizing holism/particularism in a favorable light. To be fair to the other side, though, Little's discussion of holism is also couched as a reply to those who accuse particularists of "forgetting to provide any argument for their position" (Little 2000: 277).

It might be suggested that even if context-dependence and uncodifiability are not a 'package deal,' those who concede that reasons can be context-dependent should feel considerable pressure to accept radical holism about reasons. After all, once we begin to notice some of the specific ways in which reasons can be context-dependent, we may suspect that they are so many and so various as to escape codification. We return to these issues in Chapter 7. For now, we note only that whatever the force of this argument, it is one in which holism about reasons plays no essential role. The force of the argument, whatever it may be, lies in the extent to which examples that reveal the rich complexity of morality constitute evidence of uncodifiable complexity. That is, we have here a version of what we would call the argument from cases (sometimes called the "supersession argument;" see Holton 2002), and not, as particularists have claimed, an improved alternative to that argument. Moreover, whatever the force of the argument, holism about reasons is not essential to it. An atomist about reasons could just as well be impressed by the same diet of examples and conclude that moral reasons are not codifiable. Such an atomist will not, of course, see reasons as context dependent. Such an atomist will instead take such examples to suggest that reasons are so complicated and so numerous and heterogeneous that codifying them is impossible.

## 2.4. From Particularism to Holism?

Holism about reasons provides no positive support for particularism. Given how closely associated holism and particularism have been, it would be somewhat surprising if there were no interesting connections between them. Perhaps the support runs in the other direction; perhaps particularism provides support for holism. Suppose for the sake of argument that there is a good argument for particularism that does not invoke holism about reasons. In particular, suppose that a form of particularism according to which even *pro tanto* reasons transcend codification can be established on independent grounds. Having established such a form of particularism on independent grounds, one might argue for holism about reasons by *reductio*. Suppose for *reductio* that holism about reasons is false and hence that atomism about reasons is true. Atomism about reasons plus the thesis that reasons are uncodifiable seems incompatible with the idea that an ordinary and hence cognitively finite person could ever perform an action for a good reason. For this combination of views entails that good reasons are indefinitely complex and hence presumably beyond the ken of ordinary cognitively finite people. Since it is absurd to suppose that ordinary people could never act for good reasons simply in virtue of their finitude, our *reductio* is complete and we can conclude that holism about reasons is true. Perhaps particularists are right to think holism about reasons and particularism are intimately connected but have the direction of support backwards.

To be clear, this sort of argument would not provide positive support for particularism. For this argument takes particularism as a premiss and then mounts a *reductio* against atomism about reasons on the basis of that premiss. So this line of argument would at best provide an argument from particularism to holism about reasons, rather than the other way around. Since our concern here is the argument from holism about reasons to particularism, we need not take issue with the converse line of argument. However, the argument is worth noting in its own right. Moreover, if the argument is sound then there is perhaps a wider sense in which holism about reasons does support particularism, albeit a more indirect and modest support than has been claimed by particularism's defenders. For without holism about reasons the particularist apparently would be stuck with an atomist conception of reasons, but that constellation of views seems to have the absurd consequence that no finite agent could ever act for good reasons. So even if it provides no positive support for particularism, perhaps holism about reasons helps fend off the otherwise damning objection that particularism cannot explain how a cognitively finite agent could act for good reasons, and thereby provides some admittedly indirect dialectical dividends to the particularist after all.

Seen in another light, though, this reveals a dialectical liability of particularism in comparison with generalism. Granted, the truth of holism indirectly supports particularism by blocking an otherwise damning objection but this reveals an important respect in which particularism is subject to a line of objection to which generalists as such are immune. Generalists as such can be more flexible than particularists about holism about reasons; they can take it or leave it without thereby betraying their generalism, or so we have argued. Particularists, by contrast, seem forced to defend holism about reasons. So particularists are potentially vulnerable to criticism on a front which generalists as such can simply avoid by rejecting holism outright. Particularists no doubt are sufficiently convinced of holism about reasons as to be unfazed by this relative lack of dialectical flexibility. Nonetheless, for those who are less certain about the truth of holism, the somewhat ironic conclusion seems to be that, so far from providing positive support for particularism, holism instead reveals a dialectical liability for particularists which generalists can simply avoid.

## 2.5. Summary and Preview

Particularists have done a great service by highlighting the importance of holism about reasons, which is an interesting and previously neglected thesis. Particularism itself (in its many guises) is also an important position and its apparent intelligibility should awaken generalists from their dogmatic slumbers. Nonetheless, these two interesting positions are not related in the way particularists claim. Holism about reasons provides no positive support for particularism.[16] Holism neither implies that there are no principles nor that any principles there might be would be 'cosmic accidents.' Consequently, those antecedently inclined to reject particularism need not be moved from that position even if they accept holism about reasons. If there is a relation of positive support, it goes in the other direction; there seems to be an interesting argument from particularism to holism about reasons. If this argument is sound then holism about reasons may be essential for a plausible particularist account of how cognitively finite agents can act for good reasons. In this more modest role, holism about reasons seems to bolster particularism against an otherwise damning objection, but without providing it any direct support at all.

In the next chapter, we take up a difficulty that arises for particularists. If holism is true, and (further) if just about any consideration could count as a reason given a suitable context, then particularism must find some way to distinguish those considerations which normally and regularly do provide reasons of a certain valence (e.g. pain) from those that normally and regularly do not provide reasons (e.g. shoelace color). For absent some such distinction, particularism threatens to flatten the moral landscape by suggesting that insofar as they might provide reasons all considerations are on a par.

[16] Many thanks to Jonathan Dancy and an anonymous referee at *Ratio* for helpful comments on earlier versions of this material.

# 3

# Default Reasons

*... the exception that proves the rule.* What rubbish! There are no exceptions to rules or they would not be rules.

(Jacob Aagaard)

We have seen in Chapter 2 that while holism is not sufficient for particularism, holism may well be necessary for a plausible version of particularism. The combination of holism and particularism, in turn, suggests that an enormous range of considerations can be reasons for action. Here it is worth pausing to remember some of the more memorable examples offered by particularists. Here is Margaret Little:

Depending on which case the comparison is made to, any feature may assume moral significance, from shoelace colour to the day of the week: after all, against a rich enough story, there are cases in which the change from Tuesday to Wednesday makes all the difference. (Little 2000: 291)

Of course, there is a sense in which a hardy generalist can agree with Little's comments. For example, a hedonistic act-utilitarian can admit that shoelace color or the day of the week can assume moral significance if the context is right, since shoelace color or day of the week can sometimes influence the consequences of various actions. Insofar as shoelace color or day of the week can figure in, for example, the content of a promise, a Kantian can also admit that such features can assume moral significance. In order to distinguish particularism from these hardy generalist accounts of how such eccentric features can matter, Little presumably wants to insist that such seemingly eccentric features as shoelace color can in some sense have *direct* moral significance if the context is right.

In our view, the most plausible gloss on the idea of direct moral significance is that features with such significance can figure in the content of moral reasons for action. Jonathan Dancy goes so far as to insist that "we can give no sense to the idea that we might now have finished the list of moral principles or of properties that can make a difference sometimes ... there is no limit to the number of properties which can on occasion be important" (Dancy 1993: 67). Once again, we assume that Dancy does not intend this point in the anodyne sense in which a utilitarian or Kantian could accept it. Nor should it be surprising that particularists make such strong claims about what sorts of considerations can be moral reasons for action. For if the number of possible reasons were finite and manageable, then the idea that we might codify the moral landscape would look much more plausible.

One danger that has not been lost on particularists is that their extremely ecumenical view of moral reasons for action threatens implausibly to 'flatten the normative landscape.' After all, even if we think that in the right context that shoelace color can provide a reason for action (which, to be clear, we do not), there is an important difference between considerations of shoelace color and considerations of pain, pleasure, promising, and the like. Mark Lance and Margaret Little put the worry very clearly:

In unqualified form, moral holism of the sort just outlined seems to imply that lying, killing and the infliction of pain have no more intimate connection to wrongness than do truth-telling, healing and the giving of pleasure. After all, each, in the right context, can have a positive, negative or neutral moral import. But the morally wise person, one might have thought, is someone who understands that there is a deep difference in moral status between infliction of pain and shoelace color, even if both can, against the right narrative, be bad-making. (Lance and Little 2005: 20–1)

Particularists have tried to show how they can avoid any unfortunate flattening of the normative landscape by drawing a distinction between default reasons and non-default reasons. Roughly, the idea is to privilege certain considerations as default reasons, where the status of such considerations as a reason with a given valence does not stand in need of explanation. By contrast, non-default reasons are sometimes reasons but their status of reasons cannot be assumed and always stands in need of explanation. Drawing some such distinction does seem critical to making particularism plausible, and in this chapter we explore different ways of understanding the distinction between default reasons and non-default reasons. The distinction can be given a number of different readings, and in this chapter we argue that all but the most deflationary of these various readings is either implausible or insufficient to help the particularist avoid the flattening of the normative landscape. Our own view is that the best way to avoid worries about implausibly flattening the normative landscape is to reject the particularist's extremely ecumenical conception of reasons for action and more generally of what kinds of features can assume direct moral significance, and we argue for this view in Chapter 7.

## 3.1. The Explanatory Conception

To convey an intuitive feel for the distinction between default reasons and non-default reasons, we can do no better than to quote Dancy's own admittedly metaphorical initial way of putting it. Some reasons, Dancy claims, "arrive switched on, though they may be switched off if the circumstances so conspire, while others arrive switched off but are switched on by appropriate contexts" (Dancy 2004: 113).[1] A 'default reason,' then, is a consideration whose reason giving force has a default setting. Pain, for example, might be in this sense a default reason. It 'arrives' as a reason against performing an action that would promote it, but (in the spirit of holism) can be switched off by context.

Though intuitive, the language of arriving and switching suggests that some considerations have the force of reasons independently of context. This suggestion is at odds with at least some particularists who emphasize that considerations can have reason giving force only in a surrounding context.[2] Fortunately, the familiar particularist tools of defeaters and enablers can help unpack the metaphor. A default reason is a consideration whose status as a reason does not stand in need of explanation by some further feature of the situation—it does not require an enabler. Non-default reasons do stand in need of such explanation and require an enabler.[3] Since default reasons are on this account defined in terms of the need for explanation, we call this conception of default readings 'the explanatory conception.' One interesting corollary is that one and the same consideration could be a default reason with respect to one valence and a non-default reason with respect to the opposite valence. The example of pain is a good illustration if we agree that the fact that an action would cause pain is sometimes a reason in its favor. When the fact that an action causes pain is a reason against the action, it is plausibly a default

[1] Making the same distinction in the theory of value, Dancy remarks that "some features come switched on already, as it were, though they can be switched off by other features; others do not come switched on, but they can be switched on by a suitable context" (Dancy 2003: 638).

[2] Little (2000) emphasizes this point and understands it as one of the central lessons of holism. To think that a consideration could have a reason giving force antecedent to its position in a surrounding context is, she claims, to subscribe to a dubious 'ideal model' of moral reasons.

[3] Cullity (2002) marks the distinction in a similar way. What he calls "presumptive reasons" are "pro tanto reasons unless undermined." Though Cullity does not explicitly define non-presumptive reasons, one might think that they are considerations that must first be 'enabled.'

reason, for the idea that pain counts against an action stands in no obvious need of explanation. By contrast, when an action causing pain is a reason in favor of the action its having this valence will require some enabler, such as that the pain is constitutive of athletic achievement.[4]

Dancy explicitly understands the distinction between default and non-default reasons as a metaphysical one. The idea is not simply that some considerations usually do have a particular reason giving force or that we should expect or presume them to have a given status as reasons. Instead, the distinction concerns the considerations themselves. Pain is a reason against (when it is) just because of the nature of pain. To see things this way, then, is not just to know the contingent fact that the fact that an action would cause pain is a reason against the action, but rather to know something about pain. By contrast, when the fact that an action would cause pain is a reason in favor of the action there must be an enabler which explains why this is so. This way of drawing the distinction is extremely natural for a particularist, as it builds heavily on the machinery of enablers and defeaters familiar from discussions of holism. Moreover, this approach seems to avoid flattening the normative landscape in a fairly robust way, as the distinction between default reasons and non-default reasons on this interpretation is meant to be metaphysically deep and not contingent on local circumstances.

However, the metaphysical reading of the distinction between default reasons and non-default reasons is untenable. For on any plausible version of holism *all* reasons require enablers, in which case *all* reasons are non-default reasons in this sense. Why do we say all reasons require enablers? Here we invoke the plausible idea that certain considerations need always to be present for any consideration to count as a reason but are not themselves part of the reasons which they make possible. The best example of this is that no fact can be a reason for an agent to perform an action if the agent cannot perform the action. Nonetheless, as particularists have plausibly insisted, the fact that an agent could do something is not part of the reason to do it. The reason to meet me for lunch is that you promised, not that you promised and can. If the fact that an agent could perform an action is not a reason or a part of a reason, though, then what is it? The tempting answer is to say it is an enabler for all possible reasons, and indeed we think that this answer is correct. So all reasons need at least one enabler, in which case there can be no default reasons in Dancy's canonical sense and the distinction lacks interest.

---

[4] The example is from Mark Lance and Margaret Little; see Lance and Little 2005.

The preceding objection demonstrates the untenability of Dancy's canonical formulation of the distinction between default reasons and non-default reasons. However, a very close cousin of Dancy's formulation can survive this first objection. For we can and should distinguish what might be called *global enablers* from *local enablers* and redraw the explanatory version of the distinction between default reasons and non-default reasons in terms of local enablers rather than global enablers.[5] A global enabler is a consideration which must obtain before there can be any reason for an agent to perform an action. That the agent can perform the action is a clear example of a global enabler. More controversially, perhaps there can be a reason for someone to do something only if the agent can refrain from doing it as well. The idea would be that reasons function to guide our actions but guidance is possible only when an agent has some choice between alternatives. If an agent cannot help but perform an action, then talk of guidance and reasons is simply out of place.[6] Though just which considerations are global enablers will be a controversial question (and one we will not try to settle), the idea of a global enabler is tied to the general idea of a reason for action. By contrast, some enablers (most of the ones particularists discuss) are local, having to do with specific kinds of reasons rather than with the very idea of a reason for acting as such. For example, suppose that while the fact that an action will involve pain normally is a reason against it, if the pain is constitutive of athletic accomplishment then that very same consideration can be a reason in favor of the action.[7] In that case, the fact that a given pain would be constitutive of athletic accomplishment can function as a local enabler.

This distinction between global and local enablers shows the way to a more subtle distinction between default reasons and non-default reasons which is very much in the spirit of Dancy's canonical version of the distinction but which avoids the objection from global enablers. We might give the idea of a default reason the following intuitive gloss: a default reason is a fact which does not depend for its status as a reason on any further facts beyond those required by the very concept of a reason for acting. The existence of 'global enablers' then poses no threat to the proffered distinction. For a default reason is on this account not a fact which stands in need of no enablers whatsoever to function as a reason, but rather is a fact which requires no local enablers to function as a reason.

---

[5] Dancy prefers the terminology of 'generic' and 'specific.'

[6] Kant makes a similar point in the *Groundwork* when he claims that imperatives apply only to "imperfect wills," wills capable of being determined by rational norms, but also subject to competing motivations (K 413–14).

[7] The example is borrowed from Margaret Little and Mark Lance. See Lance and Little 2005.

However, even on this more refined understanding the explanatory conception of the distinction between default reasons and non-default reasons ultimately collapses. The tenability of the distinction depends on the tenability of the distinction between the presence of an enabler and the absence of a defeater. However, this distinction itself is untenable. Suppose that we agree that the fact that an action will promote pleasure is sometimes a reason but also maintain that its status as a reason depends (in part) on whether the pleasure would be sadistic. We can then describe our view in one of two ways. On the one hand, we could maintain that the fact that the pleasure promoted would be sadistic (when this is a fact) is a defeater, preventing the fact that the action would promote pleasure from functioning as a reason in favor of that action. Alternatively, we could maintain that the fact that the action is sadistic merely serves to indicate the absence of an enabling condition, understanding the fact that the pleasure promoted is nonsadistic as an enabler which must be present for the fact that an action would promote pleasure to function as a reason. If we characterize the presence of sadism as a defeater, then we are still free to characterize the fact that an action would promote pleasure as a default reason which needs no enablers. If instead we characterize the presence of sadism as the absence of an enabler, then we no longer can say that the fact about pleasure is a default reason in the intended sense. This naturally leads to a series of questions. How do we determine which of these descriptions (needs an enabler vs. needs the absence of a defeater) is correct? This epistemological question is difficult enough, but even more difficult questions concern the logical independence of enablers and defeaters. Is there any reason in our example to think that both descriptions of our view (the one couched in terms of nonsadism as an enabler and the one couched in terms of sadism as a defeater) could not be correct? Indeed, is there any reason to suppose that claims about enablers and claims about defeaters are not really just notational variants on one another?

In our view, the answer to this last question is 'no' and this spells the end for the explanatory conception. If a consideration needs an enabler in order to function as a reason, then trivially that consideration can be defeated; the absence of the enabler is a defeater. Similarly, if a consideration's status as a reason can be defeated, then the consideration needs an enabler; the conjunction of the negation of all of its possible defeaters is an enabler.[8] Lest this seem too swift, note that enablers and defeaters are typically defined in

---

[8] One reply here is to insist that there are infinitely many defeaters for each reason, in which case it is not clear that there is any such thing as the conjunction of the negation of all of a given reason's possible defeaters. Whether it is plausible to suppose that there are infinitely many defeaters for some or all reasons is a question we take up carefully in Part II and answer in the negative. For now, though,

counterfactual terms. Here is Dancy: "in the absence of (2), (1) would not have favoured the action. In this sense, the presence of (2) *enables* (1) to favour (5)" (Dancy 2004: 39). Certainly if we understand enablers and defeaters in counterfactual terms then the fact that a consideration needs an enabler entails that it can be defeated and vice versa. Moreover, Dancy himself goes on explicitly to endorse this necessary connection: "trivially, the absence of an enabler will disable what would otherwise be a reason" (Dancy 2004: 41). Though Dancy here endorses only the inference from 'needs an enabler' to 'can be defeated,' there is no textual or rational reason (given his counterfactual definition) to suppose that he would deny the inference in the other direction.

Perhaps a purely counterfactual conception of defeaters and enablers is too crude. We might instead hold that for a consideration E to be an enabler of a fact F as a reason to x in circumstances C is for E to be a possible feature of C such that E's presence would *explain* why F is a reason to x. This refinement of the conception of enablers and defeaters does not help, though. For being an enabler means that E is a member of a set of possible features of C (E might or might not be the only member of the set) such that the absence of *all* of the features in that set would *defeat* F's status as a reason to x in C. Moreover, the absence of all of a candidate reason's enablers also would *explain* why the candidate is not really a reason. Someone puzzled about why a given consideration was not a reason in a given case could find it illuminating that none of the various further facts which would explain its functioning as a reason is present. Of course, these further facts may be too numerous to list, but we could still perhaps give our interlocutor an idea of the kinds of considerations which would have to be present for the fact to function as a reason by listing representative examples and then explaining that no such feature is present. On this way of thinking, to say something is an enabler in a given context entails that it is a member of a set of possible features, such that the absence of all of the features in that set is a defeater. So once again the fact

two points are worth making. First, it is far from obvious that there are infinitely many defeater types for a given reason. So far as we know, particularists have not given an argument for this claim and accepting Dancy's version of particularism does not appear to commit one to it. It would be enough for Anti-Transcendental Particularism if there were too many defeaters for manageable codification by creatures like us, or rather, that moral thought and judgment do not depend on there being few enough to make codification of them by creatures like us possible. The second point is that, even if there were infinitely many defeaters for a given reason, there might still be an infinite conjunction of them. Here it is important to remember that we are doing metaphysics, so the fact that such a conjunction would not be one we could grasp is beside the point. It would, in any event, be giving serious hostages to fortune to let one's reply to the 'flattening the normative landscape' objection rely on the somewhat obscure debate in metaphysics over whether there are infinitely long conjunctions (or infinitely long conjunctive facts if we prefer to cast things in this way). Thanks to Mark Lance and Margaret Little for pressing us on this point.

that a consideration needs an enabler entails that it can be defeated. Similarly, to say a consideration D is a defeater of a fact F as a reason to perform a given action is to say that its presence can explain why the feature is not a reason. This seems to entail that D is a member of a set of possible features such that the absence of all of those features *enables* F to be a reason to perform the action. For if a consideration is a reason in favor of a given sort of action unless defeated then the absence of all defeaters will explain why that consideration functions as a reason. So the fact that a consideration stands in need of an enabler entails that it can be defeated and vice versa.

The preceding line of argument is fairly abstract, but the basic point is actually quite simple. An example should help get the idea across. Suppose for the sake of argument that the status of the consideration 'it would cause pain' as a reason against an action has exactly two defeaters: (*a*) the pain is constitutive of some excellence and (*b*) the pain is constitutive of a deserved punishment. The fact that considerations of pain have these defeaters also entails that such considerations stand in need of an enabler. The enabler is the conjunctive fact the pain is not constitutive of excellence and is not deserved. For the fact that a given pain is neither constitutive of excellence nor deserved can explain why the fact that an action causes pain should function as a reason not to perform the action. Someone who was perplexed at the idea that such a fact might function as a reason could gain understanding if told that the pain is neither constitutive of excellence nor deserved. For the person might have implicitly been assuming one of those conditions was not satisfied. A full theory of explanation goes well beyond the present scope. However, we take it that on any plausible account to figure in an explanation is to track dependence relations in ways that can remove puzzlement about that which is explained. Note that explanation is a metaphysical notion on this reading, albeit a metaphysical notion which must meet certain epistemic constraints (being capable of removing puzzlement). On the toy theory under consideration, the fact that the pain is neither constitutive of excellence nor deserved does track a dependence relation. Moreover, citing those facts can thereby remove puzzlement and answer the relevant 'why?' questions. This does not mean that the fact that the pain is not constitutive of an excellence nor deserved *fully* explains why the fact that an action promotes pain functions as a reason when it does; they may provide only a partial explanation or be at best part of an explanation (these may not be the same). Since presence of the pain in question is neither constitutive of excellence nor deserved and since this fact can at least partially explain why the fact that an action would produce such pain is a reason not to perform the action, it follows that the fact that the pain is neither constitutive of excellence nor deserved is an enabler. Of course, a particularist may insist that there will be far more possible defeaters for a candidate reason than two, and our example is in this sense just a toy example; the example was given only to illustrate the basic point in a simplified context. The fact (if it is a fact) that any plausible example will involve far more possible defeaters does not gainsay our basic point. That would instead just mean that the enabler in question will be the fact corresponding to a much longer list of possible defeaters.

So far we have used our example to show how the fact that a consideration's status as a reason can be defeated entails that the consideration needs an enabler in order to function as a reason. The example also illustrates how the fact that a consideration needs an enabler entails that it can be defeated. In our example the fact corresponding to the negation of (a)—that the pain is constitutive of an excellence—can explain why the fact that the action produces pain is *not* a reason not to perform the action. Since a defeater just is a fact that can explain why a fact that would otherwise be a reason with a given valence does not function as such a reason, this means that the fact corresponding to the negation of (a) is a defeater. The same point applies, *mutatis mutandis*, to the fact corresponding to the negation of (b). So the claim that a given fact functions as an enabler in the case at hand will entail that certain other facts would function as defeaters in the case at hand. The defeater(s) corresponding to the enabler present in a given case will be the facts corresponding to the negation of each of the conjuncts of the conjunction corresponding to the conjunctive enabler. In the limiting case in which the enabler is not best understood as corresponding to a conjunction, we should say that the fact corresponding to the negation of the enabler is a defeater. The main point here is that when a fact's functioning as a reason with a given valence depends on the presence of certain facts, the absence of any one of those facts functions as a defeater and the fact corresponding to the conjunction of those facts functions as an enabler.

So any reason which can be defeated also trivially needs an enabler and vice versa. In that case, though, the distinction between default reasons and other reasons collapses into the distinction between invariable reasons and context-sensitive reasons. For the idea was supposed to be that default reasons are considerations whose status as reasons does not stand in need of explanation *in the sense that they need no enablers*. Given the preceding line of argument, the only reasons which truly need no (local) enablers whatsoever will be reasons which cannot be defeated, and those just are the invariable reasons. In that case, the distinction between default reasons and non-default reasons collapses into the distinction between variable reasons and invariable reasons. So we do not need a further distinction here; we have already marked the distinction between variable and invariable reasons more clearly in terms of variability.

More to the point, the collapse of the distinction means that the idea of default reasons (so understood) will not do the kind of work that particularists needed that distinction to do. For the distinction was supposed to mark an important divide *within* the category of context-sensitive reasons, and not to distinguish the variable from the invariable ones. Hence, drawn in this way the distinction cannot forestall the worry that particularism implausibly flattens the normative landscape. However, the distinction between default reasons and non-default reasons can be drawn in other ways.

## 3.2. The Autonomous Conception

In light of the sorts of worries pressed in the preceding section, Dancy has revised his view. He now rejects what we have called the Explanatory Conception and instead endorses what we shall call the 'Autonomous Conception.' On this account, we should not try to understand the distinction between default reasons and non-default reasons entirely in terms of the distinction between enablers and defeaters. Instead, Dancy argues, we should understand the distinction between default reasons and non-default reasons in terms of a distinction between positive and negative dependence. In "Defending the Right" Dancy illustrates this idea with a series of examples which we name and, with one slight modification, paraphrase as follows:

Bicycle: I can bicycle from home to campus in fifteen minutes if there isn't a strong headwind (the absence of the headwind does not produce any of the power required). I can bicycle from home to campus in ten minutes with a strong following wind (the wind helps; it produces part of the power required).

Stile: I can get over the stile if you don't get in my way, hinder me. He can't get over the stile without your help.

Advisee: I can write a good thesis all on my own, so long as you do not stop me. He can write a good thesis too, but only with help from his adviser. The latter case can slide imperceptibly into co-authorship.

Knowledge: My knowledge that all equiangular triangles are equilateral is not positively dependent on anything empirical; it does not need any empirical grounds. However, this knowledge is (on a Quinean view) negatively dependent on empirical considerations; I could be forced to revise this belief if confronted with empirical evidence of an equiangular triangle that was not actually equilateral.

In addition to naming these illustrative examples, we have also embellished the one we have called 'Knowledge' with a concrete example (of geometrical knowledge) where Dancy simply spoke of knowledge in the abstract. With that caveat noted, these examples are all either discussed or suggested in Dancy (forthcoming). Each of these examples is meant to remind us of our familiarity with the distinction between positive and negative dependence. In Bicycle, I am positively dependent on a strong following wind in order to bicycle from home to campus in ten minutes while I am only negatively dependent on the absence of a strong headwind in order to bicycle from home to campus in fifteen minutes. In Stile, I am negatively dependent on your not hindering me from getting over the stile whereas he is positively dependent on your help to get over it. In Advisee, I am negatively dependent on your not stopping me, whereas you are positively dependent on help from your adviser. In Knowledge, my knowledge that all equiangular triangles are equilateral is negatively but not positively dependent on experience. In discussing the last sort of case, Dancy alludes to Marcus Giaquinto's account of the distinction between positive and negative dependence in epistemology (we return to this point in a rather different context in Chapter 7).

With a distinction between positive dependence and negative dependence in hand, Dancy suggests that a default reason is one which 'needs no help' in order to be a reason with a given valence, but whose status as a reason with that valence can nonetheless be defeated; whereas a non-default reason does need help in order to be a reason with a given valence. It should by now be clear why we have called this version of the distinction between default reasons and non-default reasons the 'Autonomous Conception.' Default reasons do not need help from anything external in order to be reasons with a given valence and in this sense are autonomous qua reasons with that valence; whereas non-default reasons are dependent on something external and in this respect are not autonomous.

Crucially, Dancy now emphasizes the distinction between two distinctions: (a) the distinction between enablers and defeaters, and (b) the distinction between needing help and not needing help. Something can need enablers and the absence of defeaters and still not need help in order to be a reason with a given valence. This approach does seem like an improvement on Dancy's original account. For the idea of needing help does not seem open to the objection we raised against the explanatory account, as Dancy's illustrative examples make clear; whereas if something needs an enabler it must also need the absence of a defeater, it does not follow from the fact that something needs an enabler/absence of a defeater that it needs help. Needing a suitable sort of non-interference (e.g. a strong headwind) is a way of needing an enabler/absence of a defeater but is not a way of needing help. Moreover, the distinction is not a merely epistemic or pragmatic one, and seems to fit with Dancy's aim of providing a deeply metaphysical conception of the distinction between default reasons and non-default reasons.

We mention one technical problem with the Autonomous Conception only to put it to one side, as we do not attach great weight to it. At one point Dancy quite rightly allows that a consideration might be both a reason and an enabler for itself, as in cases in which the mere ability to act is a reason: "Walter Sinnott-Armstrong suggested to me that, in a case where the mere ability to act is a reason it is also an enabler for itself. I see no reason to deny this amusing possibility" (Dancy 2004: 40 n. 1). This seems right to us, but if this is right then we see no reason in principle why a consideration could not also be its own helper (in the sense of 'helper' relevant to Dancy's account). After all, the idea of helping oneself is familiar enough; we are often told that God helps those who help themselves. Why then should it be impossible for a reason to instantiate this structure? That is, if one and the same consideration can both be a reason and enable itself to be a reason (as in the Sinnott-Armstrong example), then why could it not also be that one and the same reason could both be a reason and help itself to be a reason? If there were any reasons like this, then it would be unclear on Dancy's account whether we should say they are default reasons.

Technically, such reasons do indeed need help in order to be reasons with a given valence, but for all we have said so far they could need no help beyond the help they provide themselves. This seems to force us to say that such considerations are *not* default reasons. However, let us also suppose that the status of such considerations as self-helpers is not subject to possible defeat, and that such considerations need only their own help in order to be reasons. Again, we see no reason for supposing that this could not be the case. In this case, though, such a considerations seem to come 'switched on,' albeit 'switched on' by themselves. So Dancy's earlier metaphorical gloss on defaults in terms of coming already 'switched on' seems to counsel in favor of saying such self-helping reasons are default reasons after all. Dancy could try to avoid these difficulties by redefining defaults as needing no *external* help, but in addition to being rather ad hoc this may generate new problems. For now take a consideration which can be its own helper but which needs an enabler to function as a helper where the relevant enabler is a distinct consideration. Intuitively we may well want to say that such a reason is not a default reason since it does need a helper and in some circumstances the relevant sort of help will not be forthcoming (as when the consideration is not enabled qua self-helper). However, if being a default is defined in terms of needing external help we will not be able to say this. In any event, we shall not put great weight on this particular objection simply because we have not yet been able to generate a clear example of a self-helping reason of the right sort. Nonetheless, the defender of the Autonomous Conception does, we think, owe either some account of why such self-helping reasons are impossible or some principled way of classifying them in one way rather than another.

Putting this technical worry to one side, what should we make of the Autonomous Conception? In our view, it faces the following dilemma. Either the appeal to the idea of 'needing help' is metaphorical or it is literal. If the appeal is metaphorical then it is fine as far as it goes, but it does not pin down the theory enough to know whether it really makes sense or indeed whether it is distinct from the fairly deflationist proposal we shall make in the final section of this chapter. Understood as a metaphor, the theory is simply too indeterminate even to understand adequately, much less assess for plausibility. On the other hand, perhaps the appeal to the idea of 'needing help' should be taken literally. On this reading, examples like Bicycle and Stile are not simply suggestive analogies, but species of the larger genus of the category of 'needing help.' The idea must be that this presumably more abstract category is broad enough to make good sense of the idea of a default reason while also figuring literally in claims about climbing over stiles and bicycling without a suitable wind and the like. Dancy seems to favor this literal interpretation and in the remainder of this section we explore some problems for this interpretation of the Autonomous Conception of default reasons.

Given a literal interpretation of the Autonomous Conception, we should pause over the literal meaning of 'help' which is most germane here. The most suitable definitions are typically cast in terms of 'assistance' and leave the basic concept unreduced. However, some sources do try to provide some further illumination of the concept. For example, the Cambridge *Advanced Learner's Dictionary* defines 'help' as "to make it possible or easier for someone to do something, by doing part of the work yourself or by providing advice, money, support, etc." (http://dictionary.cambridge.org/define.asp?key=36652&dict=CALD). If this definition gives the right analysis of helping in the relevant sense, then some of Dancy's examples must themselves be taken metaphorically. For on this definition, helping is always a relation between persons—*I* help *you* by doing some of the relevant work for you, providing advice, etc., etc. So we cannot literally speak of a suitable wind helping a bicyclist, however apt this metaphor may be. Impersonal entities and forces like winds can of course do something similar in important ways to helping by making it easier for the person in question to perform the task at hand. We should perhaps not underestimate how rife ordinary language is with metaphor, and metaphorical uses of 'help' may be commonplace, after all. Even if we extend the literal meaning of helping to cover cases like Bicycle, though, the analysis may still essentially require that *one* of the relata of the 'helps' relation is a person (the wind helps *me* bike home faster, after all). If this is right then the notion of 'helping' cannot do the work Dancy wants it to do for at least two reasons. First, the notion is one which in any literal sense holds only when that which is helped is a person, but Dancy needs the helping relation to be one which can literally hold between considerations or facts. Secondly, the notion of helping seems to be a causal one, cast in terms of X bringing it about that Y is easier in some suitable sense of 'easier.' However, Dancy's notion of 'helping' presumably is not a causal one. Suppose that the fact that the pain would be constitutive of athletic accomplishment would in the intended sense 'help' make the fact that running the race would be painful into a reason to run it. Surely this supposition should not be understood as a claim about the causal impact of the one fact on the other.

These two objections put pressure on Dancy's account but are nothing like decisive objections. For there are other cases in ordinary language in which the idea of helping is invoked but in which the idea is clearly neither causal nor interpersonal. An art critic, for example, might hold that a dab of green paint helps make the painting beautiful where the relevant notion of helping holds between non-persons (a dab of paint and painting) and also seems noncausal. Once again, we could and arguably should take this claim as metaphor rather than literal truth, but let us suppose that we should take such claims at face value. The idea might not so much be that the green dab of paint causes the painting to be beautiful as it is that the dab of paint partially constitutes its beauty. If we insist on preserving the idea that helping is a causal relation then we can here invoke the idea of a constitutive cause. For example, we could say that the molecular structure of the vase is a constitutive cause of its fragility. We think such uses of 'cause' are strained as far as ordinary language goes, but perhaps fine for a suitable theoretical purpose.

However, if this is the best we can do to extend the idea of 'helping,' then it seems unlikely to do the needed theoretical work for the particularist. For now it looks as if the idea of helping is either a causal notion (in an ordinary sense of causal) or a constitutive notion (regardless of whether we cast this in terms of constitutive causes). The crucial point is that neither of these ideas look likely to do the work Dancy needs. We have already seen why the former is problematic, but what about the seemingly more promising constitutive application of the concept of helping? Here the trouble is that the intuitions which motivate holism in the first place suggest that when one fact 'helps' another fact be a reason that this need not be because the former (partially) constitutes the latter. This may happen in special cases (see our discussion of a 'riff' on the Sinnott-Armstrong example above) but it should certainly not be part of the very definition of a helper in this context. For to build helpers into the reasons which they help is just the knee-jerk atomistic instinct which leads some generalists to insist that whatever is necessary for a fact to be a reason is actually part of the reason itself. So the defender of the Autonomous Conception should resist this route as well.

At this point, we find ourselves unable to see how the particularist can make further progress in explaining how the concept of helping (as we ordinarily understand it) can be useful in these contexts. So on pain of falling back on to mere metaphors to motivate the view, we need either some further discussion of our pretheoretical notion of helping to show how it can do the needed work or some theoretically motivated definition of the relevant sense of helping. Although we cannot demonstrably prove it, our hunch is that neither of these strategies is likely to bear much fruit. We therefore tentatively conclude that the Autonomous Conception cannot really plausibly get beyond being most charitably read as a set of very suggestive metaphors as opposed to a coherent conception of what a default reason is. Since those metaphors highly underdetermine what the best theory of the literal truth about defaults is (and, indeed, these metaphors might even be apt given our own account as developed in Section 3.4 below), we conclude that the Autonomous Conception is not likely to help (no pun intended) the particularist.

## 3.3. Defeasible Generalizations

In order to avoid the flattening of the normative landscape, the particularist needs some way to privilege considerations like those to do with the prevention of pain and the keeping of promises from more esoteric considerations which can be reasons in the right circumstances. So far we have considered attempts to make sense of this privileging in terms of what 'stands in need of explanation' and in terms of what 'needs help' to be a reason, but upon examination neither of these proposals seems to be very promising. How might we proceed from here?

One is tempted to say that the fact that an action would cause pain is *essentially* a reason against it, while shoelace color is not.[9] However, the particularist must not say precisely this, for to do so is to restrict the holism of reasons to fairly esoteric sorts of reasons like those to do with shoelace color, whereas particularists want to say that even fairly central and paradigmatic reasons, like those to do with pain, are context-sensitive. What we need, then, is a distinction within the class of variable reasons. One possibility is that we might turn to the properties of the conditions under which some kind of consideration is a reason of a certain valence. In a fascinating series of papers, Mark Lance and Margaret Little, by developing just such an account, try to supply particularism with the resources to avoid flattening the moral landscape. In this section we briefly outline the main contours of their approach and explain what seems right about it to us. We then explain why the account is unlikely to be sufficient to block the worry that particularism flattens the normative landscape.

Lance and Little draw our attention to generalizations which seem to do a lot of explanatory work but which do not hold without exception. One of their many memorable examples is the generalization that "fish eggs develop into fish." This generalization obviously does not hold without exception. Slightly less obviously, the generalization does not even hold 'for the most part' in any statistical sense. Most fish eggs end up not turning into fish. Still, the idea that fish eggs develop into fish seems to be a theoretically important generalization. Someone who did not understand that, at least in the right kinds of conditions, fish eggs develop into fish would not really understand the nature of fish eggs. Moreover, when fish eggs do not develop into fish we explain this in terms of deviations from the sorts of circumstances in which they do. In both respects, the conditions under which fish eggs develop into fish enjoy a kind of 'privilege.' By contrast, the generalization "fish eggs spin clockwise" is not (we suspect) associated with privileged conditions. Like the generalization that fish eggs develop into fish, it picks out something variable. Sometimes fish eggs spin clockwise; sometimes they do not. But there is nothing (we suspect) very significant about the conditions under which the generalization holds.

Given this start, we can define a notion of a defeasible generalization as an exception-laden generalization that holds under privileged conditions. What is it for conditions to be privileged relative to a given domain? The suggestion

---

[9]  The example of shoelace color is taken from Little 2000. Lance and Little no longer endorse this particular example (private conversation). In the text we in effect use it as a stand-in for whatever those with particularist sympathies take as their favorite esoteric reason for action.

seems to be that for any x, conditions C are privileged relative to x just in case C either (*a*) is particularly revealing of x's nature or (*b*) is particularly revealing of the broader part of reality in which x is known. To express defeasible generalizations, Lance and Little invoke an operator P which means 'in privileged conditions.' So the defeasible generalization that fish eggs develop into fish may be expressed as:

(P) (Fish eggs develop into fish).

Lance and Little call these generalizations 'defeasible' to remind us that what happens in privileged conditions need not happen in any given actual case. This all looks to be just what particularism is in need of, a distinction within the class of variable reasons.

Lance and Little discuss four main kinds of privileging moves. First, there is what they refer to as the privileging of a paradigm over a 'riff' on that paradigm. In the paradigmatic case, soccer is played with eleven players per side, but there are numerous permissible riffs on this paradigm. Sometimes, a riff is simply similar enough in the relevant ways to the paradigm to count as an instance of the same kind. Soccer is a good example. Another example from Lance and Little is found in the contrast between an ordinary chair and an ornamental chair. "Chairs are for sitting on" is a defeasible generalization in their sense, but an ornamental chair need not be for sitting on (it might be too fragile to support one's weight). Still, ornamental chairs are best understood as counting as a kind of chair in the first place only because they constitute a sort of permissible 'riff' on the more standard case. The idea in all of these cases is that in order to understand the deviant cases one must understand them in terms of their relation to the paradigm, but not vice versa. In the moral case, Lance and Little illustrate this idea with the defeasible generalization "Pain is bad." While in suitably privileged conditions pain is wrong-making, there can be circumstances in which it is not. In particular, they suggest that when pain is constitutive of athletic accomplishment that it is not bad. Still, they argue, one must understand the latter case as a 'riff' on the former. An adequate understanding of how pain can be good when constitutive of athletic accomplishment depends on an understanding of how, in privileged conditions anyway, pain functions a bad-making feature—as something to be avoided, or so Lance and Little suggest.

A second sort of privileging that Lance and Little discuss is an epistemic one. Defeasibly, appearances are trustworthy, but not if you are in the Hall of Holograms or have just taken a drug that makes things look different from how they really are. However, our justification for treating the deviant cases as deviant is epistemologically dependent on other cases in which we took appearances at face value. For without our having trusted the appearances before how could we have come to know we were in a Hall of Holograms or had just taken a drug that made things seems different from how they really are? Here we have a sort of defeasible generalization where the privileged conditions are ones in which appearances can play what we take to be their normal epistemic role. Our knowledge of deviant cases is parasitic on our having knowledge in other cases in a nondeviant way.

Thirdly, defeasible generalizations can be based on explanatory asymmetries. Pain, they suggest, is normally bad, but not if it is constitutive of athletic accomplishment. Here the explanatory asymmetry is supposed to be that we can understand why pain is not bad in the athletic case only by understanding how it is normally bad. Only by understanding that pain is normally the sort of thing one ought to avoid can we understand the value of athletic accomplishment, but not vice versa. For clearly someone could understand why pain can be bad without understanding the special role it can play in athletic accomplishment. The example is also an illustration of paradigm/riff, but this is just to emphasize that the species of privileging are not exclusive. Another example is poker. Deception is normally wrong, but not if you are bluffing in a game of poker.[10] Moreover, one must understand why deception is normally wrong in order to appreciate why it is not wrong to bluff in poker. For it is only because people freely and honestly agreed to play a game like poker that deception becomes acceptable. So the acceptability of deception in poker is explained via an agreement reached (perhaps tacitly) in a context in which deception has its normal valence, whereas the wrongness of deception in more normal cases is in no way explained by special cases like poker in which its not. Once again we have an explanatory asymmetry.

Fourthly, and finally, there is the privileging of conditions that are ideal in some way; we might call these 'valorizing' moves. In a non-defective case, the fact that it would be pleasant is a reason to do it. However, if the situation is morally defective in certain ways then this need not be the case. In particular, if the pleasure would be sadistic then the fact that it would be pleasant might even be a reason not to do it. Nonsadistic pleasure is, we might say 'valorized' when it is not sadistic or defective in some other way.

Defeasible generalizations are shot through with exceptions and cannot be applied mechanically. Part of what it is to understand the nature of something which figures in a defeasible generalization is to understand what the relevant privileged conditions are for that thing, but this is not sufficient for full

---

[10] Lance and Little use the example of the game of *Diplomacy*.

understanding. One must also understand how it functions in non-privileged conditions too. On Lance and Little's account, understanding the relevant privileged conditions is necessary but not sufficient for the latter. In addition to grasping what sorts of conditions are privileged, I must know how to navigate the heterogeneous array of deviations from the privileged in terms of the ways in which they deviate and which deviations preserve the functioning found in the privileged conditions and which do not. Here we have a robustly particularist element in the Lance and Little story. For they insist that what is needed here is a set of epistemic skills which depend on, but go well beyond, the grasp of a defeasible principle. Crucially, these further skills are not in turn well understood in terms of principles at all.

In our view, Lance and Little have tapped into some extremely interesting and original territory, and we shall not here try to assess the overall framework in the detail it deserves. Instead, we restrict ourselves to assessing the extent to which the theoretical tools provided by their account really are sufficient to avoid the flattening of the normative landscape within a particularist framework. We make three main points.

The first and most obvious point to make is that in many respects the Lance/Little approach serves to vindicate, rather than to undermine, our position. For it is only by incorporating a generalist element that their account is supposed to avoid the flattening of the normative landscape. After all, Lance and Little's position holds that some features figure in moral principles, that moral understanding requires grasping and knowing how to apply these principles, and that such principles can play important theoretical and explanatory roles. On this account, moral thought and judgment does depend on a suitable stock of moral principles, albeit what they call defeasible principles. To be clear, we do not take this to be a criticism of Lance and Little's position, for they offer their position as an important compromise between Dancy's fairly radical particularism and positions more robustly generalist than their own.[11] Moreover, their account does retain important particularist elements which we shall (in Part II) go on to reject. For we shall argue that we can and should get beyond defeasible principles in the sense laid out by Lance and Little, and articulate genuinely exceptionless moral principles which are nontrivial and can do important explanatory work. Nonetheless, it seems worth noting that their account avoids the flattening of the normative landscape only insofar as it incorporates a hardy generalist element.

---

[11] Indeed, in some moods they seem not to mind if their view is characterized as a form of generalism. As Mark Lance once nicely put the sentiment (in discussion of one of their papers in Bled), "We don't care what team we're on, as long as we're winning!"

Our remaining two points are variations on the following worry. The name of the game here is to avoid the flattening of the normative landscape. If one accepts the particularist/holist idea that just about any consideration can be a moral reason in the right context (to be clear, we do not, but we do not argue for this until Chapter 6) then one needs to draw a distinction between core and periphery such that pain, promise-keeping, and pleasure end up in the core while shoelace color, shininess, and shuffling end up in the periphery. Lance and Little have drawn a very interesting distinction between reasons which figure in defeasible generalizations and reasons which do not. We shall call the former reasons 'paradigmatic' and the latter reasons 'non-paradigmatic'. We shift terminology slightly here simply because it would be false to call the latter reasons 'non-defeasible;' if anything, shoelace color is intuitively 'more defeasible' as a reason than pain and the like. Our worry is that there is no obvious reason to think that the intuitive core/periphery distinction will map neatly onto the distinction between paradigmatic and non-paradigmatic reasons.

With this background in place, we are in a position to raise our second worry. In a nutshell, the second worry is that there will be core reasons which are non-paradigmatic in the Lance/Little sense. Recall that on the Lance/Little approach, conditions C are privileged relative to any given x just in case C is either (a) particularly revealing of x's nature or (b) particularly revealing of the broader part of reality in which x is known. The species of this genus are paradigm−riff, explanatory asymmetry, justificatory, and valorizing.

For purposes of distinguishing core reasons from periphery reasons, we think that the notion of an explanatory asymmetry is by far the most promising one. We see no plausibility, for example, in the idea that figuring in paradigm−riff relations could explain why a reason is a core reason. For a start, it is unclear to us why periphery reasons (shoelace color and the like) cannot have 'riffs' of their own. Moreover, given their emphasis on the ways in which we are constantly surprised by the complexity of morality, particularists are ill-suited to declare a priori that the right context could not provide such riffs. Indeed, if anything, one might plausibly argue that a consideration which has no permissible riffs is a sort of especially pure case of a reason, one which is so perfectly suited to function as a reason that any attempted 'riff' on this reason would be doomed to failure. The absence of permissible riffs, if relevant to the core/periphery distinction at all (which we doubt), seems if anything to suggest that a reason falls into the category of core reason rather than periphery reason. This, of course, will not do if Lance and Little are right that pain and other such intuitively core reasons have permissible riffs.

For similar reasons, we do not think that standing in valorizing relations would in itself help explain why a given consideration falls within the core rather than the periphery. For why should a consideration which does not stand in need of valorization to function as a reason not be a core reason all the same? Indeed, the fact that a consideration does not depend on special valorizing circumstances in order to be a reason might plausibly be thought thereby to be more of a pure instance of a reason than a consideration which is so dependent on external features.

Unlike the paradigm–riff and valorizing species of privileging, the idea of an explanatory asymmetry does seem potentially helpful in distinguishing core from periphery. For here we do seem to have a genuine asymmetry between core and periphery such that the periphery is dependent on the core but not vice versa. This does seem to us to promise an interesting explanation of why the intuitively core features deserve to be thought of as core and likewise for the periphery reasons.

The justificatory species of privileging might also be helpful in some cases, but we doubt its scope is wide enough to cover most of the interesting cases. The example of appearances and reasons for belief is a very special one, in our view, in that the rational formation of empirical beliefs as such presupposes that we can take appearances at face value, at least unless some special story explains why we cannot. Without this assumption we cannot even get off the ground in the business of rationally forming empirical beliefs. So there is a kind of transcendental argument for the justificatory priority of taking appearances at face value. This is very interesting, but it seems to us to be a very special case. We doubt whether there are very many (any?) interesting analogues of this in the realm of reasons for action. What is needed is a transcendental argument that rational action as such cannot get off the ground unless we take such and such consideration as a reason for acting in certain ways, at least unless some special story can be told about why we cannot take it as such a reason. Kant and others have tried to give such arguments, but we are skeptical about their success. Moreover, even if they did succeed, we are especially skeptical that they would extend far enough to cover very many of the reasons we might plausibly want to include in the category of 'core reasons.' So in what follows we focus primarily on what we take to be by far the most promising species of privileging when it comes to distinguishing core from periphery—the explanatory asymmetry species.

We think the appeal to explanatory asymmetry will work reasonably well with thick moral features like justice and courage. By contrast, we do not think this approach does nearly so well with what intuitively seem like descriptive features like pleasure and pain. Someone who does not understand that justice is defeasibly reason-giving simply does not understand the nature of justice. However, it does not seem nearly so plausible to hold that someone who does not understand that pleasure is defeasibly reason-giving simply does not understand the nature of pleasure. The same point holds for pain.

To understand the nature of pain, for example, one must understand the functional role that pain plays, that pain is multiply realizable, that pain supervenes on the physical, and perhaps must even in some sense know 'what pain is like.' However, it is not at all obvious that one must understand even that pain can be reason-providing much less that it is a paradigmatic reason in order to understand its nature. Indeed, we submit that someone could understand the nature of pain without understanding how it can function as a reason. Yet pain and pleasure, unlike shoelace color and shininess should end up in the core rather than the periphery.

An obvious reply at this stage would be that while one need not understand how pain and pleasure can function as reasons, one does need to understand how they can function as reasons to understand normative predicates like 'reason' and 'is wrong.' There are two readings of 'understand' here worth teasing apart. On the first reading, 'understand' denotes competence with the concept. On this reading, we simply deny that one must understand how pain and pleasure can function as reasons in order to be competent with these normative concepts. A species of creatures who never experienced pleasure or pain or even had the concepts of pleasure and pain could, we submit, still be competent with normative concepts. Indeed, they could well have a plausible normative outlook, albeit not a hedonistic one. They might know that it is wrong to lie, steal, and cheat. More generally they might have a very nuanced grasp of those Kantian elements of morality which concern treating rational agents with respect. It seems to us that such creatures should not be faulted with not understanding the very concept of a reason for action. We argue for this conclusion at greater length in Chapter 5.

What does seem plausible about the species of creatures we have just sketched is that they do not fully understand the nature of wrongness, which brings us to the second reading of 'understand.' Here understanding denotes something much stronger than competence with the relevant concept, but rather a substantive understanding of the nature of that which the concept denotes. Here we are happy to admit that one must be able to understand how pain and pleasure can function as reasons in order to understand reasons for action in the relevant sense. However, we would argue that this is equally true for the periphery reasons, if any there are. If shoelace color really can be a reason for action, then someone who does not understand how it can be a reason for action does not fully understand the nature of the property of being a reason for action. To be clear, we do not really think most of the so-called 'periphery reasons' (like shoelace color) really can function as reasons at all. So in a sense we agree that one does not really need to understand how they can function as reasons to understand the nature of being a reason for action. What we do not see is how someone who really does think such eccentric features can be reasons for action can maintain that understanding how they function as reasons is not essential to a full understanding of the nature of being a reason for action.

Lance and Little might reasonably complain that 'either necessary for competence C with the concept *or* necessary for a full understanding of the nature of C itself' is a false dichotomy. Indeed, we would agree that in principle there is plenty of space between these two poles. The idea would then be in that pain is somehow more essential to an understanding of the nature of reasons than shoelace color (or whatever). However, the appeal to defeasible generalizations was meant to explain this asymmetry, and not simply assume it. If we attempt to explain the sense in which pain is a paradigmatic reason by appealing to the fact that pain figures in a defeasible generalization, then we had better not in turn explain why pain figures in a defeasible generalization by appealing (in effect) to the idea that it is a paradigmatic reason. This would be to argue in a tight little circle.

Our argument here does imply that, even if pain were an invariable reason, one would not have to understand its ability to be reason-providing in order to understand its nature. For the idea behind our argument is that the nature of pain can be understood in purely descriptive terms, and this idea does not depend on the context-sensitivity of pain as a reason. Given a metaphysically necessary relationship between pain and being a reason, this might initially seem implausible. However, we must distinguish necessary features from essential features. To take a degenerate case, everything has the property of being either blue or not blue. However, one need not understand this in order to understand a given thing's nature. One might quibble about whether tautologies pick out real properties, but we can make the point in less gimmicky terms. Consider the following case. Suppose for the sake of argument that God necessarily exists and necessarily approves of happiness. In our view, this would in no way entail that one must understand (or even know about) this relation between God and happiness in order to understand (indeed, fully understand) the *nature* of happiness.

Admittedly, one might need to understand this relation between God and happiness in order fully to understand God's nature. This, however, is analogous to the thesis that one must understand how pain can function as a reason in order fully to understand the nature of being a reason for action. We have already explained why we think this move is unlikely to help the particularist.

We do not, of course, pretend to have given anything like a knock-down argument that pain and pleasure are not essentially normative in the relevant sense. Instead, we take ourselves at most to have highlighted the prima facie plausibility of the thesis that pain and pleasure are not essentially normative in the sense that someone could fully understand their nature (as opposed to their nonessential but necessary features, say) without understanding how they can provide reasons. Pain and pleasure are properties which figure in what we take to be respectable empirical sciences—psychology and biology. We take it that those sciences can in principle give a full account of the nature of pain and pleasure and we very much doubt that the account they will give will invoke normative concepts. Or rather, insofar as the sciences leave anything out here it will be the controversial 'what it is like' to experience pain which one can also know without knowing that pain and pleasure can provide reasons. Indeed, even a hardy nihilist can know what it is like to feel pain and pleasure. Just kick one sometime if you don't believe us!

We realize that this view of the nature of pain and pleasure is not entirely uncontroversial. On a certain sort of Sellarsian account of these matters, pain and pleasure and indeed all mental properties are essentially normative. Such a Sellarsian account might well block the objection we are pressing here, and indeed may well be hovering in the background of the Lance/Little view. Unfortunately, an adequate discussion of the larger Sellarsian framework which is meant to vindicate this line of argument would take us too far afield. Instead, we shall simply note that the argument to this point suggests that particularists who want to avoid the flattening of the normative landscape via defeasible generalizations may be forced to accept such a Sellarsian framework or something rather like it. For many particularists, we suspect that this will be a cost too steep to bear.

Thus, we think it plausible that not all core reasons are paradigmatic. Our third point is just the flip side of this. It is plausible that not all periphery reasons are non-paradigmatic. We are hampered in arguing here, in that we do not think that so-called periphery reasons like shoelace color really can ever be reasons for action (we return to and argue for this point in Chapter 6 at some length). Moreover, we find it rather hard to 'get inside the particularist's head' on this score, and see what follows from a charitable gloss of their view on these matters. For although particularists often seem to suggest that considerations like shoelace color can sometimes be reasons for action, they rather frustratingly never provide examples to illustrate this suggestion. We suspect that this is because any proffered example will be highly contestable—shoelace color might influence the consequences of an action but then the generalist can plausibly respond that it is the consequences that really provide the reason for action and not the shoelace color. The particularist must mean more than this. For even a hedonistic act-utilitarian or dyed in the wool Kantian can allow that shoelace color might sometimes matter morally in various indirect ways (e.g. by figuring in a promise or influencing the consequences). The more radical suggestion here seems to be that shoelace color, for example, can itself provide a reason, but no credible example has been given to illustrate this rather odd idea. Perhaps there has been a bit too much loose talk about shoelace color.

In any event, we see no reason *ex ante* to assume that if (contrary to fact) shoelace color really could sometimes provide a reason that we might not need to understand how it could so function in order to understand its true nature. Here we are of course bracketing our second point from above, for the moment, as that line of thought would imply that we do not need to understand the normative nature of shoelace color to understand its nature, full stop but only at the cost of preventing Lance and Little from making sense of how pleasure and pain can be more relevant than shoelace color. From our perspective, once we assume that shoelace color can sometimes be a reason and bracket our general thought that purely descriptive features (like pleasure and pain) can be understood independently of their moral natures, we see no a priori grounds for supposing that one need not understand the ways in which shoelace color can function as a reason in order fully to understand its nature.

No doubt this last point will seem uncharitable to the particularist, though we think it raises a fair challenge. For the particularist position is hard to assess without the provision of examples to illustrate the very odd idea that shoelace color (and other such oddball examples) really could be a reason in itself. Fortunately, we can make our point with a less controversial example—indeed with an example taken from Lance and Little themselves. Recall that on their account, pain is defeasibly bad-making but is not actually bad-making when it is constitutive of athletic accomplishment, for example. Why, though, is pain not also defeasibly good-making? In other words, why should we not privilege those circumstances in which pain is constitutive of athletic accomplishment as also being privileged in the relevant sense—as being particularly revealing of x's nature or the broader part of reality in which x is known? There needs to be a good answer to this question if we want to vindicate the intuitive idea that pain is more intimately connected with the bad than the good, but it is hard to see how it can be answered. For the fact that pain can be constitutive of athletic accomplishment does seem like an important fact about pain. Once we allow that normative functions can be essential properties, why is such an important fact not part of the nature of pain, which privileged conditions should help display?

Presumably, Lance and Little would reply to this challenge by arguing that our understanding of how pain functions as good-making is somehow parasitic on our understanding of how it functions as bad-making but not vice versa. The idea seems to be that understanding how pain can be constitutive of athletic accomplishment itself requires an understanding of how pain is in the more normal case 'to be avoided.' However, this simply seems false. The explanation of how pain constitutes athletic accomplishment surely is that it makes the accomplishment difficult—makes it a challenge, tests one's will, and the like. Lest this suggestion from two fairly nonathletic academics seem totally off the mark, we provide some evidence in favor of this interpretation from Brian Collins, the owner and program developer of Achieve Fitness and 1st Marathon: "The marathon holds a special place of reverence in society because many view it as the ultimate test of will—a metaphor for life itself" (from *SunWellness* magazine, at http://www.sun-wellness.com/articles/051feat4.html). If this is right, then pain is constitutive of athletic accomplishment because pain makes it difficult to continue, thereby testing one's will. The relevant notion of difficulty must be understood in terms of requiring strength of will rather than in purely physical terms (requiring lots of physical force, for example). We take it, though, that the notion of willpower is still a descriptive notion.[12] However, understanding how pain makes it difficult (in the sense of taxing one's willpower) to continue and indeed finish a race, for example, does not seem to require understanding how in other contexts pain is a reason to stop running. That simply seems beside the point. Even someone Stoical enough to think (mistakenly) that pain is never a reason against doing anything can, we submit, nonetheless fully understand how pain can be constitutive of athletic accomplishment and how this can be a good-making feature.

To sum up, we have made three main points about the Lance/Little proposal. First, it avoids flattening the normative landscape only insofar as it incorporates a hardy generalist element, and in this respect is grist for our mill against more radical forms of particularism like Dancy's (Lance and Little presumably would agree with this point). Secondly, the proposal can succeed in keeping the normative landscape 'bumpy' in the right way only if what seem like purely descriptive properties (e.g. pleasure and pain) nonetheless have essentially normative natures. We have tried to cast some doubt on this suggestion by arguing that the nature of pain and pleasure can be fully understood without understanding how they can function as reasons. If this

---

[12] Indeed, one which has recently been studied empirically. A number of psychologists have argued that there is an empirically real faculty of willpower and that it functions in many ways like a muscle. If we use it frequently we can make it stronger, and it can become fatigued, etc. See e.g. Baumeister et al. 1998. Thanks to Richard Holton for bringing these interesting empirical studies to our attention.

is right, then some core reasons are not paradigmatic reasons. Thirdly, some periphery reasons (e.g. pain when constitutive of athletic accomplishment) seem like plausible candidates for defeasible generalizations, in which case the core/periphery distinction will not map neatly onto the paradigmatic/non-paradigmatic distinction embedded in the Lance/Little framework. In effect, our last two points are meant to highlight a dialectical burden not yet fulfilled by Lance and Little's discussion—to explain why we should think the core/periphery distinction will map neatly onto the paradigmatic/non-paradigmatic distinction implicit in their discussion. Our arguments suggest that the two sets of distinction cut across each other, in which case we do not yet have an adequate particularist strategy for keeping the normative terrain suitably 'bumpy.'

## 3.4. The Pragmatic Reading

We have seen serious problems with three rather different ways of distinguishing default reasons from non-default reasons. However, there is one final reading of the distinction which is much less controversial—the pragmatic reading. Indeed, one might plausibly suggest that the pragmatic reading is the default interpretation of default reasons. The pragmatic reading begins with the observation that which features it makes sense to mention when offering an explanation depends on the context. In particular, facts which are known to be common knowledge need not be made explicit when giving an explanation. For example, suppose her friends ask Sally why Harry is so upset and she simply replies, "He ran into Helen today." In the right context this might be a perfectly good reply even though as an explanation it is highly elliptical. The adequacy of this concise reply relies on the fact that it is common knowledge, and known among the parties to the conversation to be common knowledge, that Harry recently went through a bitter divorce with Helen and has not gotten over her yet. Had her interlocutors not known Harry's relation to Helen, then Sally would need to make these further facts explicit. The same point applies to moral explanations. If asked why it would be wrong to invite Helen to the party, Sally might simply tell us that her presence would make Harry upset. Sally would typically not need to make explicit that inviting Helen is not the only way to stop a catastrophic terrorist attack.

This already gives us the resources to draw a distinction between default reasons and non-default reasons against the backdrop of holism and particularism. On this account, whether a given consideration is a default reason with a given valence is itself context-dependent, and in this sense in the holistic spirit of particularism itself. For the suggestion is that whether a given consideration is usefully understood as a default reason with a given valence depends on whether one's interlocutors would take it as given that such a consideration would function as a reason with that valence unless some special story was explicitly told as to why it did not so function. That an action would cause pain is in most contexts a default reason against the action. Why? Because the fact that an action would cause pain almost always is a reason against the action and this is common knowledge and moreover it is commonly known to be common knowledge. If someone was puzzled about why a given action was objectionable, we could typically dispel this puzzlement simply by pointing out that the action would cause some pain. Moreover, this does not presuppose that the person is an atomist and assumes that pain always counts against an action. For example, our interlocutor might agree that in the context of an S & M room, the fact that an action would cause some pain might well speak in favor of the action. The point then would be that such contexts are known (and commonly known to be known) to be very rare, and this is why it can go without saying that this is not the case when it is not. Hence in most local conversational contexts, that an action would cause pain is a default reason against the action but also is sometimes a non-default reason in favor of an action in certain contexts. We do not need any fancy metaphysical or epistemological background theory in order to draw a perfectly sensible contextualist distinction between default reasons and non-default reasons.

Moreover, in our view, the pragmatic reading is considerably more plausible than its rivals and not only because it avoids the objections pressed against those rivals in Sections 3.1 and 3.2. It also fits better with a reflective understanding of the sources of our own intuitions. For those intuitions themselves seem highly sensitive to contingent features of our situation. Consider a variation on an example from H. L. A Hart.[13] A world is populated by rational creatures whose crab-like bodies feature tough exoskeletons. It is very difficult to inflict pain on such a creature from the outside, and so there are very few instances of such pain. Nevertheless such creatures are prone to pain when they exert themselves in athletic competition, and most pain is like this. It seems very likely that such people would not find the idea that pain provides a default reason against an action very plausible, assuming that they all agree that being constitutive of athletic accomplishment is sufficient (metadefeaters to one side) to make pain into a reason in favor of the action which causes it. To take another example, suppose that most instances of pleasure were sadistic. If we agree with the standard particularist idea that sadism is a defeater of the reason-giving force of

---

[13] The original example is from Hart 1961: 194.

considerations of pleasure, then (metadefeaters to one side) this would entail that most instances of pleasure would not provide a reason to perform actions which would promote the pleasure. In a world in which this was the case and widely known to be the case, we submit that the intuition that pleasure provides a default reason in favor of an action which promotes pleasure would not be widely held.[14] Indeed, the opposite intuition might well be dominant. This fits perfectly with the pragmatic reading, for whether a consideration is a default reason on the pragmatic reading does depend on local conditions. This suggests that it would be a mistake to interpret our own intuitions about default reasons in a metaphysically or epistemologically grandiose way.

Is drawing the distinction pragmatically enough to save particularists from the objection that their account implausibly flattens the landscape? Perhaps. Here we must simply assume with the particularists that all sorts of considerations can sometimes be reasons for action, even though we do not actually accept this thesis. For the objection that the particularist flattens the normative landscape does not presuppose that such considerations can never be reasons for action, only that their status as reasons is in some way second-rate. Certainly *if* shoelace color sometimes provides a reason for action this is in our world very rare, whereas pleasure and pain typically do provide reasons for action. So in our world it is quite reasonable in almost all conversational contexts to treat pleasure and pain as default reasons but not treat shoelace color and other such bizarre considerations as default reasons even if we agree that in suitably weird circumstances the latter can also provide reasons for action. This avoids the charge that the particularist flattens the actual normative landscape, but is that enough? For it now seems that in a world in which shoelace color typically did provide a reason with a given valence (and was known to do so, and known to be known to do so) it would be appropriate to treat shoelace color as a default reason as well. This does indeed follow from what we take to be the best way of drawing the distinction between default reasons and non-default reasons and perhaps this is embarrassing for the particularist. However, in our view the embarrassment here stems not from the pragmatic reading of default reasons but rather from the particularist commitment to the thesis that weird considerations like shoelace color can even sometimes be a reason for action. In our view, such weird considerations can themselves *never* be reasons for action.

---

[14] One peculiarity of the case is that sadists might be unlikely to realize that their sadistic pleasures do not count in favor of an action. However, we could handle this situation by stipulating that we are now talking about a species of rational creatures most of whom are incapable of pleasure, but a very few of them are capable of pleasure albeit only sadistic ones. It might well be common knowledge amongst the members of such a species that pleasure does not typically provide a reason in favor of actions which promote it.

Hence we agree that there is a deep and non-pragmatic asymmetry between shoelace color and pain; the former can never be a (primary) reason for action while the latter can. Which is just to say that the best way to accommodate such deep asymmetries is to reject particularism's highly ecumenical account of reasons for action. However, our argument for this conclusion does not emerge until Chapter 7 in which we argue that there are only finitely and indeed manageably many possible reasons for action and that considerations like shoelace color never provide reasons for action.

## 3.5. Conclusion

Particularism and holism threaten to flatten the normative landscape, allowing no normative distinction between shoelace color and pain. Particularists typically try to avoid this conclusion by drawing a distinction between default reasons and non-default reasons, but the ambitious glosses they give this distinction are either problematic in themselves (the explanatory and autonomous conceptions) or interesting but unpromising as a way to avoid the flattening of the normative landscape (via defeasible generalizations). The distinction between default reasons and non-default reasons should instead be understood pragmatically. This might be enough for the particularist to avoid the charge that their account entails a flattening of the actual normative landscape. However, in certain counterfactual contexts particularism would, it seems, still flatten the normative landscape, the pragmatic version of the distinction notwithstanding.

In our view, the solution to this problem is simply the rejection of the particularist's highly promiscuous attitude to what kinds of considerations we should treat as legitimate candidate reasons for action. However, we do not argue for this conclusion until Chapter 6. For now, we must put the issue of flattening the normative landscape to one side and turn our attention to moral epistemology. For many particularists have claimed that their view gains support from the plausibility of the metaphor of 'moral vision' as a characterization of how we often acquire moral knowledge. In the following chapter we argue that the distinctions between different forms of particularism drawn in Chapter 1 have not been sufficiently heeded in discussions of moral vision and its putatively particularist upshot.

# 4

# Moral Vision

Every time I see a kid making a mistake and ask him why he played that move his reply starts with the words "Well, I thought ..." "Don't think," I reply. "Look."

(Richard James, chess instructor)

Moral judgment often seems not to involve the application of principles. Rather, the sensitive agent seems to discern the morally salient features of a case immediately and judges accordingly. Morality can therefore appear very different from paradigmatically rule-governed activities like the derivation of theorems in logical systems or the following of a recipe. Instead, moral judgment often seems aptly described in perceptual terms. One 'just sees' that a given action is morally wrong. This suggests a perceptual model of moral judgment according to which at least some of our moral judgments are justified in a way that is in some respects akin to perception, perhaps most notably in that the justification is noninferential.[1] Such a perceptual model of moral judgment sometimes goes under the heading of 'intuitionism,' although that term is also used in a number of other senses.

Particularism is often thought to draw at least indirect support from the metaphor of moral vision, in that the intuitionist conception of moral judgment suggested by this metaphor has no obvious need for moral principles. By contrast, according to the most prevalent alternative to moral vision, particular moral knowledge is the product of a syllogism comprising a moral principle as its major premiss. According to some, particularism is incompatible with this approach and even provides a persuasive argument against it. Of the syllogistic model, John McDowell claims, "This picture fits only if the virtuous person's views about how, in general, one should behave are susceptible of codification, in principles apt for serving as major premises in syllogisms of the sort envisaged." McDowell famously suggests that it is

---

[1] For a recent defense of moral vision that treats the noninferential character of such knowledge as essential, see Sarah McGrath, "Moral Knowledge by Perception," forthcoming.

"quite implausible that any reasonably adult moral outlook admits of any such codification" (McDowell 1979: 336).

If McDowell is correct, then particularism undermines generalism's model of particular moral knowledge, and the perceptual account in turns provides particularism with a workable epistemology. It should be no surprise then if particularism and the perceptual model are treated as an attractive package deal. And for many particularists, it seems, they do represent such a package deal. David McNaughton, for example, argues in *Moral Vision* that principles are inimical to the development of a sound moral outlook (McNaughton 1988). More recently, Little has emphasized that particularists should and must emphasize that skills of discernment lie at the heart of moral judgment, and that such skills cannot be understood as ultimately inferential skills of drawing conclusions from prior principles (Little 2000: 292−8). Jonathan Dancy, though he is rightly skeptical of a literal moral sense akin to the sense of sight, nevertheless accepts the most central tenet of the perceptual model, namely that our most basic moral knowledge is noninferential knowledge of particular moral relations (Dancy 2004: 143−8).

In the present chapter we argue that the perceptual model provides no direct support for particularism. Given the close association of particularism with the perceptual model, this is important even if particularists have not argued directly from the perceptual model to particularism. Since we have already undermined the argument from holism, it is only natural to consider whether particularism could derive any support from the perceptual model, especially given that the perceptual metaphor is both particularism's constant companion and can seem independently plausible. Our strategy is not to contest the perceptual model itself (at least so long as it is not taken literally to imply the existence of a faculty of moral sense). Instead, we first explain the plausibility of the perceptual model and then show that, like holism, it is entirely compatible with even the strongest forms of generalism we want to defend. Indeed, we argue that the perceptual model is compatible even with at least one form of generalism which is much stronger than the forms we want to defend—constitutive generalism about standards qua algorithmic decision-procedures.

## 4.1. The Perceptual Model

The idea that we can sometimes 'just see' that a certain action is morally wrong is readily motivated with examples. Gilbert Harman's famous case of someone observing young thugs pour gasoline on a cat to burn it to death is frequently cited as an illustration of the idea of 'moral vision' (Harman 1977: 3−10).

The idea is supposed to be that any morally decent person observing such a scene would just see the wrongness of what the thugs did without needing to draw any inferences.[2] We need not dwell on the dark side of things, though. For example, if I see someone in a big hurry stop to help a stranger who has just slipped, then I should likewise be able to 'just see' that the action is morally right.

Perhaps unsurprisingly, the cases in which we apparently can 'just see' the moral status of certain actions tend to be ones in which the moral verdict is not particularly controversial. The perceptual model is less plausible for cases involving more controversy and complexity. I may be able to 'just see' that killing a small child for fun is wrong but unable to 'just see' whether abortion near the end of the second trimester would be wrong in a case of pregnancy due to rape where the child would suffer from a serious form of mental retardation and where the father opposes aborting the child. We have opinions in these much more difficult cases, but for most people the phenomenology here is much less naturally described in terms of direct perception or immediate insight. Rather, a judgment is reached on the basis of comparing the case with other cases like it, looking for similarities and differences, deliberating, and then forming a judgment. In these more difficult cases there is much more room for reasonable disagreement.

Any reasonable person can agree that Harman's thugs are wrong to burn the cat but not all moral questions are so straightforward. Discussions of our duties to provide famine relief to those starving in poor nations, the moral status of a preemptive war to prevent terrorism, debates over abortion and sexual morality more generally all show that there is room for considerable reasonable disagreement on a range of moral issues. If, however, the perceptual model provided a full account of our moral epistemology, then there would seem to be no rational way to resolve these disputes. One might worry that if a given action looks morally wrong to me but looks perfectly fine to you then the perceptual model provides no rational way to resolve our differences.

---

[2] Actually, it is slightly odd that Harman's example is so frequently cited as a good example of moral vision not least of all because (thankfully!) very few people have ever actually seen a cat be burned to death so, if part of the point of the example is to indicate the familiarity of a perceptual model, then it is an odd choice. Also, it is unclear why we should be so quick to agree that the belief that what the thugs are doing is immoral involves no inference. Why should we not instead say that what we actually directly see is that the thugs are burning a cat and from this we infer that this will cause the cat to suffer and die and from this in turn we infer that the action is immoral given our more general background commitments regarding the moral significance of suffering and the death of a sentient creature? Once we bear in mind that inferences can happen very quickly and be so natural as to escape our conscious attention, at least more needs to be said to explain why this inferential account of the example is not compelling. Thanks to Walter Sinott-Armstrong for useful discussion here.

As reasonable as these worries are, it would be premature to reject the perceptual model on their strength. Here a perceptual model of moral judgment can perhaps benefit by way of analogy with a similar account of aesthetic judgment. If people do not share your aesthetic evaluation of a given work, then you can try to convince them by getting them to see it the way you do. This might involve simply pointing out a particular feature of the work they have overlooked. Alternatively, sound judgment in a given case might involve considerable training and initially be beyond the ability of the novice. The basic idea goes back at least as far as David Hume's essay, "On the Standard of Taste," where he points out that we assign more credibility to the judgments of those whose sensibilities are more sharp and acute:

A man in a fever would not insist on his palate as able to decide concerning flavours; nor would one, affected with jaundice, pretend to give a verdict with regard to colours. In each creature, there is a sound and a defective state; and the former alone can be supposed to afford us a true standard of taste and sentiment. (Hume 1985: 235)

More recently and in defense of a version of moral particularism emphasizing the idea of 'moral vision,' David McNaughton helpfully makes a similar point about jazz appreciation. McNaughton reminds us that the newcomer may well find jazz to be a "muddled confusion of noise" (McNaughton 1988: 58). The jazz expert may need to expose the novice to more simple tunes and arrangements and only gradually work up to the piece with which the discussion started. Once this training is complete, the listener hears jazz in a different way. Discussions of more complicated moral cases might seem somewhat analogous to the aesthetic case. We might initially disagree about a given case, but then you might call my attention to a feature of the case I had simply overlooked and I might then see the case in an entirely different light. For example, I might initially think that someone breaking into another person's car is clearly morally wrong, but once you bring it to my attention that the she was trying to rush a badly injured person to the hospital I might well see it in a different light and shift my judgment. In other cases changing my mind will require a more subtle appeal to a range of examples, perhaps starting with more simple ones and then building the case slowly for seeing the original example in a different light. When these forms of reasoning are successful they reveal not that one's interlocutor was irrational but rather that she had a moral blindspot which was (perhaps) corrected through consciousness-raising discussion (see McNaughton 1988: 59–60). Neither, however, does this mean that such conversations are mere arational manipulation. One can highlight genuine features of the case or its similarity to other cases without being dishonest or deceptive in any way. So the perceptual model may have more resources for dealing with difficult and disputed cases than one might have initially supposed (McNaughton 1988: 59–60).

The intuitive plausibility of the perceptual model seems most suited to establishing Anti-Transcendental Particularism. Since the perceptual model is silent on the utility of moral principles, it does not provide any obvious support for Principle Abstinence Particularism. Nor does it suggest that there are no moral principles (Principle Eliminativism) or that there is no reason to think there are any (Principle Skepticism) or even that morality as a whole is not codifiable in finite descriptive terms (Principled Particularism). For the fact that we come to make judgments about moral properties via something like perception does not yet establish anything about the possibility of comprehensively codifying the conditions under which those properties are instantiated. Indeed, one of the main defenders of the perceptual model, John McDowell, suggests that one of its virtues is precisely its neutrality on these points, leaving room for further debate as to whether particularism (apart from what we call Anti-Transcendental Particularism, anyway) is true:

> The upshot is that the search for an evaluative outlook that one can endorse as rational becomes, virtually irresistibly, a search for such a set of principles … I have a hunch that such efforts are misguided … that we need a conception of rationality in evaluation that will cohere with the possibility that particular cases may stubbornly resist capture in any general net. Such a conception is straightforwardly available within the alternative to projectivism that I have described … *I take it that my hunch poses a question of moral and aesthetic taste, which—like other questions of taste—should be capable of being argued about.* The trouble with projectivism is that it threatens to bypass that argument, on the basis of a metaphysical picture whose purported justification falls well short of making it compulsory. (McDowell 1985 in Sayre-McCord 1988: 180, emphasis added)

However, the perceptual model may still provide some indirect support for stronger forms of particularism like Principle Eliminativism. For all of these forms of particularism will stand in need of an epistemology that can explain how moral knowledge is possible without relying on moral principles, and the perceptual model looks well suited to play this role.

The fact that the perceptual model seems ill-suited to cases in which reasonable and morally sensitive people disagree about a moral verdict even when they agree on all the relevant facts suggests that the perceptual model stands in need of further supplementation. Whether the perceptual model could be supplemented in a plausible way to deal more helpfully with cases of deep moral disagreement by reasonable people without also implicitly abandoning particularism is in our view a very good question. Still, even if the perceptual model could be supplemented in a plausible and particularist-friendly way to deal with hard cases, the perceptual model would provide no positive support for Principle Eliminativism or Principle Skepticism or Principled Particularism. Rather, the perceptual model would at best insulate these doctrines from the charge that they cannot accommodate a plausible moral epistemology.

By contrast, the appeal to a perceptual model might seem to provide a more direct and positive case for Anti-Transcendental Particularism. For perceptual judgment more generally does not seem to presuppose principles. For example, the judgment that something is crimson does not seem to presuppose that color concepts could be codified in nonchromatic terms. Nor does the more refined judgment that a particular shiraz is an excellent wine seem to presuppose that such aesthetic cum perceptual judgments could be codified in more basic terms. We do rely on moral principles in teaching young children the difference between right and wrong, but this does not in itself seem likely to help mount a transcendental deduction of moral principles. For the particularist can plausibly maintain that we teach simple rules to children who have not yet developed a suitably refined moral sensibility to get by without ourselves using oversimplified and crude moral principles as a kind of crutch. The fact that a child must rely on moral principles no more suggests that moral thought as such presupposes principles than the fact we rightly tell children not talk to strangers implies that nobody should ever talk to strangers.[3] Of course, adults also rely on moral principles, but this need not in itself undermine Anti-Transcendental Particularism. For the fact that some people do use principles in their moral thinking does not imply that moral thinking presupposes moral principles any more than the fact that some chefs wear aprons implies that cooking as such presupposes aprons.

Ultimately we argue against Anti-Transcendental Particularism, but a full presentation of this argument must await Part II. In the following section we explain why the metaphor of moral vision, once suitably unpacked, does not really provide any support even for Anti-Transcendental Particularism in most of its guises. The one possible exception is Anti-Transcendental Particularism about principles understood as algorithmic decision-procedures. Since we have claimed that generalists should not conceive of principles as algorithmic decision-procedures anyway, we are happy to accept this extremely modest form of particularism.

---

[3] See McNaughton 1988: 202.

## 4.2. Moral Vision: Getting Past the Metaphors

Defenders of the perceptual model do not really think that moral vision is literally another form of sense-perception like ordinary vision, smell, taste, touch, and hearing. The perceptual model provides a metaphor and that metaphor must be unpacked in certain ways to remain plausible. In particular, unlike ordinary perceptual judgments, most defenders of the perceptual model allow (indeed, emphasize) that at least some of our moral knowledge is both a priori and based on an immediate insight that certain actions would be morally required (or morally forbidden) under given conditions. This idea is important to preserve, because we do seem capable of forming justified judgments about what would be right or wrong in merely hypothetical cases or actual cases with which we are not directly acquainted in any way. Moreover, this a priori knowledge cannot be analytic for the intuitionist, who typically endorses Moore's "Open Question Argument" against such supposed analytic truths. We discuss Moore's argument and its successors in more detail in Chapter 5. Much less can particularist forms of intuitionism allow that such moral knowledge is based on analytic truths, for those analytic truths could then themselves serve as moral principles. So the particularist defender of the perceptual model apparently must make sense of the Kantian category of the synthetic a priori.[4]

The particularist faces a dialectical problem here, though. The perceptual model seems to fit well with particularism in part because we can distinguish paradigmatically rule-governed judgments like mathematical judgments from paradigmatically perceptual judgments like those of color or taste. However, once the commitments of the perceptual model are clarified and the metaphor is unpacked, this contrast evaporates. For, given the argument of the preceding paragraph, the relevant notion of perception must allow for a priori intuitions. By way of analogy, Kant famously argued that mathematical judgments are best understood as synthetic a priori judgments based on a priori intuitions. Nor is Kant's account without its plausibility; careful reflection on a mathematical proposition can provide an a priori warrant for believing that proposition even if it is not analytic. If a practice of judgment as paradigmatically rule-governed as mathematics can plausibly be understood as based on a priori intuitions, then intuitionism no longer looks well suited to provide support even for the more modest thesis that moral thought and judgment do not presuppose the

---

[4] For a recent attempt to rehabilitate the idea of the synthetic a priori, see Bonjour 1998. Bonjour's work is frequently cited by contemporary intuitionists as providing support for their account. See e.g. the essays collected in Stratton-Lake 2002.

provision of a suitable set of moral principles. For mathematical thought pretty clearly does presuppose principles in some sense and arguably also fits well with the perceptual model, when properly understood. Any plausible argument from the perceptual model to Anti-Transcendental Particularism will need to be more subtle, at once emphasizing certain similarities between morality and mathematics while also emphasizing salient differences. So far as we know, no such argument for Anti-Transcendental Particularism has been offered, nor can we see how such an argument might plausibly be developed.

Of course, there is one sense in which mathematics is demonstrably not codifiable. Godel's Incompleteness Theorem famously shows that for any consistent set of arithmetical axioms there will be arithmetic truths within that system that cannot be derived from the axioms and first-order quantificational logic. So a moral particularist might argue that the analogy between 'moral vision' and mathematical insight strengthens rather than weakens their position. There is a good point for the particularist here, but it supports only one of the most modest forms of particularism canvassed in Chapter 1. For Godel's Theorem proves only that there is no *algorithmic* way of capturing all of mathematics. There is no suggestion that the axioms of the system *plus* mathematical insight and intuition might not allow one to determine the truth of each of the unprovable (in the algorithmic sense) Godel sentences. Indeed, the proof of Godel's Theorem itself presupposes that we can determine that the sentence in question is true in the mathematical system under consideration even though it cannot be derived algorithmically from its axioms.[5] So the analogy with mathematics might well provide some intuitive support for the conclusion that morality cannot be captured algorithmically. However, very few (if any) moral generalists have thought that morality could be codified in this extremely strong sense. In any event, we have no interest in defending algorithmic moral standards. Indeed, we take the hyper-generalist thesis that moral thought presupposes such algorithms to be extremely implausible and join particularists in rejecting it.

## 4.3. Garry Kasparov: Particularist?

The arguments of the preceding section notwithstanding, many particularists seem to think that the apparently perceptual phenomenology of morality provides support for the fairly ambitious particularist thesis that morality cannot and need not be codified. David McNaughton, for example, admits

---

[5] See e.g. Penrose 1989: 108.

that the perceptual model does not logically entail this ambitious thesis but defends a form of moral realism that emphasizes the perceptual model and claims that this form of moral realism "naturally leads to moral particularism" (McNaughton 1988: 190).

Perhaps the train of thought to which McNaughton alludes is natural but mistaken all the same. Here it is helpful not only to show how the argument from moral vision goes wrong, but to offer a diagnosis of why the argument nonetheless can seem compelling. In this section we try to make some moves in this direction by considering a practice in which the phenomenology is even more clearly and literally visual and where many experts in the domain have made a number of particularist-sounding claims—chess. Our suggestion is that it is only a failure to heed some of the distinctions drawn in Chapter 1 (most notably the distinction between principles qua standards and principles qua guides) that has given the argument from moral vision to particularism more credibility than it deserves. The analogy with chess provides a nice way to illustrate this point.

Experienced chess players often claim that while concrete calculation is an important aspect of being a good chess player, the question 'how many moves can you calculate?' is not the most apt question when assessing a player's strength. Often, the end result of a calculated series of moves is not one in which the better side forces checkmate or loss of material. More often the advantage is more subtle, and the chess players' description of their assessment of these positions is rife with perceptual metaphors. For example, a good chess player might 'just see' that the doubled pawns are a significant liability in this position while the most salient feature of doubled pawns in another position is that they provide an open file for a dangerous attack on the opponent's king or enhanced control of the center. Alternatively, a good player might be able to 'just see' that sacrificing a pawn is justified by a lead in development in this case but would 'look dodgy' in another superficially similar case.

In some ways chess is a more promising case for the idea that we can 'just see' what is best than the moral case. Visual imagination in a quite literal sense is an important part of assessing chess positions, at least for human beings; computers like Deep Blue and Hydra presumably do things differently. So it is not at all surprising that visual characterizations of the phenomenology are so apt. Whereas someone blind from birth could still be a moral saint, the visual sense modality is more metaphorical in the moral case. Moreover, the work of Dutch psychologist De Groot supports the depth and importance of visual phenomenology in chess. De Groot found that the stronger a given chess player was the more likely he or she would be to see the board in 'chunks' (e.g. castled position, central pawn structure) whereas beginners seem to take in only one or two pieces at a time.[6] Better players literally see the game differently from weaker players.

Moreover, just as many moral philosophers have grown impatient with rule-based approaches to morality, many chess theorists have grown impatient with the more traditional rule-based approaches one finds in earlier and more traditional chess manuals. John Watson's *Secrets of Modern Chess Strategy* devotes an entire chapter to the idea of 'Rule-Independence' and other modern chess masters (and grand masters) have made similar points. Here is a representative passage from Watson:

Many changes have taken place in modern chess ... but the forerunner and in some sense precursor to these changes has been a philosophic notion, now so entrenched that we barely notice it. I call this notion 'rule-independence', for lack of a more comprehensive way to express it. It is simply the gradual divestment on the part of chess-players of the multitudinous generalities, rules and abstract principles which guided classical chess, and which still dominate our teaching texts. Furthermore, a rejection of the very notion of the 'rule' has taken place, in favour of a pragmatic investigation of individual situations ... A 'feel' for positional chess is developed, just as in the old days, but one which is unconstrained (or considerably less constrained) by dogma. Hence, 'rule-independence'. (Watson 1998: 97)

Indeed, sometimes the parallels between modern chess literature and the literature on moral particularism seems so close that one imagines replacing all occurrences of 'chess' with 'morality' and thereby transforming a passage from Watson's discussion of chess into a passage from Dancy on moral particularism. Moreover, just as in the moral case, experienced chess players sometimes find rule-based approaches do not fit their own phenomenology very well. They find their assessment of a given position to consist not in the application of various principles or rules of thumb (e.g. 'avoid doubled-pawns' and 'a knight on the rim is dim') but in an appreciation of the nuances of each particular position. Furthermore, just as many moral particularists argue that an emphasis on general rules can lead us to a distorted and artificial view of the case at hand, modern chess authors argue that an emphasis on general rules can distort our appreciation of the particular position. Here is Watson again:

In the last chapter, we began to touch on a number of dogmatic views which led even the most brilliant players and thinkers to make some rather foolish assessments about certain positions. My contention was that adherence to rules and general principles played a major role in these misassessments. (Watson 1998: 97)

[6] For discussion see Rowson 2000: 35.

Watson's view here is echoed by many other chess experts. Given that in both chess and the moral case we find an appeal to a visual phenomenology as part of a case for abandoning more traditional and putatively distorting rule-based conceptions, it is worth exploring more carefully just what lessons the chess case might provide for the moral case. Moreover, this lesson has not been entirely lost on those sympathetic to intuitionist and particularist moral philosophies. Herbert and Stuart Dreyfus argue for a conception of moral expertise very much on this sort of model, arguing that:

On analogy with chess and driving it would seem that the budding ethical expert would learn at least some of the ethics of her community by following strict rules, would then go on to apply contextualized maxims, and, in the highest stage, would leave rules and principles behind and develop more and more refined spontaneous ethical responses. (Dreyfus and Dreyfus 1990: 244)

At this point, the distinctions drawn in Chapter 1 between different conceptions of principles are essential. If we consider principles as standards, then it is clear that we do have a standard in the case of chess, perceptual phenomenology notwithstanding. Success in chess quite simply is checkmating one's opponent and, failing that, avoiding being checkmated.[7] Given this conception of success, we can construct a standard for the predicate 'correct move.' A correct move is one that makes for success. [8] Moreover, it is equally clear that this standard can

---

[7] Here we should indicate that our use of 'standard' is partly stipulative and does not fit with all of the connotations associated with that term in ordinary language. As Jonathan Dancy reminds us (private correspondence) one may fall short of a standard without failing entirely, but in chess one either checkmates one's opponents or one does not (though perhaps getting a draw is a way of falling short without failing entirely). In any event, our point is that what we call a standard sets the criterion for success in the domain in question regardless of whether that standard figures very often or ever in the deliberation of an expert practitioner in that domain.

[8] One complication here concerns the issue of how our view of success in chess translates into a standard for the correctness of individual moves. Here we think there are actually two possible standards corresponding to two different approaches to the game, as well as a third model which is a hybrid of the first two. First, there is the objective criterion which would be favored by the purist. The idea behind this account is that the best move in any given position should depend entirely on the intrinsic features of the position itself; contingent facts about one's opponent are irrelevant. On this account, the correct move in any given position is determined in the following way. First, rule out all moves which allow your opponent to force checkmate; if all of your legal moves allow your opponent to force checkmate, then all of your moves are equally bad and hence equally 'correct.' Here the notion of 'forcing' must be understood objectively, so that even an extremely complicated tree of different possible continuations will count as forcing if all of them end in checkmate; a forcing sequence need not be one that any human being could recognize as such (for all we know, the opening move 1 e4 might force checkmate!). Now suppose that at least some of your available moves do not allow your opponent to force checkmate. Then of those remaining moves, if any of them allow you to force checkmate, then those moves are all equally your best move (or perhaps we should say that the most elegant way of forcing checkmate is the best move in that case). Finally, suppose that none of your available non-losing moves allows you to force checkmate. In that case, we can say that any of your

in at least some positions be action-guiding. When there is an obvious route to force checkmate (e.g. a back-rank mate in one) then a chess player's move may indeed be guided by the principle that one ought to force checkmate whenever one can. Finally, this standard is constitutive of the practice. Anyone who failed to understand that one ought to make those moves that lead to checkmating one's opponent simply does not understand the game yet.[9] So, carrying over the terms of our taxonomy from Chapter 1, here we have a form of constitutive generalism about principles qua standards. So perceptual phenomenology notwithstanding, in chess we have not only standards but action-guiding constitutive standards, and indeed uncontroversially so. This should make us suspicious of arguments in the moral case that go directly from the premiss of a perceptual phenomenology to the rejection of both standards and action-guiding standards. For in the case of chess the premiss is true (even more obviously so than in the case of morality), but the conclusion is manifestly false.

remaining non-losing moves are all equally good, and in this very objective sense of what makes a move correct this seems the right thing to say. For if you were playing a perfect opponent then always playing any of the remaining non-losing moves would still lead to a draw, and the whole point of the objective conception of what makes a move correct is to determine what move you should play assuming best play by your opponent and assuming continued best play by yourself. The second approach to the game is much more pragmatic and insists that the best move in a position is the one that is most likely to lead to victory. This criterion might well lead someone to play a move which is objectively inferior in order to increase the odds of success against a given opponent. For example, if I know that my opponent plays very poorly in closed positions, then I might enhance my winning chances by playing an objectively inferior line which forces the closing of the position where my opponent is likely to go wrong. To take another example, I might play an objectively inferior move against a weaker opponent simply because the move creates enormous complications where I suspect that my weaker opponent is more likely to go wrong than myself. Chess players are perhaps somewhat divided as to which of these two approaches to take to the game. Many players of course take the very pragmatic approach, particularly when they know something about their opponents. However, other purists favor always trying to play the objectively best move and paying no attention to the psychology of their opponent. For a proponent of the purist school, see Svetozar Gligoric's aptly titled *I Play against Pieces* (Gligoric 2002). The debate here of course echoes debates over subjective and objective conceptions of moral rightness. We officially take no position on which approach is more plausible here; our real topic is morality, after all!

[9]   We do not mean to suggest that the rules of chess at any given time are constitutive of chess per se. The rules of chess have evolved over time and it is not plausible to suppose that every time we seem to have changed the rules we have actually switched from one game to another. In some sense, we have been playing chess all along even though the rules governing the movements of pawns, the forty move rule, and other such rules have changed over time. We might not go so far as Mark Lance and John O'Leary Hawthorne (now John Hawthorne), who claim that "there is no aspect of any game that is *in principle* immune to revision without loss of identity" (Lance and O'Leary-Hawthorne 1997: 194). Perhaps a game in which checkmating one's opponent's king was not sufficient for winning the game would simply not be chess. In any event, though, we take their main point that there can be significant changes in the rules without our having simply abandoned one game for another. Crucially, the main points in the text do not require us to adjudicate this issue. For the main points in the text should be understood in terms of chess *as it is constituted at the time of our writing this*. Actually, there

That there is a standard in the case of chess is not simply a product of the fact that chess has a goal, and that one can succeed or fail relative to that goal. For there is a goal to moral action as well, one might say, namely to act rightly, and one can succeed or fail at that. This is not enough to establish informative standards, though. Particularists will urge that there are no universal standards that explain why acts are right. In chess, it is the fact that checkmate is a well-defined position relative to the legal moves of chess that allows us to construct an informative standard for the predicate 'correct move.' The standard in chess is thus not analogous to the trivial moral rule, 'Do the right thing.' 'Checkmate your opponent and avoid being checkmated' is in this respect much more like 'Maximize aggregate happiness,' for example, while 'Do the right thing' is more analogous to the equally useless 'win.'

The analogy with chess should shake our confidence in any argument from perceptual phenomenology to the conclusion that there are no standards or to the conclusion that there is no action-guiding standard or even to the conclusion that there are no constitutive standards (whether action-guiding or not). For in the case of chess we have a rich perceptual phenomenology alongside a constitutive standard. Hence intuitionism ultimately does little to support even Anti-Transcendental Particularism about standards.

What about the particularist-sounding comments of chess experts, though? What these writers call into question is not whether there are rules qua standards or even qua standards that are *sometimes* action-guiding. Rather, they call into question the idea that there is an extensive role for rules as guides. The rule, 'checkmate your opponent when you can' may be action-guiding in straightforwardly won positions, as with a textbook mate in two. However, most positions are far too complex for a finite agent to be able to see how to force checkmate even if that can be seen to be possible from a God's eye point of view. Potentially more useful as guides are rules of thumb like 'avoid doubled pawns,' 'a knight on the rim is dim,' and 'castle early.' What Watson calls into question is the idea that excellence in chess is largely a matter of adhering to such rules of thumb, and it is here that the appeal to a more perceptual methodology seems to do some work. Rather than dogmatically sticking to such general rules, the good chess player can 'just see' whether, for example, doubled pawns would be a bad-making feature of a given position or serve instead to open files for attack or strengthen the center. Inflexibly sticking to rules of thumb according to which, for example, doubled pawns

---

presumably are a plurality of ways in which chess is constituted even just now, given differences in rules from one chess federation or informal game setting to the next. We take it that understanding that checkmating the opponent's king and avoiding being checkmated oneself is critereal of success in all of these variants, though.

are always a disadvantage (at least to some degree) can and often does lead to mistaken evaluations.

Moreover, it is easy enough to see structural parallels with holism about reasons. Just as the fact that an action would make someone happy can be a good-making feature in one case but not another, backward pawns can be a bad-making feature of a position in one case but not another. Indeed, in his discussion of backward pawns, John Watson makes his point in a way that is extremely similar to things Dancy says about the holistic functioning of reasons: "[B]ackward pawns are in general less of a disadvantage than classical theory would imagine, *and in some cases, no disadvantage at all*" (Watson 1998: 127, emphasis added). However, in spite of his strong rhetoric against classical rule-based approaches, to his credit Watson does not make any quick inferences from holism about features of positions to particularism. Rather, he allows that this context-dependence may well be codifiable, albeit with far more complex rules than those we find in most classical manuals. Here is Watson again, in this case discussing a fairly subtle principle offered by Mihai Suba:

Suba's hypothesis makes a certain amount of sense to me. It would be interesting to pore over modern practice and try to come up with other such neo-principles. My guess is that most of them would prove to be highly qualified by conditions, and much more difficult to state. (Watson 1998: 139)

It is interesting to see how an analogue of the dialectic of Chapter 2 on holism is playing out here. Watson sees the importance of context-dependence in chess, and argues that it makes a mockery of classical chess principles. All the same, he goes on to allow that such context-dependence is consistent with much more sophisticated chess principles doing much the same work as the classical ones. The obvious analogy would be seeing the importance of the context-dependence of moral reasons, arguing that it makes a mockery of classical moral principles, but then also allowing that such context-dependence is consistent with more sophisticated moral principles doing much the same works as the classical ones were meant to do. Which is precisely the philosophical terrain we explored in Chapter 2.

Perhaps the analogy with chess suggests that a perceptual phenomenology supports some form of qualified particularism about principles qua guides but provides no real support for particularism about principles qua standards. The idea in the chess case would not be that principles are always completely useless, as the principle 'force checkmate when you can' is sometimes useful and will (if properly applied!) never lead one astray. With a few such exceptions, however, the idea would be that most players would be better off without much reliance on principles. Indeed, this concern about rules in chess is not really all that recent. Going back as far as 1943, Richard Reti noted that "[T]he source of the greatest errors is to be found in those moves that are made merely according to rule and not based on the individual plan and thought of the player" (Reti 1960: 121 [1943]).

The analogous position in the moral case might allow that we should perhaps sometimes rely in a very limited way on rules of thumb, but that we generally should be wary of such rules and look carefully at the salient features of the concrete situation at hand. It is not actually clear even in the chess case that this is as widely true as some of the experts suggest. Indeed, in spite of his concerns about rules cited in the previous paragraph, Reti went onto make it clear that:

It is not my intention to lay down here that principles are superfluous (I have already demonstrated their usefulness), but I do want it to be made sufficiently clear that chess rules must be subjected to careful consideration in each particular instance of their intended application. (Reti 1960: 121–2)

Moreover, even if chess geniuses like Garry Kasparov and Bobby Fischer have sensibilities well-honed enough to do without principles altogether (very doubtful), average club players might do well to rely on rules of thumb as useful heuristics. In any event, we are not convinced that the moral case is like this, and we return in Chapter 9 to the ways in which internalizing moral principles may enhance one's moral perception. At this stage we simply want to emphasize the limitations of this form of argument for particularism.

This version of particularism would be interesting but it is not as radical as it might sound. For any form of particularism which allows a role for action-guiding standards thereby opens the door for a fairly robust generalist element. For example, this line of argument is compatible with a form of consequentialism according to which we should almost never reason in consequentialist terms. There are, after all, familiar reasons for supposing that consequentialism might be self-effacing—direct reliance on consequentialism might not have the best consequences because it might encourage rationalization, reduce the likelihood of a climate of trust, etc. Typically, indirect consequentialists argue that we should instead rely on various rules in making everyday moral decisions, but this is not essential to indirect consequentialism as such. A consequentialist might hold that so long as we have a decently trained moral sensibility we should simply do what seems morally right to us after carefully considering all of the relevant features of the case on the grounds that this approach has the best consequences or best expected consequences. More generally, on any account allowing that there are action-guiding standards it seems that in some cases it will be sensible to take a step back and evaluate our more day-to-day practices, regardless of whether those everyday practices themselves are governed by rules of thumb or direct perceptions of what needs to be done.

Finally, there is the case of principles qua algorithmic decision-procedures. In the case of chess, it is demonstrably true that there is an algorithm for perfect chess. This is because there are a finite though incomprehensibly enormous number of possible games; so it is possible in principle to construct a decision tree that always leads to the best possible result from any given position.[10] However, this algorithm is so incredibly complex that we will almost certainly never be able to construct it. To give some idea of the complexity of chess, there are some 85 billion ways of playing just the first four moves for each side.[11] So while the chess case does demonstrate that the plausibility of a perceptual model is consistent with the logical possibility of an algorithm for perfect performance, defenders of an algorithmic conception of morality (if there are any; see Chapter 1) should find little comfort in this. For while such an algorithm is available in principle, the idea that we could ever formulate that algorithm or use it in real time to make decisions looks absurdly implausible. A research program aiming to articulate an algorithm for morally ideal living might well be equally hopeless. After all, as complex as chess is, life (which can include chess as a proper part) is more complex still.

These analogies with chess tell a cautionary tale for those who base the case for radical forms of moral particularism on the perceptual model. The analogies also illustrate the importance of the different conceptions of principles articulated in Chapter 1. Visual metaphors and the importance of 'just seeing' the relevant features of each situation in the right light are at least as apt in the case of chess as they are in the moral case. Nonetheless, this should do nothing to shake our confidence that there is a standard for the correctness of moves in chess. Nor should it shake our confidence that this standard can be action-guiding, as when one can see how to force checkmate. So it is unclear why the plausibility of a perceptual model in the moral case should undermine our confidence that there is an ultimate (and sometimes action-guiding) moral standard.

Furthermore, the perceptual model leaves completely open the normative question whether moral practice might even be improved by a greater emphasis on rules and principles. After all, the fact (if it is a fact) that we make moral judgments in a perception-like way does nothing in and of itself to prove that we could not codify the subject matter of those perceptions. The analogy

---

[10] For further discussion of this point see Dennett 1995: ch. 15.

[11] See "Chess Champion Faces Off with New Computer," *New York Times*, 21 January 2003, http://www.nytimes.com/2003/01/21/science/21CHES.html?8hpib.

with chess at best provides a highly defeasible and weakly analogical case for skepticism about the utility of such a project. Moreover, we know from other cases in which the perceptual model in an even more literal sense is true that codifiability is possible. For empirical science is based on literal observation but consists precisely in the articulation of general laws. Nonetheless, for the purposes of this chapter we are not calling into question the ubiquity or justification of the perceptual model, but instead exploring its implications. We return to these further questions in Chapters 6 and 7.

## 4.4. Summary and Preview

Moral judgment can in some cases (particularly cases where the right verdict is obvious) seem well described in perceptual terms—one 'just sees' that a particular action is right or wrong. Particularists have tried to draw support from this aspect of moral phenomenology. However, once the metaphor of 'moral vision' is unpacked it turns out to make morality seem much more like a rule-governed activity than one might have thought. Godel's Incompleteness Theorem shows that even mathematics is not codifiable in the very strong sense of being susceptible of algorithmic codification. So a particularist appeal to the perceptual model might benefit from an analogy with mathematics so long as the particularist aims only to critique principles qua algorithmic decision-procedures. However, this is an extremely modest form of particularism. For it is not entirely obvious that any generalist has really advocated moral principles as algorithmic decision-procedures and this would in any event be an extremely strong form of generalism which we have no interest in defending.

A consideration of the role of standards and rules in chess helps put the issues in a useful perspective, especially in light of the different conceptions of principles distinguished in Chapter 1. Chess, as much as morality, has a richly perceptual phenomenology. Moreover, a cousin of holism about reasons is plausible in the case of chess—holism about weaknesses (backward pawns and the like). This suggests that a perceptual phenomenology and holism are perfectly consistent with the existence of uncontroversial standards. Indeed, here we even have constitutive standards that can be action-guiding. So the analogy with chess provides a healthy reminder that a perceptual phenomenology does not dictate a radical particularist rejection of standards or even action-guiding and constitutive standards. On the other hand, the analogy with chess does seem to reinforce the particularist hypothesis that rules both do and should play a limited role in the deliberation of a morally virtuous agent. For there is some evidence in both cases that it is very easy to rely too heavily on such rules and apply them inflexibly to new and different cases. This support for Principle Abstinence Particularism is itself dependent on a number of further questions about how moral principles might guide a virtuous agent. We return to those questions in Chapter 9. In the mean time, and before turning to our positive account in Part II, we must first explain why we join the particularist in rejecting an extremely strong form of generalism—constitutive generalism. In the following chapter we explain why constitutive generalism is untenable, thus sharpening the particularist challenge before developing our positive proposal in Part II.

# 5

# Constitutive Generalism

Platitude: an idea (a) that is admitted to be true by everyone, and (b) that is not true.

(H. L. Mencken)

We have seen that holism, the main thesis invoked in support of particularism, actually provides no positive support for particularism in any of its guises (Chapter 2). Furthermore, we have seen how particularism threatens to flatten the moral landscape and how the standard device particularists invoke to avoid flattening the moral landscape (the idea of a default reason) is problematic unless understood in a deflationary way that is insufficient to block the objection (Chapter 3). Finally, we have seen that the idea of moral vision at best provides support for an extremely weak form of particularism which rejects principles understood as algorithms (Chapter 4). Needless to say, this leaves enormous room for some fairly robust forms of generalism. In Part II we develop an argument in favor of a form of generalism we call 'generalism as a regulative ideal.'

However, before developing and defending generalism as a regulative ideal, we consider a leading strategy for defending generalism, a strategy recently defended by Frank Jackson, Philip Pettit, and Michael Smith. Their argument is a welcome exception to the tendency of generalists to criticize arguments for particularism without developing a positive argument for their own view. If successful, the Jackson–Pettit–Smith argument would establish a form of constitutive generalism (in the terminology of Chapter 1). We argue here that their argument fails and that constitutive generalism is untenable. By contrast, generalism as a regulative ideal avoids the pitfalls associated with constitutive generalism but vindicates moral principles all the same, or so we shall argue in Part II.

## 5.1. Constitutive Generalism

Frank Jackson, Philip Pettit, and Michael Smith argue that those competent with moral concepts are thereby committed to what in our terms is a moral standard which codifies the entire moral landscape.[1] The argument begins with the premiss that insofar as moral judgment and knowledge are possible we must be capable of determining the moral status of new cases as they are described to us in purely descriptive terms. There may be indeterminate cases in which we are rightly unsure which moral predicate applies, but we must nonetheless be able to sort at least some cases appropriately and with confidence. Otherwise, the idea that we are really competent with moral concepts looks dubious. The possibility of classifying new cases in this way seems to presuppose the existence of a pattern that unifies all and only required actions, and patterns which do the same for the forbidden and merely permissible. Since the appeal to such patterns is the linchpin of the Jackson–Pettit–Smith argument we call it the Pattern Argument.

The Pattern Argument presents the particularist with the following dilemma: either the relevant pattern can be characterized in purely descriptive terms or not. Suppose that the pattern can be characterized in purely descriptive terms. In that case, the relevant descriptive characterization will provide us with a way of linking descriptive features with the application of moral predicates in a way that explains why the moral predicate applies when it does. Unlike the 'supervenience functions' discussed in Chapter 1, these patterns will not contain any extraneous features and hence will be explanatory and presumably finite. Moreover, a grasp of these patterns will be what explains a speaker's competence with moral concepts and hence the ability to make moral judgments in the first place. So on the first horn of the dilemma the particularist position simply evaporates and we are left with a robust form of constitutive generalism.

The second horn of the dilemma holds that while there is a pattern unifying all and only actions falling under a given moral predicate, this pattern cannot be cashed out in descriptive terms. Jackson, Pettit, and Smith argue that in this case the particularist must be committed to a form of Moorean non-naturalism, according to which moral properties are *sui generis*. On this horn of the dilemma, Jackson, Pettit, and Smith argue that particularism is no longer the new and exciting position it is advertised as being. Instead it is simply Moore's doctrine all over again:

If this is the particularist's view, however, then we think that they can fairly be accused of false advertising. Under examination the new and exciting thesis that there are no moral principles collapses into the jejune doctrine advanced by Moore at the turn of the century: moral properties are *sui generis*, and hence are not to be found among the descriptive. (Jackson, Pettit, and Smith 2000: 88)

---

[1]  See Jackson, Pettit, and Smith 2000.

However, this last move is a non sequitur. Perhaps particularists are committed to Moorean non-naturalism but this does not mean that particularism 'collapses into' Moorean non-naturalism. Particularism would collapse into Moorean non-naturalism and hence not represent a novel theoretical position only if particularism's content was *exhausted* by non-naturalism. This, however, clearly is not the case. Particularists may hold that moral properties are non-natural and *sui generis*, but they also maintain that there is no further purely descriptive and finite pattern with which the moral terrain can be mapped. This further commitment is not entailed by Moorean non-naturalism itself. For example, a Moorean non-naturalist could accept a very simple form of hedonistic act-utilitarianism in normative ethics on the grounds that the non-natural property of rightness necessarily is instantiated by a given action just in case the action maximizes happiness, hedonistically construed.

The Moorean could even maintain that these actions are in some way 'made right' by the descriptive fact that they maximize happiness even though 'being right' and 'maximizing happiness' pick out distinct properties on the Moorean conception. It may be difficult to make adequate sense of the perhaps initially obscure idea of 'making right' but neither is it obviously impossible. Perhaps the non-natural property of being right should be understood as a relational property holding between facts and possible actions, in which case those facts which make an action right will be one of the relata. Indeed, Moore himself embraced a form of 'ideal utilitarianism' and so was committed to a form of generalism, his non-naturalism notwithstanding. Moore's combination of generalism and non-naturalism does not seem to make his position inconsistent.

So particularists can sit comfortably on the second horn of the dilemma of the pattern argument, at least so far as the charge of 'false advertising' goes. Indeed, Jackson, Pettit, and Smith go on to recognize this point (in a footnote) themselves:

For the record, Mooreans can allow that there are descriptive patterns *in* the right acts themselves. They are simply committed to denying that the descriptive pattern provides us with a semantics for 'right'. As proof of this, witness the example of Moore himself who was, after all, an ideal utilitarian, and hence, in one perfectly good sense, a principle-ist. (Jackson, Pettit, and Smith 2000: 93 n. 11)

This, however, means that Jackson, Pettit, and Smith's accusation of false advertising in the main body of the text is a non sequitur. Perhaps Jackson, Pettit, and Smith really just think that if particularism depends on Moorean non-naturalism then it must be false because Moorean non-naturalism itself is false. In that case, this argument against particularism is parasitic on some further argument against non-naturalism. As Jonathan Dancy points out in his reply to the Pattern Argument, "It is impossible to object to a particularist form of intuitionism that it is intuitionist. One cannot object to a position merely by describing it" (Dancy 1999a: 64).

Of course, there are plenty of familiar and powerful arguments against non-naturalism. So we do not mean to suggest that objecting to particularism by objecting to non-naturalism is an argumentative dead end.[2] However, it would be dialectically unfortunate if the debate over particularism collapsed into the debate over non-naturalism in metaethics. For while non-naturalism faces rather serious problems, so do all of the other major positions in metaethics. Non-naturalism may well turn out to be indefensible, but it is not so obviously indefensible at this stage that those concerned to defend generalism should give such hostages to fortune.

## 5.2. Constitutive Generalism and the Open Question Argument

The Pattern Argument contends that there must be some principle constitutive of moral judgment, but takes no position on its content. A more direct strategy would be to argue for a specific set of principles as constitutive of moral judgment. The most obvious strategy would be to argue that moral predicates like 'morally required' can be analyzed into purely descriptive language. In this section we explain why this more direct strategy for defending constitutive generalism is unpromising. Here we rely on a version of Moore's famous 'Open Question Argument.'

G. E. Moore argued that attempts to define 'good' and other evaluative predicates in purely naturalistic terms are doomed to failure. Even supernatural properties can be naturalistic in Moore's strained sense of the term; 'descriptive' undoubtedly would have been a better terminological choice for his purposes. There has been an extensive debate about how the natural/non-natural (better: moral/descriptive) distinction is best understood and we do not here intend to enter into those controversies, but instead rest content with an intuitive understanding of the distinction. Our discussion is compatible with any of a number of ways of making the distinction more precise. For a survey of some of the main ways of drawing this distinction, see Ridge 2003b.

According to Moore, any naturalistic analysis N of 'good' (as it is used in moral contexts) is vulnerable to what is usually called the Open Question

---

[2] Although oddly enough Jackson Pettit, and Smith do not allude to any of the familiar arguments against non-naturalism in their paper; perhaps they simply cannot take non-naturalism seriously.

Argument. Moore holds that questions of the form, 'X is N, but is it good?' are always conceptually open, in the sense that asking such a question does not betray a lack of competence with the predicate 'is good.'[3] For example, a naturalist might argue that 'good' as used in moral contexts just means 'pleasant.' Moore's contention is that this definition is mistaken because the question 'I know X is pleasant but is it good?' seems conceptually open to competent speakers whereas the proposed definition would entail that this question is conceptually closed, in the same way 'I know he is a male sibling but is he a brother?' is conceptually closed. Someone might coherently hold the view that pleasure is good only if deserved, for example, or that certain kinds of pleasures (such as sadistic pleasures) are worthless or downright bad. Regardless of whether any of these views are correct or even plausible, they seem free from conceptual confusion.

Another naturalist might maintain that 'good' just means 'approved of by all fully informed and impartial spectators' but questions like 'I know that not all fully informed and impartial spectators would approve of this but is it good?' also seem conceptually open. One might deny that all fully informed and impartial spectators would unanimously approve of anything without embracing nihilism. Again, this does not seem like a conceptual mistake; the person who denies that the approval of impartial and fully informed spectators is necessary for something to be good could be a competent user of the predicate 'is good.'

Moore thinks this point tells against any naturalistic analysis. The relevant contrast is with fairly uncontroversial naturalistic definitions of nonmoral terms. Questions where it is clear that there is conceptual confusion seem very different. For example, 'I know Joe is an unmarried man over eighteen, but is he a bachelor?' simply do not seem conceptually open in the same way that analogous questions about goodness seem open.[4] The same idea motivates Moore to charge his opponents with having committed the "naturalistic fallacy" by inferring a moral conclusion from purely naturalistic premises. On the strength of the Open Question Argument, Moore argues that 'good' refers to an indefinable non-natural property. If Moore's argument works, then it can be deployed against any version of constitutive generalism according to

---

[3] In what follows, we couch the open question argument in terms of moral predicates. We ask the patience of those readers would prefer that the argument be put in terms of moral concepts. We put the argument as we do only scrupulously to avoid begging any questions against noncognitivists, some of whom would deny that there are any moral concepts.

[4] It is, however, pretty clear that, even if Moore were right that his opponents were making the mistake with which he charges them, it would be implausible to think of it as a fallacy on all fours with the fallacy of equivocation. For a very clear and persuasive discussion of this point see Frankena 1939.

which one grasps a given moral concept by understanding that it applies just in case the descriptive features mentioned in its naturalistic analysis are present.

In a classic reply to Moore, Frankena argues that the Open Question Argument begs the question. Suppose we understand the Open Question Argument as follows:

(1) Given any naturalistic analysis, call it 'N' of any moral predicate, call it 'G,' questions of the form, 'I know X is N but is it G?' will always be conceptually open. [intuitively plausible claim motivated by induction over a set of examples]

(2) If naturalism were true then for some analysis N of some moral predicate 'G' questions of the form 'I know X is N but is it G' would not be conceptually open. [from the definition of naturalism understood as a conceptual truth] Therefore

(3) Naturalism is not true. [by modus tollens]

If this is Moore's argument, then it does beg the question. Any sensible naturalist will deny (1) unless some further argument is given for it, as naturalism (understood as a conceptual truth) directly entails the denial of (1). Frankena underscores this point by remarking that "the charge of committing the naturalistic fallacy can be made, if at all, only as a conclusion of the discussion and not as an instrument of deciding it" (Frankena 1939: 465).

So whether the relevant questions really are conceptually open must be treated as a live issue. However, we can give the Open Question Argument a better run for its money by starting instead with the more modest premiss that the relevant questions at least *seem* conceptually open to most competent users of moral predicates. The Open Question Argument then proceeds in two stages. The first stage contends that the best explanation of the appearance of openness is that the questions really are open.[5] This certainly would provide a straightforward and elegant explanation of the appearances. Moreover, the fact that such questions consistently seem open to reflective and competent speakers suggests that this appearance is not due to confusion. Of course, determining whether this is the best explanation of the appearances requires a comparison with the most plausible rival explanations.

The second stage of the argument maintains that the best explanation of the openness of the relevant questions is either non-naturalism or expressivism. On either of these views moral thought will not be constituted by a set of principles which provide the truth-conditions for moral predicates in

---

[5] The idea that this is the most charitable reading of the Open Question Argument can be found in both Ball 1991 and Darwall, Gibbard, and Railton 1992.

descriptive terms. We have already seen that non-naturalists like Moore would not suppose any such principle is constitutive of moral judgment. Neither would expressivism involve any commitment to constitutive generalism. On an expressivist account, competent speakers as such must simply be consistent in their expressions of attitudes of approval and disapproval; they need not agree in attitude (approve of the same things). So whether we take the lesson of the Open Question Argument to be non-naturalism or expressivism, we have good reason to reject constitutive generalism.

The constitutive generalist's most promising strategy is to deny that the relevant questions are always open, contesting the first stage of the Open Question Argument. The constitutive generalist could try to deny the putative data, and hold that ordinary speakers do not find the relevant questions to be open. But this seems desperate. The relevant questions simply do seem open to competent speakers across a very wide range of proffered analyses of moral terms. Most likely, this is simply a fact and any plausible theory must accommodate it. Of course it remains in principle possible that at some stage a constitutive generalist will offer an analysis that does not leave competent speakers thinking the relevant questions are open, but in our view this is very unlikely.

For any naturalistic analysis of a moral predicate will, in conjunction with the relevant facts, entail what morally ought to be done in any possible circumstance in which there is a determinate fact of the matter. The fact that disagreement on moral questions is so pervasive and deep even in the face of agreement on all the relevant descriptively characterized facts strongly suggests that the relevant questions will seem open to most competent users of moral predicates. Indeed, no defender of constitutive generalism could reasonably claim that their theory is so clearly correct that it does not leave competent speakers finding the relevant questions to have an 'open feel.' It therefore seems reasonable at this stage to put this strategy to one side, albeit provisionally. If some constitutive generalist ever does 'deliver the goods,' then this issue should of course be revisited.[6]

Assuming the relevant questions do seem open to competent speakers, is the best explanation of this that they really are open? The leading and probably the only rival explanation would be that the meanings of moral predicates are for some reason not transparent to competent speakers. If even competent

---

[6] We should note, though, that even if this were eventually shown to be the case it would not decisively vindicate constitutive generalism. For the meanings of words change over time and expressivists concede that moral terms have secondary descriptive meanings. So it is possible that moral terms could come to shift their meaning over time so much that they cease to reflect genuinely moral norms or concepts as opposed to calcified purely conventional norms or concepts.

speakers are not guaranteed to recognize a correct analysis when they see it, then it should be no surprise that the relevant questions seem open. Of course, there must be some sense in which competent users of moral predicates know the meanings of those predicates. However, they might know the meanings of those predicates in virtue of having a certain kind of 'know-how' rather than knowing that the words mean such-and-such.

The ability of competent speakers to deploy the predicate 'is grammatical' provides a useful analogy. There is reason to believe that the correct rules of grammar for any natural language will be so unintuitive and complex that competent speakers will not recognize their correctness when presented them. Nonetheless such speakers know what it means to say a sentence is grammatical in virtue of having the ability reliably to categorize sentences as either grammatical or ungrammatical. The ability need not be perfect, and competent speakers are subject to various kinds of performance-based errors. Being drunk or fatigued, for example, obviously can impair one's ability to determine whether a sentence is grammatical. More interestingly, competent speakers may use reliable but imperfect heuristics to classify sentences as grammatical. These heuristics might lead to error even if the speaker is not prone to any particular impairment. One example of this phenomenon is the string 'Buffalo buffalo buffalo' which competent speakers generally hear as ungrammatical. However, when "our friendly linguist says, 'Think of it on the model, "Men admire women." '" (Daniels 1996: 68) we can see that it can be read as grammatical after all.[7]

The linguist's job is to gather data as to how competent speakers classify sentences as grammatical or ungrammatical, controlling for performance-based errors, and then articulate a set of grammatical rules that would best explain those classifications. If the job is done correctly then there is a useful sense in which the linguist's rules provide a definition of 'is grammatical in such-and-such language' notwithstanding the inability of competent speakers to recognize the soundness of that definition. The constitutive generalist might argue that we can do something similar for moral predicates. In that case, we would have a model of linguistic competence that could explain why competent speakers might not recognize a correct analysis of a moral predicate when presented with one.

On reflection, it seems that the constitutive generalist must tell some story like this. For if moral predicates can be analyzed in naturalistic terms then there must be some way to extract that analysis from the beliefs and dispositions

---

[7] In American English, 'buffalo' can be used colloquially as a verb meaning roughly 'to bewilder or baffle.'

of competent speakers. After all, natural languages are conventional, and linguistic conventions are constituted by the beliefs and dispositions of the participants. If a proposed naturalistic analysis is not true in virtue of those beliefs and dispositions, then it is hard to imagine what makes it true. A version of constitutive generalism that denied this platitude about the connection between linguistic meaning and the beliefs and dispositions of competent speakers would be very implausible. It would be tantamount to supposing that the fact that 'fern' refers to ferns has nothing to do with the fact that people are disposed to use 'fern' to refer to ferns. The challenge for the constitutive generalist is therefore to explain how we might extract a naturalistic analysis of moral predicates from the dispositions and beliefs of competent speakers. In the next section we consider what we take to be the best attempt to meet this challenge and explain why it nonetheless fails.

## 5.3. Moral Functionalism

Frank Jackson and Philip Pettit try to meet this challenge with a view they call "moral functionalism." Moral functionalism relies heavily on a parallel with functionalism in the philosophy of mind. According to functionalism in the philosophy of mind, the reference of mental terms (like 'belief,' 'desire,' 'pain') is fixed by certain input and output relations. For example, the reference of 'pain' is partly fixed by the fact that bodily damage tends to cause pain and the fact that pain tends to cause aversive behaviour. Jackson and Pettit suggest that we take all the platitudes recognized by folk psychology and replace all occurrences of mental predicates with variables. So, for example, if it is a platitude that people who are in pain want to alleviate that pain, then we can include this in the story we tell about the reference of 'pain' so long as we replace all occurrences of 'want' with the same variable. The general strategy is to put these platitudes together into a long conjunction, replace all mental terms with variables, and then use this conjunction to fix the reference of the mental predicates. The idea is that this will allow us to include moral predicates in the platitudes without making the final analysis circular. Since this idea goes back to Frank Ramsey and has been refined and defended by David Lewis, such conjunctions are often referred to as 'Ramsey–Lewis' conjunctions.

We can understand this reference-fixing in one of two ways. Because the conjunction constructed will describe a certain functional role (a set of input- and output-relations) we might suppose that a given mental predicate refers to the property of playing the relevant functional role. If we understand the account in this way then we are committed to understanding mental properties as 'role' properties. On this account, we can determine the reference of mental predicates entirely a priori. However, we can instead understand each mental predicate as referring to the property that realizes the relevant role in the actual world. In that case, we understand mental properties as 'realizer' properties and determining the reference of a mental predicate will be partly an a posteriori matter.

To take a highly oversimplified and implausible example, we might do this sort of network analysis on 'pain' and fix on the functional role of being caused by bodily damage and causing aversive behaviour. If we think of mental properties as role properties then the property of being in pain is the property of being in a state caused by bodily damage and that causes aversive behaviour and we can determine this entirely a priori. If, however, we think of mental properties as realizer properties, then we must find out what properties realize this role in the actual world. Suppose the property of causing aversive behaviour and being caused by bodily damage is realized by the property of having such-and-such fibers firing. In that case, to be in pain is to have such-and-such fibers firing. On this sort of account, the reference of 'pain' is partly a priori (fixing on the relevant functional role) and partly a posteriori (finding out what realizes that role). Finally, we can understand these terms as referring 'rigidly' or 'flaccidly' to the properties to which they refer. A term rigidly designates a property if and only if it refers to that property in every possible world in which the property exists; otherwise it refers flaccidly to that property.[8] Different versions of functionalism might go different ways on this issue.

The moral functionalist adopts the same basic strategy to fix the reference of moral predicates. This strategy promises to disarm the Open Question Argument in two ways. First, on the 'realizer' interpretation of the reference of moral terms their reference will in part be an a posteriori matter. Even if it is a priori that a given moral predicate necessarily refers to whatever realizes such-and-such role, it will still be an empirical matter just what property realizes that role. Mere competence with a moral predicate does not guarantee that one has done the empirical work necessary to discover just what property realizes the relevant role. Secondly, there is not even a guarantee that competent users of moral language will recognize the relevant functional role when presented with it. On the proposed account, competence with moral language consists in being disposed to act in accordance with the relevant platitudes. As in the case of grammatical rules, it does not follow from the fact that one is so disposed that one would recognize a complete statement of those platitudes when presented with it.

[8] See Kripke 1980.

Crucial to the success of moral functionalism is its ability to specify the platitudes in a way that determinately fixes the reference of moral predicates. Jackson and Pettit rightly emphasize that the platitudes need not be recognized explicitly. A given platitude might instead be grasped implicitly, in the sense that speakers are disposed to draw inferences in ways that would make sense only if they accepted the platitude. Furthermore, our understanding of which putative platitudes really are platitudes is defeasible. The list of platitudes with which we begin our inquiry might have to be modified as a result of further a priori reflection. Moreover, we should recognize that our ability as theorists adequately to characterize those platitudes is fallible. These are important caveats and they make the moral functionalist position much more attractive than it would be without them. Nonetheless, the claim that a given proposition is a platitude (or 'commonplace,' as it is sometimes put) is a very strong one. Pettit and Jackson are admirably clear on this important point: "The commonplaces that emerge ... are the *a priori* compulsory propositions that anyone who knows how to use the terms is in a position to recognise as true" (Jackson and Pettit 1995: 26). This sets the bar very high, but it is hard to see how anything weaker could help us provide a genuine conceptual analysis of moral terms.

Unfortunately for the constitutive generalist, the few genuine platitudes surrounding the predicate 'is a reason to' when used to indicate a reason for action are far too weak to fix a determinate referent for that predicate. First, the platitudes surrounding thick moral predicates like 'is fair,' 'is courageous,' and 'is gluttonous' are not also platitudes for the predicate 'is a reason to.' For although anyone who understands those thick moral predicates must (let us suppose) have the concept of a reason for action, the converse does not hold. Someone might well make judgments about what there is reason to do without knowing the meanings of any particular thick moral predicate. Someone who does not think in terms of justice, fairness, gluttony, modesty, honesty can still have views about what sorts of actions are worthwhile. I might suppose that there is reason to do something just in case it promotes happiness without grasping any of the preceding thick moral predicates. After all, thick moral predicates are a motley crew and reflect substantive assumptions about what is worth doing and human weaknesses that make certain character traits necessary. Someone competent with the predicate 'is a reason to' might well reject those substantive assumptions. A hedonist, for example, would reject the idea that honesty as such provides any reason for action whatsoever yet does not thereby seem guilty of incompetence with the predicate 'is a reason to.' So while the analysis of thick moral predicates like 'is fair' presumably must include platitudes about reasons, the converse does not hold.

So just what are the platitudes surrounding thin moral predicates? Here we focus on the predicate 'is a reason to' but the main points we make should carry over to other thin predicates like 'good' and 'bad' as used in moral contexts. The most plausible candidate platitudes here are fairly formal-sounding theses. For example, it is platitudinous that a consideration is a reason for someone to perform an action only if the action is 'up to her' in some sense. The supervenience of the moral on the descriptive is also platitudinous. That is to say, it is a platitude that if two possible worlds are identical in all their descriptive features then if a consideration is a reason with a given valence in one world then it is also a reason with the same valence in the other world.

Perhaps (though this is more controversial) it is also a platitude that the predicate 'is a reason to' refers to a consideration in virtue of its standing in an appropriate relation to an agent and a possible action. We might call this relation the 'favoring relation.' For example, to say that an action's having certain consequences is a reason to perform the action is to claim that its having those consequences favors the agent's performing the action. Something along these lines may be a platitude about the logical form of reasons. However, these rather formal-sounding platitudes (and others like them) are simply not jointly sufficient for a plausible reference-fixing account of 'is a reason to.' It would, for example, hardly be plausible to hold that a consideration C is a reason for an agent A to $\phi$ just in case C stands in a relation R to $\phi$ such that (a) $\phi$ing is within A's power, and (b) for anyone in circumstances exactly like A's in all other respects relation R would also hold between that person and her $\phi$ing. This analysis simply does not fix a unique reference for the favoring relation and hence does not fix the extension of 'is a reason to.' So far as this analysis goes, the favoring relation could simply be the relation of being within the agent's power, which is hardly a plausible analysis of 'is a reason to'. We certainly mean more in saying that C is a reason for A to $\phi$ than we mean when we simply say that $\phi$ing is within A's power. After all, we also mean that when we say C is a reason for A *not* to $\phi$! To think otherwise is to leave the favoring out of the favoring relation. The analysis does not uniquely pick out this relation, though, for it does not uniquely pick out any single relation. So the platitudes considered thus far fail spectacularly to fix a unique extension for 'is a reason to.'[9]

The obvious move for the constitutive generalist is to invoke more seemingly substantive propositions as platitudes about reasons. Frank Jackson, for example, claims that it is a platitude that if an action is a killing then normally it is

---

[9] Michael Smith also raises this worry and helpfully refers to it as the "permutation problem" for network analyses (Smith 1994: 48–56).

wrong and that it is a platitude that pain is bad (Jackson 1998: 130). The trouble is that these propositions simply are not platitudes in the relevant sense. The platitude about killing is couched in terms of what is "normally" wrong, which sounds like an empirical generalization, but that cannot be the right reading if it really is a platitude in the relevant sense. For platitudes here are a priori truths grasped by all competent users of moral predicates and no merely empirical generalization can be known a priori. Perhaps the idea is that the mere fact that an action is a killing is a reason not to perform it, or at least is a reason unless certain 'defeating' conditions are present. However, this also is not platitudinous. For example, a dyed-in-the-wool hedonistic utilitarian will deny that the fact that an action is an instance of killing is itself ever a reason against it. Such a utilitarian does not thereby seem to be incompetent with moral predicates. To take another example, the acceptance of nihilism does not in our view betray conceptual confusion. However, it is trivial that a nihilist would deny that facts about killing are ever reason-providing. For a nihilist insists that there are (and perhaps can be) no reasons for action.

Jackson's other proposed example of a platitude is that pain is bad. The idea presumably is that pain is bad in itself, since whether it is bad for its consequences is not something we could plausibly know a priori. However, the thesis that pain is bad in itself must at least be highly qualified to stand any chance of being a platitude. For a start, competent users of moral predicates often suppose that pain is not bad if deserved. On a retributive view, an evil person's being in pain can be good rather than bad. We could refine the platitude to accommodate this exception. The platitude would then be that pain is bad unless it is deserved. However, even this is not a platitude. Indeed, a more radical rejection of the idea that pain can ever in itself be bad is conceptually coherent. Once again, a radical form of nihilism which holds that nothing is really good or bad does not seem to betray any *conceptual* confusion. More interestingly, a virtue ethical perspective might insist that it is always character traits which are good or bad in themselves and that this explains why pain should be avoided—we should avoid being the kind of people who cause pain. Such a view would entail that pain is not bad in itself, though a disposition not to alleviate pain is bad in itself. While we find this view substantively implausible (it seems to get things back to front), those who hold it do not seem to suffer from conceptual confusion. Finally, even if it were platitudinous that pain (when not deserved) is bad in itself, this is hardly sufficient for a plausible reductive analysis of 'is bad.' For any analysis built on this platitude alone would entail that nothing other than pain is bad in itself, which is a highly controversial question and hardly one that could plausibly be held to be settled by conceptual fiat. Those who think injustice, cruelty, and dishonesty are bad in themselves, for example, do not thereby seem to be guilty of conceptual confusion. Conceptually, there are open questions about what is bad in itself. Consequently the search for suitably robust genuine platitudes is futile, and a plausible reductive analysis of 'is bad' is impossible. The same point applies to 'is a reason to' and the other thin moral predicates.

In sum, moral functionalists face a dilemma. On the one hand, they can characterize the platitudes as formal propositions like the proposition that there is reason for someone to do something only if it is within the person's power. In that case, the proposed platitudes are radically insufficient to fix a plausible and unique reference for moral predicates. On the other hand, they can characterize the platitudes as including more robust propositions like the proposition that killing is normally wrong or that pain is bad. However, once these propositions are made determinate enough to assess they are not platitudes. For there are intuitively plausible examples of people who are competent in their use and understanding of moral predicates but who reject these propositions. In a way, this should not be surprising. The appeal to platitudes is meant to finesse the Open Question Argument by invoking a set of propositions that any competent user of moral language must accept and then build a rather complicated analysis on the basis of those propositions. This is supposed to finesse the Open Question Argument insofar as the resulting analysis might be so complicated that a competent user of moral language might well not recognize the analysis when presented with it. However, if any of the putative platitudes is very substantive, then a version of the Open Question Argument can plausibly be deployed against the claim that it really is platitudinous.

We close this section by briefly revisiting an issue raised but put to one side in Chapter 3. Recall that at one point Margaret Little characterized her construal of the distinction between default reasons and non-default reasons in conceptual terms:

> mastery of moral concepts *is* mastery of defeasible generalizations. To be sure one can understand the concepts without ever stating these generalizations explicitly (and one certainly need have no thought, as such, of the terms in which they have been put). But one cannot be said to understand moral concepts without appreciating the privileging moves that lie at their heart. (Little 2001: 39)

Moreover, this move might be used to help Jackson explain how we should understand the use of 'normally' in his claim that it is a platitude that killing is normally wrong. Lance and Little's defeasible principles seem tailor-made to help someone like Jackson avoid being forced to take an implausible statistical reading of that claim.

On one reading of the preceding quotation, Little here seems committed to a form of constitutive generalism about what she calls 'defeasible principles.' Whether this is the right reading of Little depends on just how we are to read 'understand' in the quotation above. Since constitutive generalism is an especially ambitious form of generalism, this reading might seem in tension with Little's characterization of herself as a 'card-carrying moral particularist' (Little 2001: 32). However, the machinery of Chapter 1 can help sort this out. We must simply remember that there are many moral particularisms. When it comes to *non*-defeasible moral principles, Little really is a card-carrying moral particularist—a Principle Eliminativist, in fact. By contrast, when it comes to defeasible moral principles, she is a constitutive generalist on this reading. Regardless of whether Little would, in fact, claim that defeasible generalizations are platitudes in the Jackson/Pettit sense, the view occupies some interesting logical space worth exploring. We here simply investigate whether such a view could help the constitutive generalist.

It is, though, worth noting that there is a more subtle tension between the view suggested by this passage from Little and her particularist sympathies For, as we saw in the exchange between Dancy and Jackson, Pettit, and Smith, the metaethical view most amenable to moral particularism is non-naturalism. Particularists aspire to a form of moral realism and unlike naturalists they insist that the moral is not reducible to the natural. Indeed, Little herself has defended non-naturalism elsewhere.[10] Since some version of the Open Question Argument is the most powerful argument for non-naturalism, particularists should be (and generally are) very sympathetic to it. However, by embracing constitutive generalism about defeasible moral principles Little takes on commitments very similar to those of Jackson and Pettit's moral functionalism, and we have seen how those commitments fit poorly with the semantic intuitions behind the Open Question Argument.

In any event, it should be clear enough why the view suggested in the preceding passage from Little is untenable. Someone can be competent with moral concepts without embracing any of the defeasible generalizations she discusses. A nihilist can deny that pain or lying (or anything else) provides defeasible reasons or indeed any kind of reason at all without conceptual confusion. To take another example, a hedonist would deny that lying in itself provides a defeasible reason (or any kind of reason at all) but is not thereby conceptually confused. Certain forms of Kantianism and virtue ethics deny that pain in itself provides a defeasible reason (or any kind of reason at all). However, Kantians and virtue ethicists presumably are not thereby guilty of

[10] See Little 1994.

conceptual confusion. Little's so-called defeasible generalizations are fascinating but are not essential for competence with moral concepts.

## 5.4. Preview and Summary

Constitutive generalism boldly claims that certain moral principles linking the descriptive to the moral are constitutive of moral judgment. If constitutive generalism were defensible, then this would provide a powerful reply to the particularist challenge. However, constitutive generalism is itself vulnerable to a Moorean Open Question Argument, or so we have argued. Furthermore, reliance on anything as controversial as constitutive generalism to meet the particularist challenge looks dialectically unwise. For any form of constitutive generalism will inevitably be much more controversial than the more modest thesis that there are moral principles which are true, explanatory, and useful. We should therefore explore what we are calling 'generalism as a regulative ideal.'

In Part II we turn our attention to making a positive case for generalism as a regulative idea. We begin modestly in Chapter 6 by arguing that moral knowledge in particular cases presupposes the availability of a certain sort of hedged principle which we call a default principle. Then in Chapter 7 we go further and argue that the best explanation of the possibility of practical wisdom entails that the entire moral landscape can be codified with a manageable set of unhedged principles which go from descriptive antecedents to moral conclusions. Lest this all seem of merely theoretical interest, we go on in Chapter 8 to argue that there are excellent moral reasons for us to try to codify the moral landscape by articulating these principles. Finally, in Chapter 9 we explain how moral principles can and should play an important role in guiding action.

# PART II

# The Case for Generalism as a Regulative Ideal

# 6

# From Moral Knowledge to Default Principles

"I can see nothing," said I, handing it back to my friend.
"On the contrary, Watson, you can see everything. You fail however to reason from what you see. You are too timid in drawing your inferences."

(Arthur Conan Doyle, "The Adventure of The Blue Carbuncle")

We are now ready to begin our positive case for generalism. Because the issues dividing generalists and particularists are so fundamental, any argument for generalism or particularism runs a serious risk of begging central questions. Our ambition in what follows is to start from ground that is common between generalists and particularists. But where might one find such common ground? Somewhat surprisingly, the possibility of moral knowledge in particular cases proves to be a fertile shared assumption. In the present chapter we argue that the possibility of such knowledge presupposes the availability of a certain kind of hedged moral principle—a default principle. After initially presenting our argument, we will address a long-standing objection to hedged principles of all kinds—the objection that such principles are only vacuously true. Answering this important objection will require refuting a thesis that we have already seen advanced by particularists in our discussions of the argument from holism and default reasons, namely the thesis that just about any feature can be a reason, provided a suitable context. This is the first stage in our positive case for generalism as a regulative ideal.

While some may question whether moral knowledge is possible, both particularists and generalists agree about this. Particularism is not a skeptical doctrine, and particularists are keen to emphasize how well particularism fits with the idea that ordinary people very often have moral knowledge without any need for moral principles. Even if particularists and generalists sometimes disagree about the sources of moral knowledge or the character of moral reasoning, they agree that our moral thinking can yield knowledge in particular cases. We do not in this chapter take a position on what makes such knowledge possible, but instead explore the presuppositions of such knowledge. More metaphorically, our argument in this chapter begins downstream from the possibility of moral knowledge, and does not bear upon the upstream sources of that knowledge.[1]

To be clear, we do not here deny that there may be unknowable moral truths. If there are such truths, then the arguments of this chapter (and the next) do not extend to them. So our position is that we can and should codify all of morality with the possible exception of those parts of morality which transcend possible knowledge. We do not take this last caveat to be a major concession. For moral truths which transcend possible knowledge can be of no practical interest.[2]

The argument of this chapter, if sound, is already enough to refute three of the five main forms of particularism about hedged principles outlined in Chapter 1. There are moral principles, namely default principles, and we have good reason to believe there are. So both Principle Eliminativism and Principle Skepticism about hedged principles are false. Moreover, this is also a refutation of even Anti-Transcendental Particularism about hedged principles. Recall that Anti-Transcendental Particularism holds that moral thought does not presuppose the availability of a 'suitable stock of moral principles.' If the argument of the present chapter is sound then this is simply false. The possibility of moral knowledge in particular cases, and hence moral thought insofar as it aspires to count as knowledge, does presuppose the availability of a suitable stock of moral principles—namely, a suitable stock of default principles.[3]

Importantly, the present chapter does not exhaust our defense of principles. Default principles represent a bare minimum that even those with very hardy particularist sympathies must grudgingly allow. Because default principles are hedged, some may reasonably suspect that particularism lives on in the hedges. Furthermore, because our argument for default principles does not settle how many valid moral principles there are, others may suspect that particularism

---

[1]  Thomas Baldwin argues that F. H. Bradley and H. A. Prichard are best understood as filling this logical space, holding that, while focus on particular cases is epistemologically primary, the judgment we make in the particular case itself presupposes a suitable moral principle. See Baldwin 2002: 101–4.

[2]  For a more extensive discussion of unknowable obligations, see Sorensen 1995.

[3]  Of course if we take 'moral thought' as it occurs in our characterization of Anti-Transcendental Particularism to refer simply to moral concepts, then we might agree that moral concepts do not presuppose principles, even default principles. Indeed, since we reject constitutive generalism, this seems to us like the right conclusion. But by itself this would not yield a distinctly interesting version of particularism. Such a particularism would amount to no more than the rejection of analytic moral principles. So we take 'moral thought' to refer not merely to moral concepts but to the success humans display in deploying those concepts. One dimension of that success, we (and particularists) claim is an ability sometimes to know that a moral concept applies to a particular case, e.g. that a certain action was wrong.

will live on in the sheer number of principles. We address these worries and argue for the availability of a suitable stock of unhedged moral principles in Chapter 7.

## 6.1. Moral Knowledge and Default Principles

In a standard case, knowledge that a given action is wrong is based on a recognition of the moral reasons against it. Here we assume that moral knowledge based entirely on reliable testimony is parasitic on someone else having understood the relevant moral reasons. So in a standard case knowledge that a given action is wrong is based on a recognition of the relevant moral reasons, where these reasons are themselves simply descriptive facts which favor not performing the action. Could the relation between these descriptive facts and wrongness be captured in a principle? The moral reasons against an action could transcend principled articulation if they were either infinite or simply too numerous for us to articulate. However, before considering these possible barriers to capturing our reasons with moral principles, we first need to distinguish two ways of acquiring moral knowledge.

Moral knowledge can be based on description or first-hand observation. The particularist's use of the metaphor of 'moral vision' emphasizes the latter at the expense of the former, but we should not take the metaphor too literally. Indeed, any denial of the possibility of moral knowledge by description would lead to wholesale skepticism about the practical role of morality in our lives. Morality can have practical relevance only if we can have moral knowledge apart from literal observation of the candidate action. Otherwise we could not know whether our action is permissible until we had already watched ourselves perform it!

In any event, consider the case in which an agent literally sees someone performing an immoral action, and in which it is natural to say that she 'just sees' it is wrong. The central point here is that our perceptual faculties are limited. No doubt vision and the other senses tell us more than we consciously realize at the time, but nobody seriously contends that our senses tell us everything. So the features of a situation in virtue of which we just see that a given action is wrong must themselves be limited.

The case of moral knowledge by description is even clearer. If we do not directly witness a crime but only hear about it from someone else, then our moral judgment that it was wrong must be based on the finite and humanly comprehensible set of facts included in (or at least inferable from) our interlocutor's description. When we are articulate enough to say why a given action is wrong, we may cite a wide range of features of the action, but this list of features will not be so long that we could not with patience complete it. For example, consider the decision to drop a nuclear bomb on Nagasaki three days after the bomb was dropped on Hiroshima. The example is controversial, but assume for the sake of argument that the decision to drop the second bomb was morally wrong. If it was wrong, then a full account of why it was wrong may well be difficult to provide with any confidence. However, many of the difficulties here are empirical; once we have settled on all the relevant empirical facts a full account of why it was wrong to drop the second bomb plausibly would not be extremely long or perhaps even all that complex. The wrongness of the decision presumably is a function of the obvious fact that doing so caused an enormous amount of suffering and premature death, and the less obvious fact that there were alternative ways of bringing the war to a close which would not have been nearly so costly in terms of human lives and suffering. A more full and nuanced account of the decision to drop the second bomb would go into greater detail and perhaps adduce a few additional sorts of reasons. However, the idea that a full account of the moral reasons in virtue of which it was wrong to drop the second bomb would be so long as to transcend human articulation is extremely implausible. The example illustrates the plausibility of the more general idea that even in fairly complex cases we can (given access to all the relevant empirical facts, which will often be a very tall order) give a full account of the relevant moral reasons.

If we assume atomism about reasons, then this would already be enough to establish that we could articulate a suitable moral principle. For, given that the features in virtue of which the action is wrong are humanly comprehensible, atomism entails that whenever those features occur and there are no other reasons present we have an action with the same moral status. So if we 'just see' that Harry's action is wrong simply because it involves deception when no other moral reasons are present, then on an atomistic account we could deduce a principle according to which any action involving deception is morally wrong so long as no other moral reasons are present. Jonathan Dancy sometimes calls the features in virtue of which an action has a given moral status that action's 'resultance base,' and we shall follow this terminology here.

Matters are more complicated if we are holists. For given holism, we simply cannot assume that the same resultance base guarantees the same moral verdict. The fact that Harry's action involved deception may make his action wrong. If holism is true, though, this is consistent with the moral innocence of Helen's deception even if no other moral reasons are present in Helen's case. Given supervenience, this difference must obtain in virtue of some difference between the contexts. However, these differences in context are not themselves part of the resultance base as particularists understand that notion; to think they must be is to remain in the grip of atomism. So given holism, we cannot extract a principle of the form 'Whenever an action is R and there are no other reasons present then it is morally wrong' from our particular judgment that this specific action is wrong in virtue of being R. It appears that holism supports particularism after all, the arguments of Chapter 2 notwithstanding.

Appearances are deceptive, though. Holism makes things more complicated but ultimately does not undermine generalism as a regulative ideal. In forming a moral judgment we register what we take to be the morally relevant features of the case and then, assuming we have not left out any features which bear upon the ultimate verdict, we draw our moral conclusion. For example, if you tell me that a man physically assaulted someone, then it would be reasonable for me immediately to judge that what he did was wrong. However, it is easy enough to see that my judgment implicitly rests on the assumption that your description has not left out any further morally relevant facts which would undermine my judgment. If I later discover that the assault was necessary to save the lives of several people, then I would quite reasonably retract my original judgment.

Consider another example. Suppose you tell me that your friend enjoyed a movie today. If this is all I am told then I might reasonably infer that the fact that he would enjoy the movie provided him with a reason to see it. If I later discover that the movie was a snuff film, then I would reasonably exchange my original judgment for a very different one. Once again, my original judgment depends on the assumption that any further morally relevant features would not alter the ultimate verdict. Moreover, our reliance on such assumptions is perfectly compatible with holism. The fact that someone enjoys a film may be a reason in one case but not in another, depending on the context. This is consistent with the thought that if the only morally relevant feature of a case in a suitably broad sense of 'morally relevant' is that someone will enjoy it then the fact that the person will enjoy it is a decisive reason to do it. So long as we do not assume that only moral reasons themselves (and not defeaters and enablers which in the case at hand happen not to be reasons) can be counted as 'morally relevant,' none of this is inconsistent with holism.

So a claim to moral knowledge rationally commits me to the thesis that I have not overlooked any defeaters or countervailing reasons which would overturn my judgment. This is a rational commitment of anyone who claims to have moral knowledge in the sense that such a person cannot consistently deny it and continue to claim to have the relevant moral knowledge. Note that in this sense even young children who, for example, do not yet have the concept of a defeater can be rationally committed to the absence of defeaters in this way. Suppose that young Jimmy says that he knows it was wrong to hit his sister. Lacking the concept of a defeater, he will not be able to form a view as to whether he has overlooked any of them. Nonetheless, it remains true that *if* he were to judge that he had overlooked defeaters or countervailing reasons which would overturn his judgment, this would contradict his claim to know that it was wrong to hit his sister. So our argument is compatible with the possibility that someone can have moral knowledge without yet actually having the concept of a defeater.

Return now to the question of whether our moral knowledge in a given case can be captured in a principle. Perhaps we can build the rational commitments implicit in any claim to moral knowledge into a moral principle. We could do this in one of two ways. First, we could try to list all of the different possible defeaters and countervailing reasons in the antecedent and claim that none of them is present. We consider this strategy in Chapter 7. Here we take a second approach. Instead of trying to list all of the possible defeaters and countervailing reasons we could simply quantify over them.

The proposal is most easily understood through illustrative examples. Consider a case in which someone has killed a rational agent and no other feature of the situation seems morally relevant. We therefore conclude that the person's action was wrong in virtue of the fact that it was the killing of a rational agent. Given holism, our judgment's soundness depends on two theses. First, it relies on the thesis that the fact that the action is the killing of a rational agent is a moral reason not to do it in this context. Secondly, it depends on the thesis that any reasons in favor of the action do not (when taken collectively) outweigh this reason. Finally, our judgment's soundness also depends on the thesis that the moral reason in question is stringent enough to make the action morally wrong. This last thesis is not trivial; some moral reasons function to make an action's omission supererogatory but do not thereby make the action wrong. Perhaps we can capture the various theses on which the soundness of the judgment in question relies with the following principle:

(K)  For all actions (x): If (*a*) x is an instance of killing a rational agent and (*b*) no other feature of the situation explains why the fact that x is the killing of a rational agent is not a moral reason not to perform the action and (*c*) any reasons to x do not (when taken collectively) outweigh the fact that x is the killing of a rational agent, then x is wrong in virtue of being an instance of killing a rational agent.

The thesis that no other features of the situation defeats the status of killing a rational agent as a reason against an action is captured by (*b*) in the antecedent. The thesis that any reasons in favor of the action do not outweigh this reason is explicit in (c). Rather than trying to list all of the possible defeaters and countervailing reasons, the antecedent of (K) quantifies over them and claims that none is present. Finally, the thesis that killing a rational agent is the sort of reason that can make an action wrong is captured by the consequent's claim that the action is wrong.

So we can extract a default principle (K) from our judgment in a particular case. Moreover, it is easy enough to see how this extraction of default principles should generalize. The basic idea is simple enough. Particularists may be right that the verdict we take to follow from one set of facts could be overturned by further facts. We can grant this, but insist that our judgment in a given case is warranted only if we have not overlooked any further facts which would overturn our judgment. This supposition is defeasible, of course; what we thought was a case of knowledge might turn out not to be. Still, from the fact that this supposition could turn out to be false it does not follow that it actually is always false or unwarranted, and when it is true and warranted we can have moral knowledge.

At this stage someone might object that the conjunction of all of the features quantified over in the antecedent of a default principle are themselves moral features and not purely descriptive ones. If that were true, then the principles we have so far defended would be merely intra-moral ones of a sort that at least some particularists are happy to embrace.[4] The idea here is that universal quantification over all of the many possible defeaters of a given reason is effectively a long conjunction of those features. That conjunction itself arguably picks out a moral kind rather than a nonmoral kind, for the conjuncts may be a heterogeneous set from a nonmoral point of view, having nothing interesting in common apart from being possible defeaters of a certain sort of reason.

One might at this stage balk at the idea that a conjunction of properties itself constitutes a further metaproperty, but we shall not press this point here. Putting this metaphysical concern to one side, three points are in order. First, we are not committed to denying that the conjunction of the features listed in the antecedent picks out a moral property. After all, we are defending generalism, and some generalists (ones who are reductive naturalists) will hold that moral properties just *are* conjunctions of purely descriptive properties. Our point is simply that each of the conjuncts included in this conjunction, when taken individually, can be understood in purely descriptive terms. So we have a principle which goes from purely descriptive concepts to a normative conclusion. We do not here mean to deny the epistemological claims that some

---

[4] Thanks to Brad Majors for pressing us on this point.

particularists make about how moral knowledge is possible in the first place. Indeed, we take it to be an important dialectical advantage that our argument at this stage does not beg the question of whether the particularist's favored epistemology might be correct. Our concern is to show that even the sort of epistemology favored by particularists does not really support the particularist doctrines canvassed in Chapter 1.

Secondly, on our view the fact that nobody who lacked moral knowledge could construct the relevant conjunction does not undermine the idea that each of the conjuncts is purely descriptive. Consider an analogy. Someone can construct a conjunction of God's ten favorite natural properties only if she has some knowledge of things supernatural. It surely does not follow from this that each of the conjuncts is thereby not a natural property; indeed, that would contradict the claim that these are God's ten favorite *natural* properties.

Thirdly, the particularist's epistemology in no way entails that moral principles are not important. The articulation of moral principles can play an important role both in theory and in moral practice, and we have good moral reasons to articulate them. In Chapters 8 and 9 we explain in more detail how moral principles have some very important roles to play. These arguments do not depend on rejecting the particularist's favored epistemology.

So far our examples have all been cast in terms of principles about all things considered moral verdicts—principles about what is right or wrong. However, we can also have default principles about reasons. For example, the fact that an action would be pleasant might be a reason to perform the action, all else being equal. In a given case we might be warranted in supposing that all else is equal. If the pleasure would be sadistic, for example, then this supposition would perhaps be falsified. Once again we can articulate a principle which includes this supposition. For example,

> (P)  For all actions (x) and all facts (F): If F is a fact to the effect that x would
> be pleasant and no other feature of the situation explains why F is not a
> reason to x, then F is a reason to x.

Insofar as we can know that a given fact is a reason for an action, we are committed to a principle of this form. For we can know that such a fact is a reason in a given case without knowing every single fact of the situation; once again, our finitude prevents this. So our knowledge that a given fact is a reason with a certain valence relies on an assumption that none of the indefinitely many further facts we have not yet considered undermines its status as a reason with that valence.

So both our judgments about moral reasons and our judgments about all things considered moral verdicts, insofar as those judgments constitute knowledge, suffice to ensure the availability of a suitable moral principle, namely a default principle. So moral judgment, insofar as it constitutes knowledge, does presuppose the availability of a suitable stock of moral principles. Anti-Transcendental Particularism about hedged principles is thus false. Even more obviously, our case for the availability of default principles is also enough to refute Principle Eliminativism and Principle Skepticism about hedged principles. The rejection of Holton's Principled Particularism and Principle Abstinence Particularism as well as Principle Eliminativism, Principle Skepticism, and Anti-Transcendental Particularism about *non*-hedged principles requires further argument, and in the following chapters we develop such arguments. However, we must first address an important objection to default principles.

## 6.2. The Vacuity Objection

An important challenge to default principles insists that they are all vacuously true simply in virtue of their logical form. While serious, the vacuity objection is not sound, and seeing why will both clarify the content of our proposal and reveal why particularists should not be too eager to embrace default principles.

Since default principles are universally quantified conditionals, they can be false only if they have an instantiation with a true antecedent and a false consequent. The worry behind the vacuity objection is that the logical form of a default principle in conjunction with some very plausible assumptions about moral explanation entails that, whenever the consequent of a default principle is false, its antecedent will be false as well, in which case the principle itself is vacuously true. Consider the following inane default principle:

(LY) For all actions (x): If (*a*) x would be done in a leap year and (*b*) no other feature of the situation explains why the fact that x would be done in a leap year is not a moral reason not to x and (*c*) the reasons in favor of x do not explain why x is not wrong in virtue of the fact that x would be done in a leap year, then x is wrong in virtue of the fact that x would be done in a leap year.

(LY) is clearly absurd. For an action is wrong in virtue of a given fact or set of facts in the intended sense of 'in virtue of' only if the fact(s) in question is (or are) moral reason(s) not to perform the action which carry the day. We take it that the fact that an action would be done in a leap year could never be a moral reason to perform the action (those who find this assumption problematic will find a defense of it in Section 6.3). So (LY) had better come out as false. The vacuity objection, however, insists that (LY) turns out to be trivially true. Moreover, the objection continues, the reason (LY) is true extends to any default principle.

(LY) is a universally quantified conditional ranging over possible actions and hence is false only if it has a possible instantiation in which its antecedent is true and its consequent is false. Presumably its consequent is necessarily always false—no action could be made wrong in the relevant sense by being done in a leap year—the fact that an action is done in a leap year could never in itself be a reason not to perform an action. So the crucial issue is whether any of its instantiations also has a true antecedent. The antecedent is itself a conjunction and hence will be true only if both conjuncts are true. However, the objection runs, the second of the three conjuncts ((b) above) will always be false. We are taking it as given that the leap year fact is not a moral reason, but the objection insists on general grounds that it is implausible to suppose that there is no explanation of its failure to be a reason. Moral facts are not arbitrary, at least in the extremely minimal sense that whenever something is or is not a reason there will be *some* explanation of why this is so. Even someone who thought that morality was a direct function of the arbitrary will of God should admit this much, since we will on such an account always be able to explain moral differences in terms of differences in God's will even if we cannot go on to explain why God willed one way rather than another. So moral differences can always be explained. Hence, the argument concludes, clause (*b*) in our default principle will always be false, which is enough to make the antecedent false and so enough to make the conditional trivially true.

An adequate understanding of why the vacuity objection is unsound requires careful attention to a detail of our account we have so far not discussed. The vacuity objection goes from the premiss that every time a fact is not a moral reason there is some explanation for its failure to be a reason, to the conclusion that some further feature of the situation explains this failure. However, this inference is valid only if it is valid to go from 'there is some explanation of p' to 'some feature of the situation explains p.' In fact, this inference is invalid. The inference would be valid only if we understand 'feature of the situation' so broadly that any possible explanatory fact can count as a feature of the situation. This is not an intuitive understanding of 'feature of the situation,' nor is it the reading we intend. Hence the vacuity objection is unsound.

For purposes of our own positive proposal, a feature of a situation must be a contingent fact. Necessary facts apply equally to all possible situations and hence are never features of any particular situation in our sense. This is already enough to accommodate the plausible idea that every moral fact has an explanation of some kind while blocking the vacuity objection. For quite plausibly, the moral facts in question will be explained by some necessary fact. Perhaps the explanation in the leap year example is simply that leap year facts can never be reasons for action. That explanation is perhaps not the most illuminating one, but it is a kind of explanation and it is an explanation given in terms of a necessary fact. An alternative (and more controversial) explanation might hold that a given fact is a moral reason only if it is a fact about how the action bears in some way on welfare or treating people with respect. This is a very controversial explanation, but our point is simply that if the main premiss of this explanation (a kind of pluralism involving utilitarian reasons and deontological reasons) is true, then it very plausibly is a necessary truth. Once again, the fact in question does indeed have an explanation but it is not explained by a feature of the situation. So we need not reject the plausible suggestion that every moral fact has some explanation to refute the vacuity objection. (Of course some will reject that assumption, but if they are right then the vacuity objection was unsound all along!)

More importantly, no contingent feature of the situation could plausibly figure in an explanation of why the leap year fact is not a reason in a given case. Indeed, because the leap year fact could *never* be a reason its failure to be a reason here will in no way depend on any of the contingent features of this case. If the leap year fact were sometimes a reason, then things would be very different. For in that case the contingent features that distinguish the situation in which it is a reason from those in which it is not a reason could intelligibly figure in an explanation of why the fact is not a reason here. Moreover, if asked to cite some particular contingent feature of the situation that explains why that fact is not a reason here, any sane moral agent would simply be perplexed.

So for any default principle citing a patently absurd candidate reason (and whose consequent is not necessarily true) there will be possible instantiations of that principle in which the antecedent is true and the consequent is false. This line of argument is perfectly general, so we can conclude that any principle citing a putative reason in its antecedent which could never actually be a reason and whose consequent can be false will turn out to be false.[5] The only reason to doubt that the antecedent would sometimes be true was the thought that the 'no feature of the situation explains ...' clause is always trivially false. Since we have seen this rests on a failure to distinguish explanations in general from explanations cast in terms of contingent features of a situation, we can safely conclude that default principles are not vacuously true simply in virtue of their logical form.[6]

[5] Principles with tautologous consequents will be trivially true on any account, of course.

[6] Interestingly, Paul Pietroski and Georges Rey have independently developed an account of *ceteris paribus* laws in science and why they are not vacuous that is in many ways similar to our account

## 6.3. Can Any Consideration be a Reason?

Our reply to the vacuity objection assumes that not all possible facts can be reasons for action. For our reply relies on the premiss that arbitrary facts like the fact that an action would be done in a leap year could never be reasons for action. The premiss is very plausible, but we should verify its truth. We begin by drawing some distinctions which should undermine what we take to be some of the main reasons for resisting the premiss. We then explain why two seemingly plausible conceptions of how promises and desires generate reasons which would undermine the premiss are actually not all that plausible. Along the way, we explore the interesting yet ultimately misguided suggestion (made by some moderate particularists) that we should draw a distinction between so-called primary and secondary reasons.

In testing the plausibility of the premiss that not any old fact can be a reason for action, it is crucial to distinguish reasons for action from reasons for belief. More accurately, the distinction is between theoretical reasons and practical reasons, since arguably there can be practical reasons for belief. For example, if believing in God ensures a happy afterlife, then on some accounts that is a practical reason to believe in God. We do not wish to prejudge the possibility of such reasons here. We shall not offer a reductive definition of what it is for something to be a theoretical reason for belief, but the basic idea should be clear enough. Theoretical reasons for belief count as reasons in virtue of having

of default principles in ethics. Very roughly, on Pietroski and Rey's account, a *ceteris paribus* law of the form *ceteris paribus*, (x) (Fx $\Rightarrow$ ($\exists$y)Gy) is true if (*a*) 'F' and 'G' are otherwise nomological, (*b*) any case in which something is F but not G is such that not-G can be explained by some factor which has independent explanatory power, and (*c*) the law in conjunction with the fact that some x has been F actually have done some explanatory work (Pietroski and Rey 1995: 92–3). Clause (*b*) is the most interesting and distinctive feature of Pietroski and Rey's account, and it is obviously similar to the 'no feature of the situation explains ...' clause of a default principle. On both accounts, a hedged generalization is understood as being true if any putative exception can be explained by some further fact.

On the other hand, our accounts also differ in a number of important ways. Our account includes nothing like their (*a*) or (*c*). The predicates which figure in a moral principle may, for all we have argued here, not be kind predicates which occur in any natural science. Nor do we see any reason to suppose a moral principle must have done some actual explanatory work in order to be true; in fact, we are unsure why this is plausible in the scientific case, so long as we sharply distinguish the truth of a law from our justification for believing it. Finally, we do not require that a fact which explains away an apparent exception to a moral rule must do some independent explanatory work. As far as we can see, it is at least conceptually possible for a fact to function as a defeater in certain kinds of contexts without having any moral explanatory force in other possible scenarios. We agree with Dancy that defeaters and enablers need not be reasons in their own right, and would add that they need not even be capable of being reasons. This may mark an important contrast with the scientific case, where it does seem plausible that only another cause can interfere with the operation of a causal force. In other words, perhaps only causes can block the operation of other candidate causes, but non-reasons can block the normative force of other candidate reasons.

a suitable connection to the truth of the belief for which they are a reason; they are the sorts of reasons which can sometimes yield knowledge. Neither of these constraints hold for practical reasons for belief (if any there are). For expository reasons we shall continue to speak simply in terms of reasons for belief, but this should always be understood as shorthand for 'theoretical reasons for belief' which may or not be a proper subset of the class of all reasons for belief.

Although there is some controversy on this point,[7] reasons for belief should be carefully distinguished from reasons for action. For example, the fact that a virtuous person told me that lying to save my friend's feelings would be wrong may well be a very good reason for me to believe I should not lie. However, the fact that my friend told me this is not amongst my reasons not to lie. My reasons not to lie presumably would instead be facts like the fact that lying shows a lack of respect for one's interlocutor. That my friend thinks I ought to tell the truth or remain silent is a reason for believing I should not lie and not a reason not to lie.

The distinction is perhaps even more clear in cases in which a reason to believe one ought to do something is itself a reason not to do it. For example, suppose that my perverse enemy is carefully monitoring me today and has credibly threatened to kill my family unless I do not fulfill any promises today. In this context, the fact that I promised to meet you for lunch today is an excellent reason to believe I should not meet you for lunch. However, the fact that I promised to meet you is not a reason not to meet you. On the contrary, that fact remains a reason to meet you (we may stipulate that there are no relevant defeaters present), albeit a reason which is massively outweighed by the contrary reason that meeting you would result in the deaths of my loved ones.

With a little ingenuity we can imagine many cases in which what seems like a morally arbitrary fact would be a reason to believe an action would be wrong. For example, if we knew that Jones was always at work on a construction site on Tuesdays but always in a hospital on Wednesdays, then the fact that he performed the action on a Wednesday might be a reason to believe Jones's detonating some dynamite was wrong. The fact that we can construct cases in which just about any fact could be a reason to believe some action would be wrong (or right) may give false plausibility to the idea that just about any old fact could be a moral reason for action.

We suspect that a great deal of the apparent plausibility of the idea that just about any old fact can be a moral reason for action in the right context stems

---

[7] In her book *Goodness and Advice*, Judith Thomson at some points seems to want to reduce reasons for action to reasons for believing one ought to act in a certain way. See Thomson 2001. For discussion, see Ridge 2003a.

from a failure to heed the distinction between reasons for belief and reasons for action. For example, Jonathan Dancy suggests that in the right context the fact that someone asks you for the time is a reason to tell her. In our view, the fact that the person asked you for the time is a reason to believe you ought to tell her and not itself a reason to tell her. The reason to tell the person presumably is something like the fact that telling her would be polite, or the fact that it would satisfy some desire of hers, would undermine her anxiety, or would help her achieve some (morally permissible) end. If telling the person the time would do none of these things then there may be no reason to tell her even though there may still be reason to believe you ought to tell her. Of course, we could count the fact that she asked as a further reason to tell her in addition to all of these other reasons, but this seems like one reason too many; a point to which we shall return in more detail below. This is just one example, but the particularist literature is rife with examples of supposed reasons for action which are better understood as reasons for belief about what should be done.

Moreover, we are willing to allow that just about any old fact could in the right context be a reason for *belief* even though we reject the analogous claim about reasons for action. This contrast gets some support from common sense. When asked to generate a list of all the different kinds of considerations which could be reasons for action, we suspect that most people would find the task very daunting but not obviously hopeless. However, the request to list all possible reasons for belief most likely would lead to an incredulous stare, as if we had asked the person to list all the prime numbers. What might explain this asymmetry? Intuitively, a fact F is evidence that p and hence a reason for believing that p just in case F is a reliable indicator of p. On a more subjective conception of reasons for belief we should instead say that a fact F is a reason for agent A to believe that p just in case F reliably indicates that p *by A's lights*. The phrase 'by A's lights' in turn could be understood in terms of whether F would reliably indicate that p if all of A's other beliefs were true (perhaps idealizing in some way to iron out contradictions) or perhaps in some other way. Our point here should survive any reasonable way of making this rough and ready idea more precise.

The plausibility of the basic idea is perhaps best illustrated with examples.[8] The fact that there is smoke is evidence of fire and hence reason to believe that there is fire because the presence of smoke reliably indicates the presence of fire. On a more subjective interpretation of reasons for belief, the fact that there is smoke is reason for me to believe that there is fire, given that my

---

[8] Thanks to Pekka Väyrynen for pressing us on the importance of a subjective conception of reasons for belief here.

background beliefs entail that smoke reliably indicates fire. Something along these lines is extremely plausible. Any plausible accommodation of this basic idea about reasons for belief as indicators should be enough to explain why just about any possible fact could (in the right circumstances) be a reason for belief. For which kinds of facts reliably indicate which other kinds of facts (or reliably indicate them by a given agent's lights) is a highly contingent matter, depending on the laws of nature, initial conditions, and perhaps chance (or simply on a given agent's beliefs, which are themselves highly contingent).

The only obvious and serious difficulty here is with reasons for believing necessary truths, which arguably are equally well reliably indicated by everything. So an adequate epistemology must deal with the difficulties associated with necessity; not all facts are reasons to believe $2 + 2 = 4$. So long as we restrict ourselves to purely contingent matters, though, we have an explanation of why just about any fact could in the right circumstances be a reason for belief. The fact that some kinds of reasons for belief are not best understood as indicators in any straightforward counterfactual sense does nothing to block the suggestion that reasons for believing contingent truths nonetheless should be understood in this way.

The crucial point is that no analogous explanation of how any possible fact could be a reason is available in the case of reasons for action. For a fact to be a reason for action cannot plausibly be understood in terms of that fact's reliably *indicating* anything, not even reliably indicating that the action ought to be done. For example, let us suppose that the fact that an action would give someone pleasure is typically a reason in favor of the action. This in no way entails that the fact that an action would give someone pleasure reliably indicates the rightness of the action. To see that this entailment does not hold, simply imagine a world in which whenever one person gives another person some pleasure a perverse demon causes (and is known to cause) great pain to some innocent person.[9] Here we have an illustration of how being a reason for action and being a reliable indication of the rightness of the action can dramatically come apart. Nor should this be any surprise. For a fact to be a reason for action is for that fact to count in favor of the action, but a fact's favoring an action is not well understood in terms of mere reliable indication of some further sort of fact even the fact that the action is morally right.

Reasons for action will, of course, often reliably indicate other facts, but their status as reasons for action in no way depends upon this. If this is right, then we now have an explanation of the proposed asymmetry between reasons for

---

[9] Dancy at one point makes a similar objection to one reading of W. D. Ross's account of prima facie duties; see Dancy 1993: 99.

action and reasons for belief. Just about any possible sort of fact can be a reason for belief precisely because reasons for belief (in contingent matters, at least) are reasons at least in part in virtue of reliably indicating the relevant proposition. By contrast, being a reason for action is simply not well understood in terms of indicating further facts, so this explanation will not go through in the case of reasons for action.

In addition to heeding the distinction between reasons for action and reasons for belief, we should also distinguish facts that explain the moral status of an action from facts that are reasons for or against the action. For example, the fact that this shirt is red might partially explain why I ought to buy it for my friend if my friend prefers red shirts. In this case, the fact that this shirt is red is not the reason to buy the shirt, though. Rather, the fact that buying this shirt would make my friend happy is my reason to buy it. The fact that the shirt is red explains why my friend would like it. However, it is the fact that buying it would make my friend happy that is my reason for buying it. Note that in this case the fact that the shirt is red might also be a reason for me to believe that I ought to buy it, but we have already seen that reasons for belief should be distinguished from reasons for action. Even an atomist should admit this much. Holism makes it even more obvious that features of a situation can bear on the moral status of an action without themselves being reasons for action. For if holism is true then enablers, defeaters, intensifiers, and diminishers can all figure in moral explanations in ways that should by now be familiar without thereby being reasons for action.

The preceding distinctions notwithstanding, there are a couple of specific grounds for thinking just about any fact could in the right context be a reason for action. On some apparently plausible ways of understanding how promises generate reasons, promises can transform any otherwise morally irrelevant fact into a moral reason for action.[10] For example, suppose I promise to buy you a plaid baseball cap. On the interpretation of how promises generate reasons on offer, the otherwise morally irrelevant fact that this baseball cap is plaid will then be a moral reason to buy it. On this interpretation, when someone makes a reason-generating promise it is a fact corresponding to the content of the promise which is the reason for the person to perform the relevant action, and not the fact that the action would fulfill a promise.

However, this interpretation of how promises generate reasons is not plausible. Consider again the suggestion that when a promise generates a reason for action the reason is simply a fact corresponding to the content of the

---

[10] The caveat 'just about any' is necessary since promises to do independently immoral things (like a promise to murder someone) plausibly can never generate reasons for action.

promise. The crucial contrast is with the view that the reason to perform the action is simply that it would fulfill a promise. Returning again to our example, on the view under consideration, if my promise to buy you a plaid baseball cap generates a reason, then it will be the fact that this baseball cap is plaid that provides me with a reason to buy it and not the fact that buying it would fulfill my promise. The apparent plausibility of this view stems from the fact that is very easy to imagine an agent who made such a promise being appropriately guided by her belief that a given baseball cap is plaid. It is easy to imagine someone who made such a promise casting her eyes over a large display of differently colored caps, then noticing a plaid one and saying to herself, "That one is plaid, so I'll buy it," and straight away buying it. Moreover, this train of thought and action seems eminently rational. Since we tend to suppose that a rational action just is an action done for a reason, it is easy enough to infer that the fact that the cap in question is plaid is a reason for the agent to buy it.

However, it should not be too hard to see how this line of thought goes wrong. First, it is simply not true that a fact which rationally guides an agent to perform an action is thereby a reason for action. People can rationally act on the basis of all sorts of facts which they perversely or simply mistakenly take to be reasons but which actually are not reasons at all. Rationality is a kind of internal norm, which roughly speaking requires that we act in ways that make sense by our own lights, but this is compatible with the judgments which constitute 'our lights' being badly mistaken.[11]

Secondly, even when an agent has no false beliefs about her reasons for action, the mere fact that she rationally acts on the basis of a given fact does not entail that the fact is a reason. Often it can be rational to act on the basis of rationally acquired habits or reasons without always (at the time of action) consciously thinking about the reasons which made the habit or intention rational to adopt in the first place. A rational agent should be able to take advantage of the goods of timely and efficient action in this way.

Thirdly, even if the thought, 'this cap is plaid' did figure in the deliberation of the agent at the time of action as a reason, we need not understand it as her reason for action. We could instead understand that thought as her reason for belief. In particular, the thought that the cap is plaid might be one of her reasons for believing that she ought to buy that cap. Although the agent's conscious thoughts might simply go, 'that one is plaid so I'll buy it,'

---

[11] We should emphasize that in our view rationality in belief formation is not sufficient for one's belief being epistemologically justified, much less is it sufficient for knowledge. Someone can rationally form beliefs in our sense of 'rational' even though they have such poor reasoning and perceptual skills and abilities that we should not classify the resulting beliefs as warranted or knowledge. Thanks to Brad Majors for drawing us out on this point.

we need not assume that these thoughts fully capture her line of reasoning. Her conscious thoughts might instead be understood as enthymatic. When fully spelled out this argument might instead go something like, 'This baseball cap is plaid, I promised to buy my friend a plaid baseball cap, I have good reason to fulfill this promise, so I ought to buy it; therefore I will buy it.' One justification for understanding an agent's thoughts in this way would be that she would articulate the premises of the argument if pressed for an explicit justification.

So the fact that an agent could be rationally motivated by a fact does not entail that the fact is a good reason for action. Intuitively, a moral reason for action is a fact which morally favors the action. A moral reason for action is therefore a fact in virtue of which the action in question would be sure to seem morally attractive to an ideally virtuous agent. Eccentric facts like the fact that the action would be the buying of a plaid baseball cap for someone are hardly guaranteed to make the action seem morally attractive to a virtuous agent. Imagine trying to explain to a morally wise but puzzled agent who does not know about your promise why you are buying a plaid baseball cap simply by saying, "Look, this is the buying of a plaid baseball cap! Oh, and no other feature of the situation explains why that fact is not a good moral reason to buy it." Rather than finding this answer illuminating and helpful, your interlocutor probably would begin to wonder what sort of bizarre moral sensibility guides your actions. By contrast, a morally wise agent presumably would find the buying of the cap attractive because it is the fulfilling of a promise, assuming no other features of the situation explained why this was not a reason (e.g. the promise was not coerced). So it is much more plausible to suppose that in all of these cases the agent's reason for action is that the action would fulfill a promise and not that it has the features corresponding to the content of the promise.

At this point someone might insist that we have relied on a false dichotomy by assuming that either the fact that the action would fulfill the agent's promise or a fact corresponding to the content of the promise is the reason for action, *but not both*. Why not instead take an ecumenical view, according to which both kinds of facts are reasons for action? This view might be bolstered by a version of the distinction which is sometimes drawn between primary and secondary reasons. Here we must briefly digress in order to introduce the version of the distinction which is most helpful to the particularist in the present context.

The distinction between primary and secondary reasons was originally introduced by J. L. Urmson,[12] but has been more recently emphasized by

---

[12] See Urmson 1975.

David McNaughton and Piers Rawling.[13] The distinction is usually drawn in roughly the following way. A primary reason is a consideration which is always a reason for action no matter what the context. By contrast, a secondary reason's status as a reason depends on the presence of a primary reason. In Dancy's terms, primary reasons are atomistic whereas secondary reasons are holistic.

While those sympathetic to atomism may find this a helpful way of drawing the distinction, the basic idea behind the distinction does not require an atomistic interpretation of primary reasons. For the basic idea is one of an asymmetric dependence—secondary reasons are dependent for their status as reasons on the presence of primary reasons but not vice versa. This sort of dependence can hold even if the considerations which themselves are primary reasons are not themselves always reasons. Primary reasons may depend on certain enablers in order to count as reasons, but these enablers need not themselves be reasons much less primary reasons. For example, the fact that my action would be the breaking of a promise might be a reason not to perform the action only if (a) it is possible for me to refrain from performing it and (b) the promise was not coerced but (a) and (b) need not themselves be reasons for action. So there is a holism-friendly way of glossing the distinction between primary and secondary reasons in terms of asymmetric dependence.

Any version of the distinction between primary reasons and secondary reasons raises the question of what explains their asymmetric dependence. In our view the distinction itself is best understood in terms of the constitution of some facts by other facts and this in turn should give us the resources to explain the asymmetry between primary and secondary reasons. For a start, the constitution relation is asymmetric; some clay might constitute a statue while the statue does not constitute the clay. Moreover, the constitution approach seems to fit well with the most plausible examples of the distinction between primary and secondary reasons. The idea would be that if one fact constitutes a second fact, where that second fact is a primary reason for an action then the first fact is thereby a secondary reason for that action. Primary reasons are then simply facts which do not depend for their status as reasons on their constituting some other fact which is also a reason.

One reservation about this way of drawing the distinction is that it threatens to entail that esoteric facts about subatomic particles are reasons for action, since on a physicalist metaphysic facts about subatomic particles presumably constitute all the other contingent facts and even on a non-physicalist metaphysic such facts will probably constitute all the other nonmental contingent facts. However, the distinction can perhaps be salvaged against this objection if we

---

[13] See McNaughton and Rawling 2000.

add a further necessary condition according to which a fact can be a secondary reason for a given agent only if that fact could rationally guide the agent in the right way. Since creatures like us can almost never be rationally guided by facts about subatomic particles, this may be enough to deflect the objection.

Moreover, in those rare circumstances in which we could be rationally guided by facts about subatomic particles those facts do not seem so implausible as candidate reasons for action. For example, suppose that someone tells me that the lead-coated room next door contains a certain number of plutonium atoms. This is a fact about subatomic particles but, given my knowledge of the relationship between such atoms and radiation poisoning, it would not be a terrible stretch to conclude that this fact about subatomic particles is a reason for me not to go in the room in the sense the defender of secondary reasons has in mind. Of course, one could still object in this case that this supposed secondary reason is really just a reason to believe I should not go in the room and not a reason for action at all. My reasons for action instead presumably are such facts as that going in the room will cause me to suffer intense pain and that going in the room will cause my death. Needless to say, we are very sympathetic to this objection but we are now trying to see whether the distinction between primary and secondary reasons might ultimately help meet it. To be clear, the analysis of primary and secondary reasons in terms of constitution is our own gloss on it which we offer so as to make the idea more precise without presupposing an atomistic account of all primary reasons. However, the objections we will raise to the distinction itself do not depend on this particular and perhaps controversial interpretation of the distinction.

With the distinction between primary and secondary reasons in hand we are now in a position to return to the ecumenical account of how promises generate reasons for action. Recall that on the ecumenical account, a promise to X which I have the opportunity to fulfill by performing a given action produces two reason for action—(a) that the action would fulfill my promise to X and (b) that the action is an instance of X-ing. The suggestion is that (a) is a primary reason while (b) is a secondary reason. The defender of the ecumenical account may admit in a given example that (a) and (b) are both reasons for belief—reasons to believe I ought to X—but insist that it is just a false dichotomy to infer from this that both facts might not also be reasons for action.

The deeper problem with the ecumenical account is that it simply yields too many reasons. Intuitively, in the original example of a promise to buy someone a plaid cap the agent's promise only generates one reason to buy the cap. However, the ecumenical account entails that the promise generates at least two reasons—the fact that buying the cap would fulfill the promise *and* the fact that buying it would be the buying of a plaid cap. Since these facts are numerically distinct (we can have the one without the other), we now have two reasons to buy the cap. If this is right then whenever a promise generates a reason it will generate at least two reasons—the fact that the action would fulfill a promise and the fact which constitutes its fulfilling the promise.

However, the suggestion that promises always generate two reasons for action is implausible. Suppose I am trying to decide whether to buy the hat, and I tentatively arrive at the conclusion that the balance of reasons is evenly divided. On the one hand, buying the hat would fulfill a promise but on the other hand buying the hat would leave me with no bus fare to get home, forcing me to walk across town in the rain with no umbrella. I consider the fact that buying the hat would allow me to keep my promise (this is my last chance to buy the hat before you leave the country) to be identical in its normative force to the normative force of the fact that buying the hat in this context would cause me a great deal of displeasure as I despise long walks in the rain with no suitable protection from the elements. I then suddenly realize that I have overlooked a reason. For in addition to the fact that buying the plaid hat would fulfill my promise there is also the fact that doing so would be an instance of buying a plaid hat. Suddenly my quandary is resolved! Having found an additional reason for action, I conclude that it is clear after all that I must buy the hat. What initially seemed like an evenly balanced set of reasons turns out not to be so evenly balanced after all. Though absurd, this train of thought seems to follow inevitably from the proposed distinction between primary and secondary reasons.

So far as we can see, the only way to block this objection would be to insist that secondary reasons provide no additional normative force over and above the primary reasons to which they are related. However, this makes the idea that so-called secondary reasons really are reasons at all begin to look very dubious. For now a so-called secondary reason is a reason which does not itself speak in favor of the action for which it is supposed to be a reason. We seem to be stuck with the idea of a reason with zero weight, but that sounds to us like no reason at all.

So we should reject the distinction between primary and secondary reasons and with it the ecumenical account of how promises generate reasons. What we should instead say is that in addition to facts which are reasons for action there also are facts which constitute those reasons. Both reasons and facts which constitute those reasons can play a role in moral decision-making. For example, noticing a fact which constitutes a reason for action might usefully prompt an agent to perform the action ('this one's plaid, I'll buy it'). We can allow that such facts perform important functions in our deliberations without going on to say that they thereby instantiate some further species of reason for action, namely secondary reasons.

For those who remain unpersuaded by our objection to the distinction between primary and secondary reasons there is another way to defend default principles which does not require the abandonment of that distinction. For we could simply revise our canonical statement of default principles about reasons so that such principles are cast explicitly in terms of primary reasons and not in terms of reasons more generally. This would be enough to insulate the proposed account from the vacuity objection. For no defender of the distinction between primary and secondary reasons would claim that any old fact can be a primary reason for action. That would defeat the whole point of drawing the distinction in the first place. It will remain true on this way of thinking that a full and complete set of default principles will not capture all the possible reasons for action but will instead 'only' capture all the primary reasons.

In our view, this is not a very deep objection since secondary reasons are entirely parasitic on primary reasons and never provide any normative force over and above the primary reasons upon which they are parasitic. So an agent who always recognized and properly weighed all the primary reasons would never go wrong; so-called secondary reasons are in this way entirely epiphenomenal when it comes to reliable moral decision-making. So a codification of morality which captures all the primary reasons but leaves out the secondary reasons seems entirely sufficient from a practical point of view. Therefore the tenability of the distinction between primary and secondary reasons would not really undermine the practical significance of our positive proposal.

Indeed, it is not even clear that the tenability of the distinction would undermine our proposal in any theoretical way. For once we know all the primary reasons we will be in a position to deduce of any other fact whether it is a secondary reason in a principled way as well—we just (a) determine whether the fact in question constitutes any primary reason and (b) if so, whether the fact could be rationally action-guiding for some agent. This seems to give a principled way of determining whether any given fact is a secondary reason, once we know all the relevant primary reasons. So the tenability of the distinction between primary and secondary reasons fails to pose a deep challenge to default principles. Nonetheless, our considered view is that the distinction between primary and secondary reasons is not tenable and should be abandoned. We therefore do not see any need to revise our account of default principles in this way.

We now consider a second challenge to the premiss that not any old arbitrary fact can be a reason for action. This second challenge is posed by the relationship of desires to reasons. Suppose an agent's desire that p generates a reason to do A, where A will bring about p. On the view we are considering, it is the fact that the action would bring about p that is the agent's reason, rather than the fact that the action would lead to the satisfaction of a desire. On this view, if I want to take the train, my reason to buy a ticket is the fact that buying a ticket will bring about my taking the train. If this account of the relationship between desires and reasons were allowed, then the only limit on what kinds of facts can be reasons for action will be the limits of what states of affairs can be desired. The objection is structurally parallel to the objection from promises. In each case the idea is that a fact's being the content of something else (either a promise or a desire) is sufficient to transform that fact into a reason. Unsurprisingly, our main lines of reply are similar. We should not be misled by the fact that it can be rational to be guided by the contents of our desires into thinking the content of one's desire is one's reason. The discussion of promises should make it clear that we can be rationally guided by facts which are not good reasons for action.

In any event, we should reject this account of how reasons are generated by desires. Here we must distinguish two kinds of desires. First there are desires we simply find ourselves with and which are not based on good reasons. Secondly, there are desires which are based on good reasons.[14] For example, a whim to tap one's toes may be based on no reason whatsoever. By contrast, a desire to phone a friend may be based on the thought that calling her would make her happy and the thought that in this context the fact that it would make her happy is a reason to call her; in this case one's desire is based on a reason. This latter category—of desires based on reasons—can be further divided into two categories. First, there are desires based on real reasons. Secondly, there are desires based on what agents wrongly take to be reasons. What we should say about an agent's reason for action will depend on which of these three cases (not based on a reason at all, based on a genuine reason, and based on what is wrongly taken to be a reason) we have. Suppose we have a desire which is not based on any reason at all. In that case, it is plausible to suppose that if the desire provides any reason at all then the reason just is that performing the action would satisfy the desire. After all, if pressed for a justification for tapping one's feet most people would say something like, "I just felt like it;" by contrast, very few people would think that the fact they were tapping their feet was any kind of justification.

Now consider cases in which the agent's desire is based on a reason. Consider again my desire to call my friend, which is based on the thought that this

---

[14] Here we roughly follow Thomas Nagel's distinction between brute desires and motivated desires. See Nagel 1970.

would make her happy and the thought that in the context there is reason for me to make her happy. If pressed for a justification of my action, I would not say, "I just felt like it," but instead talk about how the call would cheer up the friend. This, however, suggests that the desire in these kinds of cases does not actually provide the reason in any interesting sense.[15] The reason for calling the friend in this case is that it would make someone happy and this reason would remain even if I had no desire to call my friend.

Consider another example. Suppose I want to catch the train so I can make it to a lecture which I think I ought to attend. The train is about to leave and I must run to get there. What is my reason to run? It might seem reasonable to say that my reason to run is that running is the only way to catch the train. We might in turn try to explain why this is a reason in the context simply by citing my desire to catch the train. However, we should not read any substantial conclusions into the theory of reasons from such cases. For if we pressed an agent on why it mattered that he caught the train he would tell us about why he ought to make it to the lecture, and here he presumably would tell us about how the lecture is intellectually stimulating or promotes some other valuable end. He might then be rather easily convinced that the real reason to run was to ensure that he would gain intellectual edification or gain certain goods he associates with a thriving career. After all, if the person ran to catch the train and the lecture turned out to be a useless bore then he might well say, "I practically killed myself sprinting to make the train *for no reason at all*—what a waste!" We take the fact that these further comments would be so natural and plausible to suggest that the original reason was not simply that the agent would catch the train by running. Indeed, unless we try to resurrect the distinction between primary and secondary reasons, we take it that the fact that the agent would catch the train by running is not any reason at all to run (though the fact that he wants to catch the train might be).

The preceding might seem to imply that a wide variety of ordinary language claims are confused or just plain false. In fact, our account does not force us to take issue with the garden variety statement that the fact that the train was leaving was his reason to run. For we can understand such statements as really suggesting that the agent *treated* the fact that the train was leaving as a reason to run. It was in this sense 'his' reason; it functioned as a reason for him. An agent may treat a fact as a reason without the fact being a reason and even without the agent really (on reflection) believing it is a reason. To treat a fact as a reason to perform a given action is simply to be motivated by it to perform that action. In other words, to treat a fact as a reason is to be motivated in a way that would

---

[15] Scanlon (1998) makes similar claims.

make sense if it really were a reason. This account of such remarks gets further corroboration when we consider a case in which someone ran to catch the train simply because a trusted friend advised him to do so. In this case it would be equally natural to say that "his reason for running was that his friend advised him to do so." However, unless we reject the distinction between reasons for action and reasons for belief altogether, this should not lead us to conclude that the fact that his friend advised it really was a reason for his action.

So neither desire-based reasons nor promise-based reasons, when properly understood, are evidence that any old fact can be a reason for action. Moreover, if we are careful to heed the distinction between reasons for action and reasons for belief, and if we confine reasons for action to those considerations that favor our action the idea that any old fact can be a reason for action looks extremely implausible. We therefore conclude that the main premiss of our reply to the vacuity objection is true and that our reply is therefore sound.

## 6.4. Summary and Preview

We have argued that default principles are available to us insofar as we have moral knowledge in particular cases. Moreover, the details of our account explain why default principles are immune from the vacuity objection. So there are nontrivial moral principles and we have reason to believe that there are. Hence Principle Eliminativism and Principle Skepticism about hedged principles are false. Furthermore, ordinary moral thought insofar as it aspires to count as knowledge presupposes the availability of default moral principles. So Anti-Transcendental Particularism about hedged principles is also false.

For all we have said so far, though, there might be infinitely or unmanageably many moral principles, in which case Holton's Principled Particularism would be true (see Chapter 1). Nor have we done anything to show that there must be nonhedged moral principles. In the following chapter we explain why we should be confident that there are only finitely and manageably many moral principles and indeed that we can move from hedged default principles to principles which are not hedged. By the end of Chapter 7, therefore, we will have provided an argument against Principle Eliminativism, Principle Skepticism, Anti-Transcendental Particularism, and Principled Particularism where those doctrines are understood in terms of nonhedged principles and not merely in terms of hedged principles like the more modest default principles defended here.

# 7

# Beyond Default Principles:
# Trimming the Hedges

The key to wisdom is knowing all the right questions.

(John A. Simone, Jr.)

We have argued that moral knowledge presupposes the availability of default principles. This is already enough to refute Principle Eliminativism, Principle Skepticism, and Anti-Transcendental Particularism about hedged principles. Nonetheless, important particularist challenges remain. First, our argument so far has been limited to default principles, but default principles are insufficient to guide action without an independent ability to judge whether relevant defeaters are present. So without some reason to think we can trim the hedges of our default principles, particularists might reasonably complain that we have at most scored a Pyrrhic victory.

Secondly, we have not yet provided an argument against Principled Particularism. Recall that Principled Particularism allows that every moral verdict can be understood in terms of a principle, but insists that no finite (much less manageable) set of principles could map out the entire moral landscape. The fact that every piece of moral knowledge presupposes a corresponding moral principle is perfectly consistent with morality's being so complex that no finite set of principles could codify the whole of it. Richard Holton motivates this version of particularism by way of an analogy with mathematics in light of Godel's Incompleteness Theorem. The point is that there may be a principled proof for every truth of mathematics even if no finite and consistent axiomitization can yield all mathematical truths. Principled Particularism just makes the analogous claim about morality, albeit without the benefit of a proof.

Each of these important challenges suggests that the spirit of particularism survives even if the argument for default principles is successful. As we noted in Chapter 6, if the hedges inherent to default principles can never be finitely explicated in descriptive terms, one might reasonably worry that particularism lives on in the hedges. In this respect, a potentially infinite or incomprehensibly large set of default principles alone may seem to be too light a timber for the ambitions of traditional moral philosophy. Many of the most familiar moral theories seek to articulate what is morally relevant in a few interrelated categories. The goal of moral philosophers has often been to make morality manageable by showing how seemingly diverse moral phenomena can be explained in terms of a few basic factors.

So we need to meet these twin challenges. We need to show that the number of valid moral principles is manageable, and we need to show that that whatever hedges they may contain can be explicated in manageable terms. In this chapter we argue that the best account of the possibility of practical wisdom entails that the person of practical wisdom is a person of principle. More specifically, the best account of practical wisdom entails that practical wisdom involves the internalization of a finite and manageable set of non-hedged moral principles which together codify all of morality. Thus insofar as practical wisdom is possible, these remaining challenges can be met.

We give three complementary reasons in favor of our account of the possibility of practical wisdom. As a point of contrast, the particularist claims that:

> our account of the person on whom we can rely to make sound moral judgements is not very long. Such a person is someone who gets it right case by case. To be consistently successful, we need a broad range of sensitivities, so that no relevant feature escapes us, and we do not mistake its relevance either. But that is all there is to say on the matter. To have the relevant sensitivities just is to be able to get things right case by case. (Dancy 1993: 64)

The first reason to prefer a generalist account of practical wisdom is one of scope. A generalist account can make sense of practical wisdom's extending to more unusual circumstances much more easily than particularism. This in turn fits better with the plausible idea that our moral outlook can be refined and improved through engagement with the right sorts of fiction, where some of the right sorts of fiction may involve wildly different situations from those we normally face.

The second advantage of our account is epistemological. The particularist account of practical wisdom faces a dilemma. It must either understand moral knowledge as straightforward empirical knowledge or hold that moral knowledge is contingent a priori. We argue that each of these options is problematic. By contrast, a generalist account of practical wisdom provides a very plausible division of moral knowledge into a priori and a posteriori components. The knowledge of a given moral principle is a priori, while the knowledge that the antecedent of that principle is satisfied is a posteriori.

The third advantage we claim for our account is intuitive. On reflection, the idea that there are an infinite number of morally relevant considerations is not very plausible. This is evidenced by the reception enjoyed by theories that attempt to specify a finite range of morally relevant considerations. Though no such theory commands universal assent, neither are they thought to have embarked on a hopeless mission. Together these three considerations speak heavily in favor of a generalist account of practical wisdom.

Assuming that practical wisdom is indeed possible, these three considerations dramatically expand the scope of our refutation of Principle Eliminativism, Principle Skepticism, and Anti-Transcendental Particularism. For now we have a refutation of those three doctrines not only about hedged principles (specifically, default principles), but also a refutation of the corresponding three doctrines about unhedged principles. If successful, our argument also refutes the Principled Particularist thesis that no finite set of principles can codify all of morality. For the person of practical wisdom is a person in command of a set of finite and unhedged principles which codifies all of morality (or at least, the entire portion of morality of which knowledge is possible) in descriptive terms. So if practical wisdom is possible then morality can be captured in a finite set of unhedged principles with purely descriptive antecedents.

## 7.1. Scope

The person of practical wisdom must exhibit a complex set of sensitivities. If holism about reasons is true, practical wisdom involves at least three sensitivities. First, the practically wise person must successfully identify candidate reasons. Secondly, the practically wise person must successfully identify whatever relevant defeaters and enablers are present. Thirdly, the practically wise person must successfully identify what there is most reason to do when a multitude of undefeated reasons point in incompatible directions.

An agent who completely lacked any one of these sensitivities could not come close to instantiating practical wisdom. To be clear, we do not here assume that practical wisdom is necessary for moral virtue. We do not wish to rule out views of moral virtue according to which a virtuous agent may rely on fairly crude heuristics and need not have a very deep understanding of moral reasons. Such people may be the very salt of the earth and nothing we say here should be taken to suggest that such people are lacking in moral virtue. This caveat to one side, how should we understand practical wisdom itself?

Consider sensitivity to reasons. For the person of practical wisdom, this is more than recognizing a consideration as a reason when it is recognized to be present. It also comprises the disposition to inquire whether some normally reason providing consideration is present. The practically wise person does not merely recognize a reason to stop when he finds out that what he is doing is hurting another person. He is also someone who knows to ask, "Does that hurt?" The same could be said for sensitivity to defeaters and enablers. The person of practical wisdom must know what to look for and must reliably find it if it is there to be found.

There are cases where even a practically wise person may fail to make important judgments about her reasons. If someone is unwittingly infected with a deadly and contagious disease then she has reason to avoid mingling with people in the train station. The fact that she has not recognized these reasons does not count against her being practically wise since her failure is not a failure either to know what to look for or to recognize its significance. In other cases, a practically wise person may fail to make important judgments about her reasons because the cognitive abilities upon which her wisdom depends are temporarily inactive. A person who fails to wake her family when the house is on fire because she is asleep and unaware is not for that reason lacking in practical wisdom.[1]

It is important to be clear about the sort of reliability at stake here. Consider the following analogy. Imagine a bomb detection device that is reliable in the following sense. If it detects an object, it can reliably determine whether that object is a bomb. The device is easily fooled, however. It cannot detect objects that are shielded by tinfoil, and so it cannot determine whether such objects are bombs. The device is merely conditionally reliable. If an object is available to it (if it is not shielded by tinfoil), then it reliably detects whether it is a bomb. With respect to objects behind tinfoil, though, the device is blind. The person of practical wisdom is not like this. The person of practical wisdom goes through life with a view of her reasons that is, by and large, accurate. The person of practical wisdom is not merely conditionally reliable and does not have such systematic blind spots. This is why practical wisdom is such a valuable achievement, and why for most of us it is an ideal that can only be approximated.

---

[1] As should be clear, our discussion assumes that the epistemic availability of a consideration is not a necessary condition on that consideration counting as a reason. Put another way, epistemic availability is not an enabler. This seems to fit the spirit of thinking that reasons are considerations that favor various responses. A response could be favored even if we could not know that it is favored. While our discussion assumes that epistemic availability is not an enabler, our argument does not require it, and could readily be adapted if we decided that a consideration's status as a reason depended upon that consideration being epistemically available to the agent whose reason it is. In fact, if it were true that only epistemically available considerations could count as reasons, then this would only aid our argument, since it would radically limit the range of considerations that might be reasons.

How is it possible for an agent reliably to judge that a consideration is a reason? First, the agent must reliably detect whether the consideration is present. Having detected the presence of the consideration, the agent must reliably detect whether it is defeated. This, in turn, requires that the agent reliably detect the presence of any potential defeating conditions, and whether those potentially defeating conditions are in fact defeating.[2] What makes this possible? Our contention is that the best explanation of the possibility of such reliability is that the number of potential defeaters is finite and manageably short. If there were an infinite or even vast number of diverse considerations that could function as defeaters or enablers (or metadefeaters or metaenablers), then it is difficult to see how an agent could reliably judge when a consideration is a reason. We shall argue that those explanations of reliability which are consistent with unmanageably many defeaters implausibly impoverish the scope of practical wisdom.

Now consider reasons themselves. The person of practical wisdom will succeed in reliably judging not only whether some consideration is a reason. The person of practical wisdom also must reliably determine what there is most reason to do.[3] The best explanation of how a person of practical wisdom can reliably know what there is most reason to do will invoke the idea that she already knows all of the kinds of considerations which can function as reasons, defeaters, enablers, intensifiers, and diminishers and indeed understands how they interact. Such knowledge is essential if the person of practical wisdom is to know what to look for.

In typical cases of moral knowledge by description, the practically wise person need not deploy all of this knowledge. For in such cases some of the potential reasons, defeaters, and the like may be known by the agent to occur very rarely or to have too little force to matter, at least in the circumstances with which she is familiar. However, the practically wise person should be able to have moral knowledge about circumstances which are novel and atypical. The possibility of practical wisdom so understood is best explained by the hypothesis that the person of practical wisdom already knows and indeed can articulate all of the potential reasons, defeaters, etc. which might be in play in order to ask the right questions even about extraordinary cases.

This argument faces a *tu quoque* objection according to which the generalist must also give an account of how we deal with a huge number of reasons. Both in the case of reasons and in the case of defeaters and enablers we should

---

[2] This will require sensitivity to higher-level defeaters and enablers.

[3] The same could be said of any of the deontic predicates, wrong, right, permissible, etc. In the text, we present the argument in terms of the predicate, what there is most reason to do, but the same arguments could be given, we believe, for any of these other predicates.

draw a distinction between types and tokens. Even if possible reasons fall into a limited number of types, there might still be a vast or infinite number of tokens of those types in a given situation. If the person of practical wisdom must be properly sensitive to a potentially infinite number of token reasons, then why would it be more difficult to be sensitive to an infinite number of types?

First, this is not a problem for moral philosophy in particular. For the issue here is really how we can come to know certain kinds of purely descriptive facts—the facts which constitute the token relevant moral reasons of a given type. We somehow manage to do this, and though it may be a puzzle how we manage to do it, the puzzle is ultimately not a problem for moral generalists any more than anybody else. Rather, if this is a puzzle at all, then it is a general puzzle in epistemology.

Secondly, there is in any event a significant difference between a vast multitude of types and a vast multitude of tokens. So long as there are a limited number of types of reasons, we can proceed to inquire what specific reason tokens there are. We have a manageable sense of what to look for. If, by contrast, there were a vast number of types, then it becomes hard to know what to look for. A pilot can know that he has good reason not to crack jokes about engine failure over the intercom because this is likely to cause distress to passengers. Even if the pilot does not know just how many tokens of this reason are present (perhaps a few of his passengers enjoy dark humor), he can know that it is likely to cause distress to many passengers and that this is of greater significance than the entertainment value his jokes might have. It is not clear that the pilot could reach such a conclusion if there were a potentially infinite number of types of reasons. With a huge number of tokens of the same type we can at least quantify over those tokens and have some rough sense of how strong those reasons are. On the other hand, if there were a huge number of radically different types of reasons it is much harder to see how we could get a sense of the overall balance of reasons. Quantifying over them will not solve the problem since the variety of types of reasons means that their overall force may well not sum so neatly.

There are two main nonskeptical particularist alternatives to our approach. First, the particularist might insist that there is an infinite or unmanageably vast number of morally relevant considerations which often matter in our local circumstances. Such a particularist then owes some account of how this supposition leaves room for practical wisdom. Secondly, the particularist might more modestly claim that only a limited number of the unmanageably many potential moral reasons (and defeaters, enablers, etc.) are ever instantiated in our local conditions. On this account, the person of practical wisdom is reliable within his local circumstances by being sensitive to a limited number of morally relevant considerations.

The first of these alternatives is not very promising. We simply do not have any clear model for how normal human beings could be properly sensitive to each of an infinite (or even incredibly vast) number of distinct types of morally relevant considerations. As we emphasized in our argument for default principles, our cognitive capacities are limited. In fact, particularists have not (so far as we know) tried to provide a model of how human agents could be sensitive to an infinite number of morally relevant considerations. Instead, they have strived to square moral reliability with our limited capacities. Here, for example, is Jonathan Dancy:

> Given that the cycle of enablers and disablers may continue indefinitely, are we ever going to be in a position to determine how things actually are in the world of reasons? This sort of worry needs to be firmly put aside, on pain of driving us to overall moral (and other) scepticism. Competent moral judges do not need to be aware of everything that just <u>might</u> make a difference in order to determine whether it does or not; they don't even, I would claim, need to be aware of everything that does make a difference, any more than the competent chess player needs to be aware of all the indefinitely ramifying contributions of the different aspects of the position in front of her in order to reach a responsible judgement about what move there is most reason to make. We don't have to know everything before we can make a start at all. (Dancy 2004: 142)

Dancy is surely right that reliability does not require us to be sensitive to every reason that is present in our circumstances. This is not enough to dispel the worry that a sufficiently vast number of distinct reasons would preclude reliability. Take, for example, a case in which what Dancy says about the competent chess player is most clearly correct. Suppose that my position leaves me only one move that avoids the capture of my queen. Even if I am quite insensitive to the presence of other aspects of the position, I will (if competent) reliably make the proper move and avoid the capture of my queen. The most ready explanation in this case, however, is that there are very few considerations that could ever outweigh the loss of my queen, and if I am a competent player I have already been sensitive to them. For example, I have looked to see if saving my queen gives my opponent a ready checkmate. Having looked for these dangers, I have no need to be sensitive to minor positional features, as none of these will outweigh the loss of my queen. When we turn to cases in which the reasons are more closely balanced, though, it becomes less clear that a player can reliably make the proper move unless he is sensitive to all of the positional factors. The chess expert must be reliable not just in the easy cases, when one factor obviously predominates. He must also be reliable in more finely balanced positions.[4] So Dancy's analogy notwithstanding, we do not see how agents could be suitably reliable if there were an infinite number of morally relevant considerations present in the circumstances they regularly face.

Let us then turn to the second particularist alternative to our account. Particularists might claim that, in the circumstances we actually face, only a limited number of morally relevant considerations are typically present. If this were the case, then a limited set of sensitivities might nevertheless achieve reliability. This might seem to compromise the spirit of particularism. For it leaves open the possibility of codifying those morally relevant features which are at all likely to matter in our own circumstances. However, the position at least does not compromise the letter of many forms of particularism. For it may still be maintained that the number of morally relevant considerations which could matter is still vast.

One critical question to pose for this version of particularism is whether it does not implausibly limit the scope of practical wisdom. If the person of practical wisdom's reliability is possible because she only ever (or typically) faces a limited subset of the vast or infinite number of morally relevant considerations, then her reliability is limited in two related ways. First, her reliability is limited to her local circumstances. If she were to leave her local conditions and enter circumstances in which more or different morally relevant considerations were present, she would cease to be reliable. Secondly, the agent's reliability is contingent on local circumstances not changing in the wrong ways.

The question is whether we think the scope of practical wisdom really is and indeed must be limited in this way. The answer to this question appears to us to be no, and this tells forcefully against the particularist's second alternative. While there are significant obstacles to extending our moral judgment to new and unfamiliar cases, the person of practical wisdom can do so. For the person of practical wisdom, the challenge posed by novel circumstances is the challenge of identifying what morally relevant considerations are instantiated. The person of practical wisdom should know what to look for, even in radically novel or unusual circumstances.

Consider the following thought experiment. Our hero Wanda, interstellar journalist and person of practical wisdom, is covering the recent happenings

---

[4] Dancy's discussion concerns the 'competent player' and Dancy's conclusion is that we do not need to be perfectly sensitive "to make a start at all." In both respects, Dancy is setting the bar lower than we are. It may be enough for competence that one be capable of reliably avoiding gross errors. It may be enough to "make a start," that one be able to do better than one could by random guessing. But we are assuming that it is possible to be more than minimally competent. We are assuming that it is possible to be practically wise, and this requires making reliable judgments even when things are not obvious.

in an entirely alien culture. Recently, the government of this culture has been rounding up members of the general population and surgically removing a small appendage. Wanda wants to tell her readers the whole story, both what is happening and whether it is morally objectionable. Her only source is a very well informed member of the native population. Her source is entirely honest and forthcoming in all respects save one. He will not tell Wanda whether what is happening is wrong or offer any other moral evaluation of it.

Wanda has her practical wisdom, and a perfect source for the nonmoral facts, and a very accommodating editor who will allow her to take as much time and ask as many questions as she likes. Is this enough? Our inclination is that the answer is yes. Wanda would know what to ask her source. Are these appendages a threat to their welfare, or are they important for healthy functioning? Have they consented to the procedure? If the procedure is not performed, does this create dangers for others? Are we watching a system of universal health care removing cancerous tumors or a forced sterilization program targeting an ethnic minority? If she can get answers to these (and other) questions, then Wanda, given her practical wisdom, will be in a position to tell her readers the whole story. She will be able to tell them what is happening, and whether it is morally wrong.

Our optimistic assessment of Wanda's prospects does not depend on a naive view of the challenges of anthropology. Perhaps it will be very difficult for Wanda to get an accurate picture of what is happening (construed nonmorally) in an alien culture. If she is unable to do this, then she will not be in a position to render a reliable moral judgment. Our point is that insofar as these descriptive facts are forthcoming the practically wise person could reliably determine the moral facts as well.

It is possible, of course, that Wanda will overlook some relevant question. Perhaps there are some reasons that are seldom instantiated in her world but which are frequently instantiated in the alien culture. Perhaps some reasons normally (in her world) have so little force that they rarely make a difference. Given their infrequency or weakness (in her world) she has a habit of not asking about them. Faced with a novel culture, her old habits rule the day, and she forgets to ask about (what turns out to be) a very prevalent or weighty reason in the alien environment. This would undermine her reliability, but it also seems to count against her being practically wise. The practically wise person must know that novel circumstances demand uncommon scrutiny. Moreover, this limitation on Wanda's practical wisdom is open to correction. If, for example, Wanda were the regular beat reporter for moral affairs in alien cultures, then she would learn not to assume that the distribution of morally relevant considerations is constant across different worlds.

It might be argued that Wanda will never be able to render reliable moral judgments about the alien scenario unless and until her source relents and provides her at least with the sort of moral information conveyed by 'thick' moral predicates. How, after all, will Wanda know if the surgical removal of these appendages is morally acceptable unless she knows whether those who are subjected to them have been *coerced*? It is often suggested that it is these thick moral concepts that simply cannot be characterized in descriptive terms.[5] If this is right, then whether we think of reasons holistically or atomistically, finite principles specifying reasons will not be able to take us from a descriptive characterization of situations to a conclusion about what reasons there are. We are left with what David McNaughton and Piers Rawlings have called "thick intuitionism" (McNaughton and Rawling 2000).

Consider the following principle:

For all actions x and agents A, (If A promises to x and A's promise to X was not coerced, then A has reason to x in virtue of the fact that A promised to x.)

For the record, we do not suppose this principle is true; coercion is not the only possible defeating condition for promising.[6] The example is meant only to help focus attention on the concept of coercion.

When we judge that someone ought to do something because she promised to do it, we presuppose that the relevant defeating conditions do not obtain in the case at hand. Let us now restrict ourselves to the judgment that a particular promise was coerced. Particularists will be keen to emphasize that coercion is a moral concept, as A coerces B only if A threatens to infringe B's moral rights.[7] We do not mean to contest this claim. Rather, we think the right strategy here is to redeploy our recipe for generating default principles, but now with the target moral concept being coercion. When we judge that a promise was coerced, we judge that it was coerced in virtue of its more specific descriptive features. If we are asked what was coercive about a particular promise, we are

---

[5] McNaughton and Rawling 2000 and Little 2000. It is also sometimes argued (Crisp 2000) that these considerations tell against holism. Rather than say that we have reason not to tells lies (except when doing so is not dishonest), we could just say that we have reason not to be dishonest. Just how particularist 'thick intuitionism' is depends not upon whether it is holistic or not, but on whether dishonesty can be spelled out in finite descriptive terms.

[6] David McNaughton and Piers Rawling (2000) note that promises to do something immoral are also not reason-providing. It is also at least arguable that sometimes coerced promises are binding, if the coercion was legitimate. In this case, we would say, there must be some further feature that explains why the coercive nature of the promise does not defeat its reason giving force.

[7] This is how, for example, Charles Fried defines coercion. See Fried 1981. Thanks to Brad Hooker for drawing us out on this important point.

expected to be able to answer this question if we understand the case. So, for example, it might be a default principle that if I threaten to kill you unless you make a certain promise and no other feature of the situation explains why this is not an instance of coercion, then my threatening you in this way is a form of coercion. Moreover, it is plausible that there are only manageably many such default principles. For there are only manageably many moral rights and hence only manageably many forms of coercion.

If we are right that coercion is grounded in descriptive features in this way, then the possibility of knowing whether coercion is present presupposes the viability of certain principles regarding what descriptive features ground coercion and in what contexts they do so.[8] The person of practical wisdom can reliably identify coercion on the basis of the descriptive features upon which it is grounded. Our contention must then be that the possibility of this reliability is itself explained by the fact that only a limited number of descriptive features count as coercive and that the context-sensitivity of these features itself can also be captured in descriptive terms. If that is right, then (given time) Wanda should be able to identify what thick moral concepts are applicable by querying the descriptive nature of the situation. In that case, the reference to coercion in the antecedent of Wanda's moral principle could eventually be replaced with a specification of the various ways in which a promise can be coerced. On reflection, this does not seem implausible. If Wanda's source refused to characterize situations with even thick moral concepts, this would make things more difficult, but she need not despair and start writing horoscopes.

This does not guarantee that Wanda, even if she is practically wise, will never be ignorant of some morally relevant consideration. We are not claiming that the practically wise person is sensitive to every potentially relevant consideration. Our position is fallibilist. If Wanda is reliable, however, then she must not be ignorant of too many of the morally relevant considerations. If her reliability extends—given an awareness of the nonmoral facts—even to quite strange and alien worlds, then this suggests that she must be sensitive not just to most of the morally relevant considerations that frequent her local conditions, but to most of the morally relevant considerations that there are, period.

Those with particularist sympathies might at this point dig in their heels and insist that it is simply true that human practical wisdom even in its ideal form does not extend to exotic circumstances like the one facing Wanda. On the particularist account, practical wisdom is a local and contingent affair and of

---

[8] Sometimes the argument from holism is applied directly to the case of thick concepts. As Little puts it, "Whether [particular examples] qualify as cruel depends irreducibly on the context in which they are situated" (Little 2000: 280). We find such an argument unpersuasive for the same reasons we found the original argument from holism unpersuasive (see Ch. 2).

course must be shaped by the features which tend to matter morally in our local environment. From this perspective, the fact that someone who is practically wise could not discern the moral facts in a situation like the one facing Wanda should not seem especially surprising or disturbing. On this view, Wanda's inability to derive the moral facts should bother us no more than the possibility that an expert on human emotions could not discern an alien's emotions from the same evidence that these aliens use to detect each other's emotions.

In our view, this assessment of the potential scope of practical wisdom has little independent plausibility. Pretheoretically, the idea that practical wisdom for creatures like us at least *can* have a very wide scope is indeed a plausible one. We should be reluctant to reject it simply on the strength of a philosophical theory like particularism. However, we can go beyond this appeal to pretheoretical intuition. To do so we should reflect upon our engagement with morally laden fictional scenarios. The moral instruction of young children typically relies heavily on fables and parables, and this point might even seem to favor particularism. After all, people seem to remember morally loaded Bible stories better than lists of rules like the Ten Commandments. Notably, particularists have taken the importance of parables and stories as evidence for their own view, since a narrative-based approach provides a model of moral learning which does not invoke principles. Here, for example, is David McNaughton: "What the great moral teachers of the past, such as Buddha and Christ, have done is to bring us, by parable, story and paradox, to see the world in new and revealing ways. What we need is not a better set of principles but better moral vision" (McNaughton 1988: 205).

So the idea that we might gain new moral knowledge by engaging with fictional scenarios is not one particularists should reject out of hand. Particularists and generalists will divide on whether this new moral knowledge is best understood in terms of acquiring new principles. However, the moral benefits of engaging with fictional scenarios is not entirely limited to the acquisition of new moral knowledge. For engagement with fictional scenarios can also function to deepen our appreciation of familiar moral norms. For example, a moral principle which forbids torture (save perhaps in very extreme situations) may acquire new meaning for someone after engaging with a narrative which vividly describes the torture of an innocent person. Moreover, engagement with such fictional scenarios may not only deepen our appreciation of the force of a norm; it may also play an important epistemic function by justifiably increasing our confidence in the norm itself. We have put this point about deepening our appreciation in generalist terms, but an analogous point is available to particularists. For particularists can (and should) urge that engagement with fictional cases can deepen our appreciation of the moral force a certain sort of consideration can have in the right context. For this deepening of appreciation to be broadly speaking a rational one, our judgments about fictional cases must not be mere guesswork, but rather constitute moral knowledge.

So there are very good non-question-begging reasons for thinking that we can have moral knowledge about fictional scenarios. Once this much is conceded, though, it is natural to ask what limitations there might be on the sorts of fiction from which we might draw important moral lessons. Obviously, a work of fiction which somehow managed not to raise (even indirectly) any moral questions would be of very limited utility, but this is a fairly trivial constraint. The real issue we want to explore is whether our moral sensibility can reap benefits only from stories set in fairly familiar environments. Instead, we shall argue that we can reap moral dividends from much more fantastical scenarios of the sort one finds in some science fiction.

In our view, it would be implausible to declare *ex ante* on the basis of one's allegiance to a philosophical theory that people cannot deepen their appreciation of moral considerations from fantastical fictional scenarios. After all, many ordinary people certainly think they actually have reaped moral benefits from reading the right kinds of science fiction, watching the right kinds of science fiction movies and television shows, and even considering the right kinds of fantastical thought experiments. If this is right, then we should believe we are able to have moral knowledge about extremely fantastical scenarios. For the kinds of scenarios we find in science fiction are often very strange indeed. So we should favor an account of practical wisdom which has greater scope. For such an account fits better with the plausible idea that we can reap moral benefits from engagement with fiction, including very exotic forms of science fiction. So the greater scope of a generalist account of practical wisdom is a significant advantage.

Consider just one example. In the science fiction classic *Flatland*, Edwin A. Abbott describes a two-dimensional world inhabited by various two-dimensional shapes. But these are no mere shapes. The line segments, squares, and hexagons of Flatland have feelings, beliefs, notions of moral right and wrong, and in short are recognizable as moral agents. Moreover, part of the point of Abbott's novel (often lost on his readers) is to provide a satirization of the sexist and classist norms which so dominated Victorian England at the time (*Flatland* was written in 1884). So here we have a nice example of some fairly bizarre science fiction (is it even metaphysically possible for a two-dimensional shape to have a mind and perform actions for reasons?) which is supposed to expand our moral (as well as geometrical) horizons. The class system described in *Flatland* is based on the number of sides a shape has. A square is higher up the social ladder (to use a three-dimensional metaphor to describe a two-dimensional world!) than a mere triangle, but an octagon is higher up the social ladder still. At the top of this caste system are the so-called circles, who in reality are just figures with so many sides that they 'approximate' genuine circles. At the bottom of the social hierarchy are women who are mere line segments. It is part of the mythology of Flatland that each male child has exactly one more side than his father, but we learn in the sequel to *Flatland*, *Flatterland* (written much more recently by a different author, Ian Stewart) that, in reality:

Most male children had the same number of sides as their fathers. A tiny proportion had fewer, usually just *one* fewer. A roughly equal proportion had an extra side; a very tiny proportion indeed had two or more extra sides. This 'random walk' of polygonal sides had, over time, led to a small number of 'Circles', while the overwhelming bulk of the population were equilateral triangles, squares, pentagons, or hexagons. This, at least, was what happened in the regular classes. With the irregulars, mainly triangles, a similar story was played out but with changes to the lengths of the sides. (Stewart 2001: 16)

Parents in Flatland want their children to move up the class hierarchy as much as possible, and this fact, in conjunction with some of the technology available to Flatlanders of suitable means, has some morally significant consequences:

Our physicians have discovered that the small and tender sides of an infant Polygon of the higher classes can be fractured, and his whole frame re-set, with such exactness that a Polygon of two or three hundred sides sometimes—by no means always, for the process is attended with serious risk—but sometimes overleaps two or three hundred generations, and as it were doubles at a stroke, the number of his progenitors and the nobility of his descent.

Many a promising child is sacrificed in this way. Scarcely one out of ten survives. Yet so strong is the parental ambition among those Polygons who are, as it were, on the fringe of the Circular class, that it is very rare to find a Nobleman of that position in society, who has neglected to place his first-born in the Circular Neo-Therapeutic Gymnasium before he has attained the age of a month.

One year determines the success or failure. At the end of that time the child has, in all probability, added one more to the tombstones that crowd the Neo-Therapeutic Cemetery; but on rare occasions a glad procession bears back the little one to his exultant parents, no longer a Polygon, but a Circle, at least by courtesy: and a single instance of so blessed a result induces multitudes of Polygonal parents to submit to similar domestic sacrifices, which have a dissimilar issue. (Abbott 1952: 45 [1884])

On our view, it should be possible for a person of practical wisdom to determine whether the social practice described in this passage is morally acceptable, at least if certain further descriptive features of the situation left underdetermined by the text could be specified. Simply imagine that we can ask the author for more descriptive facts when this is necessary, and that he always has a ready answer for us.

A generalist should have no trouble explaining how a practically wise person could determine the moral status of this practice on different specifications of the relevant details. Of course, the exact details of this determination will depend on the details of the true moral theory, and we take no stand on that substantive issue here. For example, if the extreme pro-life position on abortion is correct, then the mere fact that these infant Polygons are potential persons will settle the question. On this view, unless subjecting them to such a known and high risk of premature death is somehow necessary to prevent some enormous disaster, doing so is wrong. On a more moderate rights-based account, the moral standing of the infant Polygons may depend on whether they have attained certain features deemed essential to personhood, such as sentience or self-consciousness. Abbott's text is silent on these descriptive features of the situation, but we are here assuming that we could probe the author with questions about such matters.

On yet other moral theories, the morality of the practice will depend on facts about the utility of a social practice allowing such procedures. It would be tedious and we suspect unnecessary to run through a whole host of different plausible moral theories to show how this point generalizes. The generalist account of practical wisdom has no difficulty in explaining how we might have moral knowledge about fantastical situations like the one described by Abbott.

By contrast, how might a particularist accommodate the idea that we could have moral knowledge in such cases? The particularist might try to borrow the generalist strategy of having a kind of checklist of morally relevant features which they could use to generate questions about the situation such as 'do the infants have self-consciousness?', 'is having more sides really correlated with natural talents and abilities or is this just social mythology?', 'does this practice promote general happiness?' However, for particularists, any such checklist will never contain every possible reason, defeater, and enabler. As Dancy at one point puts it, the idea that we might somehow have a complete list of "moral principles or of properties that can make a difference sometimes" makes no sense for "there is no limit to the number of properties which can on occasion be important" (Dancy 1993: 67).

Perhaps the particularist can maintain that in ordinary life this presents us with no insuperable problems. For, the particularists argues, some of the properties which can be morally relevant in the right context "are more commonly important than others; and therefore some properties should be viewed as more 'central' than others, i.e. as having a natural right to figure early in one's list of principles" (Dancy 1993: 67). Principles here are understood as mere reminders of which considerations can sometimes matter and the idea of a full codification of morality is dismissed as generalist fantasy. This point about which considerations are more commonly reasons in the actual world is fine as far as it goes. However, there is no reason to assume that the properties which are often important around here will also be important in situations as different from our own as Flatland. So whereas on a generalist account we can have moral knowledge about such fantastical cases, it is very hard indeed to see how a particularist account could deliver these epistemological goods.

To be clear, our argument does not depend on the idea that there are no important analogies between fantastical societies like Flatland and our own. Indeed, Abbot's point in writing Flatland was to satirize Victorian England. Our point here is not that there are no important points of commonality between our world and Flatland. Instead the point is that the text does not provide any clear idea of just how far these points of commonality extend and where the relevant differences begin. On a particularist account, this makes it hard to see how a person of practical wisdom could ever be rationally confident that there was not some further reason or defeater lurking in the background that she had not asked about. On a particularist model, just about anything can be a reason or a defeater if the context is right, and this makes it very hard to judge when one knows enough about a truly exotic situation to stop one's inquiry and make a decision.

For example, perhaps our world and Flatland are similar in that in both worlds a certain consideration is sometimes a reason. This point of similarity notwithstanding, it might also be true that there is a defeater for this reason, a defeater that is rare in our world but common, for example, in Flatland. The point, then, is not that there are no important analogies between our world and Flatland. Rather, the point is that there are also massive disanalogies which make it impossible to predict in advance whether a consideration which is usually a reason here will be a reason there. This, in turn, makes it impossible for a particularist moral sage ever to determine reliably that she knows enough about Flatland to make a sensible moral judgment.

One might object to our use of this example on grounds that our knowledge of the author's intentions is sufficient evidence that there are no relevant defeaters. Because Flatland is a satire, we can be relatively sure that the author intends that certain of the practices he describes are immoral. In this case, we can infer that the situation is not one in which some unmentioned defeater explains away the apparent wrongness of the practice. However, we can abstract away from this detail of the actual case and the main point still stands. Simply consider a reader of Flatland who has no idea of the author's intent. Many of Abbott's actual readers have mistakenly thought that Abbott was an apologist for sexism and classism. Alternatively, just consider a hypothetical case in which Wanda comes into contact with a source from Flatland, where Flatland is now construed as real (in our hypothetical case). In either of these two cases, a person of practical wisdom should be able to have moral knowledge about the practices in Flatland if given enough time to ask the right purely descriptive questions (of the author or of the source). Since these versions of the Flatland scenario rob the person of practical wisdom of any quick and easy inferences based on authorial intent, our main point stands.

In one of the few particularist discussions which touches on particularism and fictional cases, Dancy argues that it is easy to overstate how much new moral knowledge we can gain from engagement with fictional scenarios. Dancy's main target here is the idea that we can use our intuitions about fictional cases to help us resolve otherwise perplexing actual cases. Strictly speaking, we can concede this point. For our argument does not rely on the idea that we can learn new moral lessons from fictional cases but instead relies only on the idea that our knowledge about fictional cases can sometimes deepen our appreciation of reasons or norms with which we are already familiar. However, generalism as a regulative ideal goes beyond this particular argument. In any event, we do not concede that we cannot learn from fictional cases.

Dancy's main argument here comes in the form of a dilemma. Either the fictional case does or does not include all of the morally relevant details that we find in the actual case it mirrors. If it does include all of the moral complexity of the difficult actual case, then Dancy contends that it is hard to see why we would not find it at least equally difficult to resolve the fictional case. If, by contrast, the fictional case does not include all of the morally relevant complexity of the actual situation it mirrors, then any inference from the fictional case to the actual one is dubious.[9]

The only apparent way to make progress here would be if we somehow knew in advance that our judgment was distorted in the actual case by some morally irrelevant feature. We could then stipulate that this irrelevant feature is absent in the fictional case. However, if we already knew that our judgment was being distorted in this way by some morally irrelevant feature, Dancy argues, we would not need the fictional case to help us decide the actual case in the first place. As Dancy puts the point, "How can an imaginary case help, if essentially we have to make up our minds *before* we can come to a view about whether the imaginary case is, after all, a reliable guide?" (Dancy 1993: 69).

---

[9] See Dancy 1993: 68–9; see also Dancy 1985 for a more elaborate case against the use of fictional scenarios in moral theorizing.

To be absolutely clear, Dancy's argument is aimed at those whose main point is that we can use fictional cases to learn about actual cases. Our argument for generalism in this section does not presuppose this (though we think this is true and part of the reason that fictional cases are important). For the purposes of our argument it is enough that we can at least have moral knowledge about even fairly strange fictional cases and Dancy's argument here does nothing to undermine this premiss. Nor would conceding Dancy's point necessarily rob such knowledge of its moral and philosophical interest. As we have already seen, engagement with fictional cases might well deepen our appreciation of moral facts about the actual world. Moreover, it might be interesting in itself to see how some moral norms extend quite naturally to very alien situations whereas others seem more plausibly to be limited to situations close to our own in various relevant ways. Here it is germane to recall that any logically valid argument in some sense already contains its conclusions in its premisses, yet it can be useful and instructive all the same to follow a valid argument to its conclusion. Something analogous might hold in the case of considering fictional scenarios. They bring our prior commitments into sharp relief.

Secondly, Dancy's argument that we cannot really use fictional cases to help resolve otherwise perplexing actual cases is too swift. For a start, we might simply have a *hunch* that some morally irrelevant feature of the actual case is misleading us. On the basis of this hunch we might construct a pair of thought experiments. In the first we might describe a situation which is structurally similar to the actual case, but in which the suspected distracting feature is absent. The second might be similar to the first, but include the distracting feature. Forcing ourselves to confront less familiar situations in this way might serve to confirm our hunch that the relevant feature of the actual case was distorting our judgment.

Also, hypothetical cases can throw into sharp relief certain morally relevant features which otherwise might not get the attention they deserve.[10] Judith Jarvis Thomson's often-discussed example of the 'famous violinist' is arguably

---

[10] To be clear, a hypothetical case differs from a fiction in its logical form in the sense that a hypothetical case invites the reader to suppose its contents for the sake of argument and think about what could reasonably be inferred from those contents. A fiction as such need not invite the reader to suppose anything for the sake of argument, though it might. With fiction we may just engage our imagination instead of supposing anything for the sake of argument and e.g. thinking about its implications. While this distinction is an important one, we do not think it undermines the main point we make in the text. For the issue is how, given particularism, one could know what questions to ask about an underdescribed case to make one's mind up assuming one does decide to form a moral verdict about it. One can of course engage one's imagination to do this once one gets the relevant information, but our point is the prior one of how someone would know just which questions to ask. Thanks to several of the participants at the Bled conference on particularism (2005) for emphasizing the distinction between hypotheticals and works of fiction (in discussion).

a good case in point (see Thomson 1971). In Thomson's example, someone is kidnapped and hooked up to a famous violinist who needs to use the person's body for nine months to survive. The plausibility of the premiss that it would not be wrong to unhook from the violinist in this situation arguably can help us resolve the morality of abortion, at least in the case of rape. The case of rape is most analogous to the violinist case in that both involve a clear lack of consent to be hooked up to someone who needs you to survive. We do not here want to defend Thomson's argument, but only to illustrate how arguments of this form can actually be very helpful.

One potential advantage of Thomson's example is that the 'host' need not be a woman. Insofar as latent sexism might explain at least some opposition to abortion, controlling for this morally irrelevant factor might help purge our thinking of such distortions. Someone who at a conscious level rejects sexism but is being influenced subconsciously by it might see this influence when confronted with Thomson's example. The example also helps make vivid that the fetus is using someone's body without that person's consent by drawing on analogies in which some may find this description more natural. The mere fact that pregnancy is a natural process may also subconsciously distort people's judgment, leading them to think of it as somehow not aptly described as one in which the fetus is literally using the mother's body without her consent. Being forced to confront the case of the famous violinist might make this latent commitment explicit; and once it is made explicit it might well be one that we would (for familiar reasons) want to reject. Again, the dialectical point here depends not on the success of Thomson's argument in particular, but of the logical space for an argument like hers using hypothetical scenarios to help us with actual cases. Our suggestion is that there are ways of understanding how Thomson's example at least *could* help us with the actual case which suggest that Dancy's critique is too swift.

Finally, Dancy does try to accommodate the idea that we can benefit from engaging with fictional cases, albeit to a limited extent. Here is Dancy:

An imaginary case might be an abbreviated sketch of a situation where a property can be seen to be important: where the importance it can have is revealed. I think this especially effective as an account of what is going on in some of the parables in the New Testament, or in the morals attached to Aesop's fables. (Dancy 1993: 69)

This is very close to our point about how engagement with a fictional case might deepen our appreciation of morally relevant considerations. The issue we want to raise, though, is whether as a particularist Dancy really can accommodate the possibility of such benefits in fictional cases. Perhaps the particularist can, as Dancy suggests, accommodate our ability to learn from at least *some* fictional cases—ones in which it is plausible to assume that the scenario is embedded in a world which is in most important respects like our own. This assumption would allow the particularist to be reasonably confident that a sensibility which gets things reliably and systematically right in the real world will also reliably and systematically get it right in the fiction precisely in virtue of the similarity of the fictional scenario to the actual world. Here we *can* reasonably assume that what is commonly a reason in the actual world will also be a reason in the fictional world.

For our purposes the point to be made is that this assumption of similarity to the real world grows increasingly implausible as the fictional scenario being described grows increasingly distant from our own world. (Aesop's fables already include talking grasshoppers!) In strange science-fictional examples, it is hard to see how the idea that the fictional world is like our own in all ways not ruled out by the text can do any important work. For in some of these cases the explicit disanalogies with the actual world are so great that the assumption of similarity in all other respects is itself an extremely thin reed on which to build a particularist epistemology of these cases.

Indeed, in some cases, it is hard even to give much sense to the idea that the fictional world under consideration is, in all other respects, like the actual world. Here one is reminded of Roderick Firth's description of the ideal observer as someone who is "omniscient with respect to non-ethical facts, omnipercipient, disinterested, dispassionate, perfectly consistent and *in other respects normal*" (Firth 1952). In just the way that it is actually hard to make much sense of Firth's "in other respects normal" clause given the fantastical attributes he has given the ideal observer, it will also be hard in some science fiction cases to make much sense of the implicit 'and in all other respects it is like the actual world' idea. In sum, then, Dancy's attempt to make sense of how we can learn from fictional cases is fine as far as it goes but it does not go far enough.

Before concluding this section, we should return to the point that the form of particularism we are considering significantly compromises the spirit of particularism. Typically, particularists have advanced their view as the best account of the moral world in which we find ourselves. However, a form of particularism which holds that it is only in very exotic circumstances that we would expect very unusual features (like shoelace color) to function as reasons or defeaters begins to look less like a form of particularism anyway. For the particularism in such a view would in effect turn out to reside in worlds strange and different from our own—or in the constellation of our own world and these other strange worlds where our practical wisdom would run out. Whatever particularists have been meaning to claim, it presumably is not that *our* moral world is safe and predictable and populated by a manageably small number of reasons. So a further point against the particularists here stems from the fact that they must either maintain that our actual local environment is one in which moral reasons can behave in very unexpected ways or not. If they do allow for such strange behavior of reasons in our actual environment then it becomes hard to see how they can make sense of practical wisdom in the actual world—forget about science fiction. If, however, they do not allow for unexpected behavior of reasons in the actual world then their view is particularist in letter but not in spirit.

The preceding account of practical wisdom and the argument based upon it is, importantly, consistent with a familiar particularist refrain. It is often claimed that, no matter how exhaustively we identify what considerations can count as reasons, it will always be possible that some further consideration might come along and turn out to count as a reason too. No matter how well we mapped the moral terrain, it might still surprise us. This is true, but it does not undermine our argument. For this just underlines the anodyne fact that we can always be mistaken. Given new evidence or experience, we might be led to revise our view of what considerations are morally relevant. We would then revise our view of who has practical wisdom. Even if we perfectly identified all of the considerations that can ever be morally relevant as well as how they interact, we might not be certain that we had done so. Thus when McDowell speaks of moral principles as "something whose correctness we could try to make out independently of their application to particular cases" (McDowell 1988: 94) and goes on to cast doubt upon them, he is criticizing a conception of principles that we are not here defending. Our sense of what principles are correct must be shaped by our judgments in particular cases, and new experience may prompt revision of received principles.

## 7.2. Epistemology and Modality

While it is not our intention to present a full moral epistemology, it is worth sketching the outlines of the epistemology that is suggested by our account, and contrasting it with the most promising particularist models. Doing so lends further credence to our view that the best explanation of practical wisdom invokes principles. This is because generalism fits well with a plausible account of the epistemology and modality of basic moral facts. The picture is a familiar one, and this is no accident. Indeed once generalism has been rejected the available accounts of the epistemology and modality of basic moral facts start to look pretty bleak. This is the second advantage of our account of practical wisdom over its particularist rivals.

Suppose that we know that some particular action was morally right. According to generalism as a regulative ideal, this knowledge can be based on our a posteriori knowledge of the morally relevant contingent facts and our presumably a priori knowledge of a suitable and necessarily true moral principle. Given that our knowledge is based in part on a posteriori premisses, our conclusion that the particular action was morally right will be a posteriori on any plausible way of drawing the a priori/a posteriori distinction. We take this to be just the right result. *Of course* my knowledge that, for example, Bush's decision to go to war in Iraq was wrong is a posteriori knowledge of a contingent fact. That knowledge may well be based in part on some a priori moral principle, but that alone should not lead us to conclude that the knowledge is a priori. For my knowledge of the contingent facts in virtue of which the relevant principle applies will still be a posteriori. A piece of knowledge is not a priori simply because it is *partly* based on some a priori premiss(es). Rather, knowledge is a priori only if its status as knowledge does not depend on its drawing any positive support from a posteriori sources.[11] Since our knowledge that some specific action was right (or wrong) or that some specific fact was (or was not) a reason with a given valence will depend on various a posteriori premisses for positive support, such knowledge is clearly a posteriori. We take this decomposition of moral knowledge into the necessary a priori principle and the contingent a posteriori facts to provide a plausible explanation of why our moral knowledge always seems to have some a priori element.

While this combination of views is not mandatory for the generalist, it is a traditional and plausible way to understand moral knowledge. While generalism is consistent with the thesis that our knowledge of fundamental moral principles is a posteriori, we find this version of generalism considerably less plausible. Some of our reasons for preferring an a priori conception of our knowledge of fundamental moral principles emerges in our discussion of the problems facing a particularist epistemology.

How should a particularist understand basic moral facts and our knowledge of them? There seem to be two main options here. Since the particularist eschews moral principles, basic moral facts presumably must be facts about particular cases, such as that the fact that it would promote pleasure was a reason for her in her actual circumstances. This knowledge must not itself be based on some antecedent moral principle which would apply to other cases. Such basic moral facts are of course contingent. It need not have been the case

---

[11] In thus distinguishing a priori and a posteriori knowledge or justification we follow Bonjour (1998: 2).

that her action would promote pleasure at all. And if holism is true then even the fact that it would promote pleasure might not have been a reason. On the plausible assumption that knowledge of contingent facts is a posteriori, we are led to the conclusion that knowledge of basic moral facts must itself be a posteriori knowledge.

The problem with this approach is that it leaves no room for nontrivial a priori moral knowledge, and this is implausible. Some naturalists may hold that our moral knowledge is entirely a posteriori, but we take this view to be implausible *when combined with particularism*. For given particularism, moral properties are not reducible to descriptive properties; otherwise there would be a principle linking the predicates which refer to the relevant descriptive properties to the moral predicate in question. So if our moral knowledge is entirely a posteriori, then we must have a posteriori knowledge of the instantiation of *irreducible* moral properties. Moreover, given particularism, this *a posteriori* knowledge cannot be even partly based on the a priori knowledge of a suitable moral principle.[12] However, this combination of views is highly implausible. We certainly do not directly perceive moral properties, understood as irreducible features of a situation. That really would be to take the metaphor of moral vision too literally. We do not have a special moral sense which allows us to detect such irreducible moral properties. This, however, leaves it mysterious how we could reliably track the presence of such irreducible properties.

The only obvious purely a posteriori alternative would be to hold that such irreducible properties figure in the best explanation of our experiences. The epistemology of moral properties on this account becomes much like the epistemology of unobservable entities (and their properties) in science. Following Harman (1977: 3–10), we think this explanatory thesis is problematic. We need not insist on that, though. For there is a more basic point which has often been overlooked in these debates, and which is enough for our purposes. That point is that whether moral properties figure in the best explanation of our experiences is not germane to our ability to have moral knowledge. The very idea that my knowledge that lying is wrong depends on its wrongness figuring in the best explanation of my experiences is simply alien to ordinary moral practice. Morality should be consistent with science, but fundamental moral knowledge is not itself scientific knowledge. We do not go out into the field and do actual (as opposed to thought) experiments to determine that lying is wrong-making.

Suppose the particularist agrees that the purely a posteriori account of basic moral knowledge is indefensible, at least when combined with particularism.

---

[12]  Generalist versions of reductive naturalism need not embrace this further constraint.

Indeed, Dancy agrees that we should reject a purely a posteriori understanding of our knowledge of basic moral facts, by which he means facts "about what is a moral reason for what" (Dancy 2004: 141). What alternative epistemology is available to the particularist who rejects the idea of a 'moral sense?' Dancy argues that basic moral knowledge is a form of judgment and that our basic moral knowledge is a priori. However, he agrees that as a particularist he must also understand basic moral knowledge as knowledge of contingent facts about particular circumstances.

In admirably Leibnizian fashion, Dancy follows his initial assumptions where they lead and concludes that our knowledge of basic moral facts is a priori knowledge of contingent facts. Dancy realizes that the category of the contingent a priori will seem, as he puts it, "alarming" (Dancy 2004: 147) and indeed it is rather alarming. After all, the idea that contingent knowledge simply must be a posteriori in order to be responsive to the relevant contingent facts in the right way is very powerful. As Wesley Salmon puts the challenge, "But how could we conceivably establish by pure thought that some logically consistent picture of the world is false?" (Salmon 1967: 39). It is no coincidence that so many historical treatments of the a priori have taken it as obvious that whatever we can know a priori must be necessary.

Before turning to the reasons Dancy offers for accepting basic moral knowledge as contingent a priori, we want to emphasize just how steep a hill the particularist must climb. For while Dancy is not alone in defending the contingent a priori, other defenses of the contingent a priori would not be sufficient for the purposes of particularism. Such defenses either fail to establish knowledge of the right kind of contingencies, or else they fail to inspire confidence that we could have enough contingent a priori knowledge to provide a basis for ethics.

Perhaps the most famous recent (putative) example of contingent a priori knowledge has been offered by Kripke, who claims that propositions such as "The standard meter stick is one meter long" are both knowable a priori and contingent (Kripke 1972). Such a claim is supposed to be knowable a priori because someone who fully understands the term 'meter' understands that its reference is fixed by a particular object in the actual world—the standard meter stick. Yet there are other possible worlds in which that very object is not one meter long, so what is known is contingent. Whether such examples are genuine instances of contingent a priori knowledge is controversial,[13] but

---

[13] Lawrence Bonjour provides a dissenting view arguing with some plausibility that what is knowable a priori is not a claim about a particular object but rather a claim about the length of whatever object is used to fix the length of a term such as 'meter.' See Bonjour 1998: 12–13.

it is not a controversy which we need to decide here. The truth (in the actual world) of 'The standard meter stick is one meter long,' while contingent, simply derives from the semantics for 'meter.' We simply assume for the sake of argument that Kripke and his followers are right about the semantics here.[14]

Clearly this kind of case, even if it is rightly counted as contingent a priori knowledge, cannot serve as a basis for particularism's epistemology of basic moral knowledge. For, emphatically, particularists do not wish to claim that the truth of our basic moral knowledge (in the actual world) is derivable simply from the semantics for moral terms. In arguing against constitutive generalism, we have sided with particularists on this score. Moreover, even if we turned out to be wrong about this, there is the worry that any semantics for moral terms which is analogous to the familiar semantics offered for terms such as 'meter' would bring in its wake moral principles. For example, if the standard of rightness were simply fixed by reference to the reactions a particular and actual virtuous person—call him Fred—then,

Whatever Fred approves of is right

would be a kind of valid moral principle. Of course the principle would be contingent. In other possible worlds, Fred might react very differently, and thus approve of things that are not right. The difficulties with such an understanding of moral language are familiar. Just as obviously, though, this picture of moral facts is not at all the kind of picture that particularists have been trying to paint.[15] What particularists need is a very different kind of contingent a priori knowledge.

Following Evans (1985), we can distinguish between deeply contingent truths and superficially contingent truths. Deeply contingent truths are such that there is no semantic guarantee of their truth in the actual world. What particularists need, then, is a priori knowledge of deeply contingent truths. Such truths will not be knowable simply in virtue of understanding the semantics of the relevant terms because those semantics leave open whether there is any world in which the sentence is true. The elements of basic moral knowledge that Dancy would count as contingent a priori are facts about what is a reason for what in particular circumstances. For example, we may know that the fact that Sue consoling Jill would bring pleasure to Jill is a reason for Sue to console Jill. Assuming that we have such knowledge, what is known

---

[14] Sometimes this point is put in terms of Gareth Evans's distinction between 'superficially contingent' and 'deeply contingent' truths. See Evans 1985: 178–213.

[15] As Dancy puts it, "But nobody could suppose that knowledge of a basic moral fact is gained purely by examining one's concepts, nor by thinking about the meanings of words" (Dancy 2004: 148).

is deeply contingent because the fact that Sue consoling Jill would bring Jill pleasure is itself deeply contingent.

Recently, John Hawthorne (2002) has urged that the obstacles to a priori knowledge of deeply contingent truths are not insurmountable. Hawthorne asks us to reflect not only upon a priority and contingency, but also on the concept of knowledge. He notes that, "We feel a defeasible propensity to ascribe knowledge when presented with various reliable methods of belief formation. We then feel reluctant to ascribe knowledge insofar as various kinds of mistakes are made to look saliently similar to the case at hand" (Hawthorne 2002: 268). To see more clearly what Hawthorne has in mind, consider one of his tentative examples. Swampscientist has an "innate storehouse that correctly represents the basic principles of interaction between physical bodies" (2002: 252). Although he does not represent such principles as expressing necessities or have (or believe himself to have) any experiences to confirm the principles, Swampscientist can use his storehouse of principles to generate beliefs about the behavior of physical objects.

Interestingly, Hawthorne suggests that our intuitions about whether such beliefs count as knowledge are driven largely by whether we see salient similarities between the beliefs of Swampscientist and a range of ways things could go wrong. If we think of Swampscientist as doing something analogous to consulting a watch, we are more inclined to count his beliefs as knowledge. Though watches are often faulty, we discount this possibility and readily ascribe knowledge to someone who consults an accurate watch. If we think of Swampscientist along with other more typical scientists, there is little urge to ascribe knowledge. In this context we do not ascribe knowledge to scientists whose beliefs are not based on sufficient evidence or who have failed to consider relevant alternative theories.

We shall not pass judgment on Hawthorne's examples. For even if one takes a favorable view of them they are unlikely to be of service to the particularist. Hawthorne's examples all have two features that are conspicuously absent in the case of particularism. First, the objects of knowledge in Hawthorne's examples are all knowable a posteriori, without any basis in contingent a priori knowledge. Secondly, the putative knowers in Hawthorne's examples all employ some inferential method. In the case of those versions of particularism which understand basic moral knowledge as always contingent a priori, though, neither of these features is present. In the first instance, though such particularists can allow a posteriori knowledge of basic moral facts (as in the case of reliance on testimony), such knowledge is parasitic upon someone having contingent a priori knowledge. In the second instance, Dancy himself emphasizes that contingent a priori moral knowledge is not reached via inference.[16] These two features are relevant because it is in virtue of them that we can even make sense of salient resemblances to other cases of knowledge. It is by comparing the method of Swampscientist to the method of either the person consulting a watch or the method of the successful working scientist (both themselves a posteriori methods!) that we pump our intuitions as to whether Swampscientist has knowledge. By contrast, if we have no sense that there is any method by which someone reaches a piece of putative contingent a priori knowledge, and if there is no independent way to achieve the same knowledge, then it is hard to see clear and salient resemblances between such putative knowledge and other cases of knowledge. If anything such putative knowledge would look more like a purely arbitrary judgment.

On the other hand, to the extent that there is a method to particularist judgment, it seems to be a posteriori—or at least to contain an a posteriori element. For it is only upon learning that Sue consoling Jill would bring welcome comfort to Jill that we judge that this fact provides a reason. If the judgment that Sue's action will provide welcome comfort provides part of the basis for drawing a conclusion about our reasons, then we have some discernible method, but just as obviously the resulting knowledge is a posteriori.

Our purpose in discussing Kripke and Hawthorne has not been to evaluate Dancy's defense of the contingent a priori, for he does not appeal to their arguments. Nevertheless, our discussion of these other defenses of the contingent a priori reveals just how radical Dancy's suggestion must be. For what Dancy must really be proposing is that deeply contingent a priori knowledge that is not the result of any discernible method nevertheless forms the basis for a whole branch of human knowledge. That is far more alarming than the suggestion that there may be some penumbral cases of contingent a priori knowledge. However, before abandoning the contingent a priori we should consider Dancy's own defense.

Dancy offers two reasons for supposing that widespread alarm at the contingent a priori is misplaced. First, he draws a distinction between positive and negative dependence, a distinction also defended by Marcus Giaquinto

---

[16] See Dancy 2004: 101–8. As Dancy rightly notes, we have no generally agreed upon account of what movements of thought deserve to be called inferences. The critical point we make here, however, is able to sidestep this partly terminological issue. For on Dancy's view, there is no method at all, inferential or otherwise, by which we move from our knowledge of the descriptive fact, that Sue consoling Jill would bring welcome comfort, to a piece of moral knowledge, that the fact that Sue consoling Jill would bring welcome comfort is a reason to console. As Dancy puts it in speaking of basic moral knowledge, "In fact, there doesn't seem to be a *method* of acquiring that sort of knowledge at all" (2004: 148, emphasis in original).

(1998).[17] Dancy appeals to this distinction to argue that a belief that would be abandoned if experience became awkward for it need not therefore be a posteriori. Such a belief may be only negatively dependent on experience, Dancy claims. However, Dancy suggests, a belief is a posteriori only if it is positively dependent on experience. Dancy then maintains that with the contingent a priori we have mere negative dependence on experience but no positive dependence. So, the argument concludes, the tendency to assume that all contingent knowledge must be a priori rests on a failure to distinguish positive from negative dependence on experience.

Dancy's defense of the contingent a priori is highly elliptical. Recall that for Dancy basic moral knowledge is knowledge of the form, "Fact F is a reason for A to $\phi$." Clearly, our knowledge of such propositions does depend on experience, in that our knowledge that F is indeed a fact in the first place is dependent on experience, the experience which provides our evidence that F. Dancy's idea seems to be that this is mere negative dependence on experience, which does not entail that our knowledge that F is a reason for A to $\phi$ is a posteriori. It would follow that the knowledge is a posteriori in Dancy's (and Giaquinto's) sense only if certain experiences served as *grounds* for the belief.

How, though, do we determine when a given experience serves as grounds for a belief? Presumably if we know that F is a reason for A to $\phi$ then we know that F, where F is some contingent fact which we know through ordinary a posteriori methods. For example, F might be the fact that A's $\phi$ing would promote pleasure. Why do the a posteriori grounds for F itself not also constitute grounds for the judgment that F is a reason for A to $\phi$? Presumably, F is a presupposition of the proposition that F is a reason for A to $\phi$. After all, we can accept Giaquinto's distinction without denying that the grounds for a presupposition, so to speak, 'leak through' as grounds for the propositions for which they are presuppositions. We can think of presuppositions as epistemic 'enablers' of our reasons to believe the proposition which makes the relevant presuppositions, or we can instead think of presuppositions as part of the grounds for belief in those propositions. Dancy's discussion simply emphasizes the legitimate distinction between enablers and grounds without providing any reason for classifying presuppositions as mere enablers rather than grounds. So perhaps we should return to Giaquinto's original discussion.

Giaquinto is interested in the epistemology of 'the obvious'—noninferential knowledge which we typically acquire in a kind of 'Aha!' experience in which everything suddenly seems clear and distinct. His leading example is of the slave boy in the *Meno*, who suddenly learns certain geometrical facts by being

---

[17] The distinction has also been drawn and emphasized in Sommerfield 1991 and Burge 1993.

exposed to certain experiences (drawings of squares and the like). For two reasons this paradigm is not helpful for Dancy. First, geometrical knowledge is knowledge of necessary truths and secondly basic moral knowledge is not always obvious or acquired in an 'Aha!' experience. Put these disanalogies to one side, though. The question is why, according to Giaquinto, the experiences which prompt the slave boy to draw his geometrical conclusions do not provide grounds for those conclusions, in which case his knowledge would be a posteriori. Giaquinto's plausible answer is that the boy's knowledge does not depend on the veridicality of his experiences or even upon his taking them as veridical: "those experiences do not serve as reasons or grounds for the belief, because the believing does not depend on the believer's taking the experiences to be veridical" (Giaquinto 1998: 199). If Socrates' drawings were not perfect squares (and they almost certainly were not) then the boy's experiences of them as perfect squares would not be veridical, but this would not undermine the status of his geometrical conclusions as knowledge.

It is a complex question in epistemology and indeed psychology just how exposure to such drawings might rationally prompt someone to grasp and accept some new geometrical truth. However, Giaquinto's basic idea that the status of one's geometrical conclusions as knowledge does not depend upon the veridicality of the original experiences is extremely plausible, and this does seem to vindicate the 'taken as veridical' criterion. So let us suppose with Giaquinto that this is the (or at least *a*) way to distinguish positive from negative dependence. Now return to the moral case in which I have basic moral knowledge in Dancy's sense. Suppose I know that the fact that her action would promote pleasure is a reason for her to do it. For me to know this I presumably must also know that her action would promote pleasure, but Dancy will insist that this is an enabler and not a ground for my belief that this fact is a reason for her to do it. However, Giaquinto's criterion does not support this conclusion. My knowledge that her action would promote pleasure is a posteriori and depends on some experience, call it E, perhaps my having seen her perform similar actions in the past and having also seen these actions as producing pleasure. The crucial point is that in this case my believing that the fact that her action would promote pleasure is a reason for her to do it does indeed depend on my taking E to be veridical. If I thought the relevant experiences were not veridical, then I would not have so much as thought that it was a fact that her action would promote pleasure, much less would I have thought that this putative fact is a reason for anything. The case stands in sharp contrast to Giaquinto's case of the slave boy, where the boy's believing as he did really did not depend on his taking the experiences to be veridical. The slave boy could have agreed with Socrates that there are no perfect squares in the world of appearances but still learned his geometry lesson from Socrates' drawings.

At this point Dancy might argue that Giaquinto's criterion provides only a necessary condition on an experience's counting as grounds for a given belief and that there may well be other such necessary conditions. But this would require argument that Dancy has not provided, and it is unclear to us how such an argument might plausibly go.

In addition to invoking the distinction between positive and negative dependence, Dancy also offers a 'companions in guilt' argument:

However, there are companions in guilt, and once we realize this, most of our worries will subside. There are unmysterious examples of a priori knowledge that not only requires antecedent a posteriori moral knowledge ... but is also acquired using no method at all, so far as one can tell. Consider our ability to assess similarities. We have four things, A, B, C, and D; we can ask whether the first two are more similar to each other than are the second two. Let us say that A is a house designed by Frank Lloyd Wright, B is a house designed by Le Corbusier, C is an apartment block by Frank Lloyd Wright, and D is an apartment block by Le Corbusier. Is A more similar to B than C is to D? Are the two houses designed by these architects more similar to each other than are the two apartment blocks? In order to answer this question we need a posteriori knowledge of the independent nature of the four buildings; but that knowledge is not in itself enough. Nor would it be enough to have listed the points of similarity and dissimilarity on either side of the two comparisons. The difficulty is that some similarities are more telling than others. No list of points of similarity will suffice for a judgement about which of these points is most telling in the present comparison. The matter is reserved for judgement, perfectly properly, and that judgement is one for which there is no method; but such judgements can yield knowledge. So here we have a more or less perfect analogy, and one which, I would claim, takes the mystery out of the situation. If this sort of knowledge can be thought of as a priori, so can knowledge of basic moral facts. (Dancy 2004: 148)

We doubt we are alone in thinking that that this example hardly inspires confidence. It is not clear that we have here a case of a priori knowledge. Why not classify it as a slightly odd case of a posteriori knowledge? Without good reason to count this a case of a priori knowledge, this is a rather thin reed on which to base one's case for a thesis as ambitious as the thesis that there can be a priori knowledge of contingent facts, much less that all basic moral knowledge is contingent a priori. Dancy's main reason for thinking that our knowledge that the two houses are more similar than the two apartment blocks is a priori that which dimensions of similarity are most salient in a given context of comparison is itself a priori. Is this true, though? By way of analogy, when comparing two keys' similarity, shape rather than color typically will be most salient since we presumably will be interested in opening doors. However, knowing that this is the relevant dimension of similarity seems be a posteriori knowledge of the purposes for which we are making the comparison.

More generally, one might think that understanding the predicate 'more similar' consists in grasping the right function from contexts of comparison to fairly specific (albeit implicit) conceptions of which dimensions of similarity matter and how much each matters relative to the other. We then come to know that one pair is more similar than another in a particular context of comparison by going from the context and our knowledge of the meaning of 'more similar' to a conception of weighted dimensions of similarity which we then apply to the case at hand in virtue of our empirical knowledge of the features of the case. Crucially, on this model, our knowledge of which dimensions of comparisons matter and how much they matter in a given context will (and indeed must) be based on our knowledge of the context of comparison, for example our knowledge that what matters when it comes to keys is shape and not color. This knowledge is itself a posteriori. We know this only because of our a posteriori knowledge of both how keys work around here (they typically work via shape and not color) and our a posteriori knowledge in a particular context of comparison that the speakers are interested in comparing the keys in terms of their function rather than (say) their aesthetic appeal. Since our knowledge of the context of comparison is (and indeed must be) a posteriori, our knowledge that one pair is more similar than another will (and indeed must be) based on an a posteriori premiss and hence is itself a posteriori.

Even more decisively, though, even if knowledge of which dimensions of similarity are most salient is a priori, this will not entail that our knowledge that, for example, the two houses are more similar than the two apartment blocks is a priori. At most, it shows that our knowledge that one pair is more similar than the other is grounded *in part* on an a priori premiss. We have already seen, though, that this is not sufficient for our conclusion to be a priori. So long as my knowledge also is (and indeed must be) based in part on some a posteriori premiss or form of reasoning which is not a priori valid, the knowledge in question remains a posteriori in spite of also being based *in part* on an a priori premiss. By way of analogy, the inference 'Joe is a bachelor, all bachelors are unmarried, so Joe is unmarried' invokes a premiss which is a priori true and deploys an a priori valid form of reasoning, but the conclusion clearly is not a priori in virtue of the first premiss' status as a posteriori. So even if we can know a priori which dimensions of similarity are most salient, inferring from this that we can know a priori which pair is more similar is a non sequitur.

Dancy's conclusion would follow only if the other grounds for our belief about which pair is more similar were also a priori, and Dancy does nothing to argue for this further premiss. Indeed, Dancy explicitly allows that our knowledge of the natures of the different buildings involved is a posteriori and this must be correct; we can know the height and shape of a particular building only a posteriori. So it is hard to see how Dancy could think that the resulting knowledge is a priori unless he thinks that our knowledge of such facts does not provide grounds for our conclusions of relative similarity. However, this is itself highly implausible and moreover we have good independent reasons to resist it if our *reductio* of the contingent a priori is sound.

So we now have two reasons to favor generalism as a regulative ideal's account of practical wisdom. First, the generalist account has a much wider scope, as the case of Wanda illustrates. We should not be too quick to limit the possible scope of practical wisdom, especially given the moral importance of engagement with fiction. Secondly, the generalist account allows for a plausible division of our moral knowledge in particular cases into an a priori component (the moral principle) and an a posteriori component (the contingent features of the situation in virtue of which the moral principle applies). By contrast, the particularist must either hold that moral knowledge is entirely a posteriori or make sense of how a whole branch of human knowledge is founded upon the contingent a priori. Each of these alternatives is problematic.

We are now in a position to revisit how the plausibility of a principled account of practical wisdom entails the rejection of the various forms of particularism canvassed in Chapter 1. Consider first Anti-Transcendental Particularism about unhedged moral principles. Our argument goes as follows:

(1) The best explanation of the possibility of practical wisdom entails that practical wisdom is partly constituted by one's having a set of unhedged moral principles (which go from descriptive antecedents to moral consequents) which codifies all of morality save those parts (if any) of morality which transcend possible knowledge available to one. [an explanation that entails this is best because it gives a wider scope to the person of practical wisdom's knowledge and also sorts the a priori from the a posteriori in a more plausible way than the leading particularist account without collapsing into an implausible purely a posteriori particularist account which is vulnerable to other objections]

(2) Practical wisdom is at least possible. [unargued but shared assumption in this dialectical context; particularists and generalists reject moral skepticism]

(3) Therefore, practical wisdom is partly constituted by one's having a set of unhedged moral principles (which go from descriptive antecedents to

moral consequents) which codifies all of morality save those parts (if any) of morality which transcend possible knowledge available to one. [from 1 and 2 by inference to the best explanation]

(4) Moral thought and judgment presuppose the possibility of our having practical wisdom. [simply because any domain of thought and judgment presupposes the possibility of our having knowledge in that domain]

(5) Therefore, moral thought and judgment presuppose the possibility of our having available to us a set of unhedged moral principles (which go from descriptive antecedents to moral consequents) which codifies all of morality available to us. [from 3 and 4]

Pretty clearly, the conclusion of this argument just is the denial of Anti-Transcendental Particularism about the relevant sort of unhedged principles. The bulk of the argument of this chapter has been devoted to the defense of (1). (2) is common ground between generalists and particularists. The inference from (1) and (2) to (3) is a perfectly ordinary instance of inference to the best explanation. We have not really explicitly argued for (4) but it is extremely plausible. It is a commonplace that belief in some sense aims at the truth. This is part of what distinguishes belief from pretense and supposition for the sake of argument which themselves also are representational states. It is also likely to be part of what explains our inability to 'believe at will.' Moreover, belief aims not only at truth but at nonaccidental truth, in the sense that in believing that p one is in some sense aiming to know that p. It is not even clear whether someone can believe that p and still truly be completely indifferent as to whether this belief constitutes knowledge, but if this is possible it clearly is a sort of intellectual vice. In this sense all belief aims at knowledge, and to aim at knowledge is to presuppose that knowledge is at least possible. For someone who claims to be aiming at something and at one and the same time claims that hitting his target is literally impossible is caught up in a sort of pragmatic contradiction. Since the person of practical wisdom just is the person of practical knowledge, (4) seems to follow very naturally from this line of thought, given that moral knowledge is a form of practical knowledge.

However, there is one difficulty with the preceding case for (4). Someone might allow that moral thought and judgment presuppose the possibility of moral knowledge in the sense that believing that p (for any moral content p) presupposes the possibility of knowing whether p. However, this falls short of allowing for the possibility of practical wisdom. For someone might allow that while each moral truth can be known, no one person can know them all. For one might argue that some moral truths can be known only from a certain perspective and that some of the relevant perspectives are mutually incompatible.

At this point generalism as a regulative ideal's emphasis on morality as a collective project is relevant. For although this is not entirely uncontroversial,[18] we think it is very plausible that we can gain moral knowledge via testimony of those we know we can trust. Here we rely not only on the testimony but the arguments of Julia Driver and Karen Jones.[19] Driver offers a debunking explanation of our hesitance to endorse the idea of moral expertise; roughly, that moral judgment is often difficult and the stakes are often very high so we are reasonably nervous about relying on the testimony of the moral expert. After all, even a moral expert may sometimes fail to transmit her moral knowledge impartially, and we must therefore also have some clear indication that we can trust our interlocutor's testimony more generally even if she is a moral expert. For there can of course be a theory/practice divide here. Knowledge of moral theory sadly does not prevent immoral behaviour, including lying about morality. However, there is no reason to suppose that we could not in a given case have sufficient evidence of the honesty of a person of practical wisdom, so this point does not cut too deeply. Jones reminds us that children could never acquire moral knowledge if trust in the moral expertise of others was not sufficient for knowledge. She also discusses a nice example to bolster the idea that second-hand moral knowledge is possible, appropriate, and important for moral adults as well (a discussion of her example would take us too far afield here, unfortunately). If second-hand moral knowledge is possible, then people of practical wisdom ought to be able to identify and learn from one another. In which case, the need for different and incompatible perspectives in order to have moral knowledge in some areas in the first instance is no insuperable barrier to the possibility of a more thoroughgoing practical wisdom. We just have to put our heads together.

So we now have an argument against the most robust form of Anti-Transcendental Particularism. Pretty clearly, we also have an argument against Principle Eliminativism about unhedged moral principles and Principle Skepticism. These forms of particularism concern the *theoretical* importance of moral principles. We have not yet turned our attention to forms of moral particularism (like Principle Abstinence Particularism) which emphasize practice rather than theory. In Chapters 8 and 9 we rectify this omission. First, though, we offer one last argument for the thesis that morality can be codified in a finite and manageable set of unhedged moral principles with purely descriptive antecedents.

---

[18] See e.g. Wolf 1970.    [19] See Driver forthcoming and Jones 1999.

## 7.3. The Intuitive Case

Each of the arguments for generalism as a regulative ideal given in the preceding sections depends upon specific philosophical premisses. There are assumptions about the scope of practical wisdom, the content of our moral experience, and the division between a priori and a posteriori knowledge. Like any philosophical theses, these are liable to dispute, and if our conclusion were deeply alien to ordinary moral thought, then we might be suspicious even of arguments that seem sound. Fortunately, the conclusion of our argument actually fits quite nicely with ordinary thought and practice, or so we shall argue. This in itself provides a further independent argument for our conclusion.

Upon reflection, there is an intuitive and fairly direct case for rejecting the view that there is a vast or infinite number of morally relevant considerations (moral reasons for action, defeaters, etc.). Those who have made a serious effort to generate a comprehensive list of the kinds of features that can function as moral reasons have produced relatively short lists. W. D. Ross, for example, defended a list of seven fundamental moral considerations that he called "prima facie duties" (Ross 1930). Ross himself allowed that his list was revisable; perhaps he overlooked a few further prima facie duties. This possibility, however, falls far short of any reason for thinking that Ross's list is radically incomplete and represents only a few of the millions or even infinitely many prima facie duties. Nor is Ross alone in having made this effort, though we shall here focus on Ross's classic attempt. For example, Thomas Nagel, Bernard Gert, and Brad Hooker have also all tried to provide a similar catalogue of fundamental moral reasons.[20]

Admittedly, Ross's categories of prima facie duties are in many cases themselves characterized in thick evaluative terms. So one might object at this stage that there are indefinitely many possible reasons corresponding to each of these thick evaluative terms. However, although this logical space is available in principle, it is not very plausible. Consider first Ross's example of duties which rest on previous acts of one's own. Ross divides these into two categories, duties which rest on a promise and duties which rest on a previous wrongful act. Unless we conflate reasons for belief with reasons for action or adopt an implausible conception of how promises generate reasons, the first of these will correspond to just one sort of moral reason—that the action fulfills a promise. The second category is more interesting in that the reason to provide reparations does seem irreducibly moral—the fact that I did something immoral is the reason to

---

[20] See Nagel 1979: 128–41; Gert 1966, 1998, and 2004; and Hooker 2002.

provide reparations. However, even if this is the right interpretation of the case it need not undermine generalism as a regulative ideal. For it is compatible with this reason that there are only finitely and manageably many forms of moral wrongness (failing to provide required reparations being an additional one) and finitely and manageably many reasons corresponding to those different forms of wrongness. Furthermore, it is not entirely clear that the reason to provide reparations in any actual case is the fairly generic fact that one acted wrongly, since that fact holds when one has broken a minor promise as when one has tortured and murdered someone's wife. Perhaps the real reason in any given case to provide reparations will be the fact(s) corresponding to the moral reason in virtue of which the original immoral action was wrong. For example, my reason to provide you with reparations might be that I broke my promise to you. Of course, this fact is a reason only because my promise-breaking was morally wrong (let us suppose), but that is just another instance of holism in the theory of reasons. Either of these two interpretations of reasons for reparations is compatible with there being finitely and manageably few moral reasons for action.

A similar point can be made about Ross's category of the prima facie duty of gratitude. The reasons here may be either the generic fact that the person did something good for you or a more specific fact to the effect that the person provided a specific kind of good for you (hedonistic or nonhedonistic, say). The first interpretation is analogous to the first reading of reasons of reparations while the second reading is analogous to the second reading of reasons of reparation. So long as there are only finitely many fundamentally different ways of doing good for someone, either of these readings is compatible with there being finitely and manageably many moral reasons. What these examples bring out is that Ross's prima facie duties are deeply interrelated, so that whether reparations are owed will depend, for example, on whether an injustice has been done. This interdependence does nothing to suggest that the total set of types of moral reasons for action is not itself both finite and manageable. Although we shall not engage in the level of Ross exegesis necessary to vindicate this reading, we take it at least to be a sufficiently natural and plausible reading of his text for our purposes. For our point (borne out by experience with undergraduates who read Ross for the first time) is that people who read Ross both think that what he is roughly trying to do is provide a finite and manageable list of kinds of moral reasons and that this project is in no way obviously hopeless. This, in turn, suggests that the thesis that there are only finitely and manageably many kinds of reasons is not at all far from common sense.

It may be suggested that Ross generated such a short list only because he embarked on his project assuming that that is what he would find. Perhaps this left his imagination cramped, and he then overlooked entirely some prima facie duties or mistakenly grouped several distinct types of prima facie duty under a common heading. We doubt this is the case, however. The better explanation of the shortness of Ross's list is simply that there are, in fact, relatively few types of consideration that actually can function as a reason. It is striking that students introduced to Ross's list seldom respond that his whole project is misguided, like the project of listing all the odd numbers or the list of all possible reasons for belief (see Chapter 6). Moreover, when we try to draw up a list of potential reasons ourselves, it is difficult to produce a list much longer than Ross's. Ross might have been badly wrong; perhaps there are another few dozen or even (though this seems very unlikely) several hundred further prima facie duties. Nonetheless, the idea that there might be infinitely many or even an overwhelmingly vast number of prima facie duties looks implausible.

Of course, Ross himself seems for the most part to have been an atomist.[21] He supposed that the fact that an action would be dishonest is always a reason against performing it, and so on for all of the prima facie duties. However, once the idea of a default principle is taken seriously, it is easy enough to revise Ross's position so that it is perfectly compatible with holism. Where Ross would have a principle intended to convey that dishonesty is always a reason against an action, we could instead formulate a principle which held that dishonesty was a reason against an action unless some further feature of the situation explained why it was not. The same move could be made for each of Ross's so-called prima facie duties. Whether a Rossian account must be tailored to holism is irrelevant to whether a Rossian approach rightly treats the potential number of moral reasons as limited. As we have already argued in Chapter 6, the question of whether reasons behave holistically or atomistically is orthogonal to the question how many possible kinds of reasons there are.

This intuitive case about the number of reasons can be readily extended to their defeating conditions. Again, consider some examples. The fact that something would be pleasant may be a reason unless the pleasure would be sadistic, so sadism is a defeater of pleasure as a reason, roughly speaking. Perhaps there are a few other defeaters of pleasure, but the idea that there might be dozens of such defeaters already looks very implausible, much less the idea

---

[21] Even this piece of conventional wisdom about Ross is not entirely obvious. In his discussion of pleasure in *The Foundations of Ethics* he argues that while pleasure usually provides a prima facie duty, when the pleasure is a manifestation of a bad moral nature it does not generate even a prima facie moral duty. He also argues that one's own pleasures, even when innocent, do not provide prima facie moral duties for oneself. See Ross 1939: 271–3. These passages raise interesting exegetical issues which for present purposes we must put to one side. Many thanks to Pekka Väyrynen for reminding us of the significance of these passages.

that there are indefinitely many such defeaters. We suspect that any effort to demonstrate otherwise by actually listing defeating conditions for pleasure would quickly run out of steam. The fact that an action would cause someone pain is normally a reason not to perform the action, but not if the person deserves it or if the person's pain is due to some moral vice.[22] Again, there may be further defeaters of pain's status as a reason against actions but the idea that there are indefinitely many such possible defeaters simply looks hopelessly implausible. We think that intuitively this sort of point holds across the board for defeaters, including metadefeaters. The attempt to generate more and more plausible examples of metadefeaters after even just a few iterations can easily seem strained and desperate.

Moreover, even when these continued iterations are plausible, they will often simply be further tokens of some type of metadefeater that has already been catalogued at a lower level of analysis. For example, the fact that I am threatening your life if you don't make a promise typically means that I am coercing you, and hence is typically a defeater. However, this defeater can itself be defeated. For example, if I am threatening you in this way to prevent you from killing someone else, then perhaps my threat does not count as coercion after all. However, this is a token of a type of metadefeater which can arise as a first-order defeater as well. In particular, the fact that an action is an instance of threatening someone's life is typically a strong reason not to perform it (as well as a defeater for any promise one might thereby extract), but the fact that threatening them in this way is a necessary means to preventing them from killing someone else can perhaps defeat the status of this fact as a reason. On reflection, it seems likely that metadefeaters will very often simply be reappearances of the same kinds of facts that constitute first-order defeaters and reasons. This should provide us with some confidence that a catalogue of all the different kinds of defeaters and metadefeaters need not be forever beyond our ken.

It is not quite so obvious that we will also be able to survey all of the ways in which these metadefeaters can function. However, even here there are grounds for optimism. For there do seem to be recognizable patterns which emerge when reflecting on the ways in which these defeaters and metadefeaters function. For example, it is easy enough to see why on a rule-utilitarian theory we should make an exception to the duty to keep promises for cases of coercion. However, we can just as equally well see, in rule-utilitarian terms, why that exception should be suspended if the coercion was necessary to save a life. Kantians also have plausible stories to tell about such defeaters and metadefeaters in terms of what rules would be selected by the members of a kingdom of ends.

---

[22] Dancy gives the example of Satan being pained by every right action (Dancy 1993: 61).

Moral philosophers should always be open to the possibility of some further reason or defeater they have overlooked, but this does not mean they should take seriously the idea that there are indefinitely or even unmanageably many reasons and defeaters. Once again, we suspect that a failure to distinguish reasons for belief from reasons for action could give false plausibility to the particularist hypothesis that there are indefinitely many moral reasons for action.

## 7.4. Summary and Preview

We have now concluded our defense of principles conceived as unhedged standards. We have argued in the present chapter that morality can be codified with a finite and manageable set of unhedged moral standards, the antecedents of which are purely descriptive. We have given three main arguments for this conclusion—the argument from the scope of practical wisdom, the argument from epistemology, and the intuitive argument.

However, our larger defense of generalism as a regulative ideal remains incomplete. Traditionally, moral theorists have thought not only that there are moral standards, but that it is important to articulate them. They have also thought that moral principles have an important role to play in guiding the deliberations and choices of virtuous agents. For all we have said so far, these assumptions remain to be vindicated. In Chapter 8 we turn to the important but often neglected question of the value of articulating moral principles. Then, in Chapter 9, we defend the claim that moral principles have a valuable role to play in guiding action.

# 8

# Generalism as a Regulative Ideal

> To have examined one's own first principles is the mark of a civilized man.
>
> (Oliver Wendell Holmes, Jr.)

If the arguments of Chapters 6 and 7 are sound, then there are moral principles. At a bare minimum, moral knowledge presupposes default principles (Chapter 6). However, our account of the role of principles in morality goes well beyond default principles. Morality also presupposes the availability of unhedged principles, principles whose defeating and enabling conditions have been fully and finitely articulated in descriptive terms (Chapter 7). The prospect of such principles is no mere hope since they figure in the best explanation of our capacity for practical wisdom and fit well with a natural resolution of moral knowledge into a priori and a posteriori components. The possibility of such principles also has intuitive plausibility. Indeed, we have argued that the entire moral landscape can be codified in finite and manageable terms by such principles. Having vindicated such a robust role for moral principles, is it time then for generalists to declare victory? Not on all fronts.

Even if particularists conceded the arguments of Chapters 6 and 7, meaningful forms of particularism remain. Without questioning the existence of moral principles, particularists might nevertheless challenge their assumed centrality to moral practice. Of course, moral principles seem in fact to play a prominent role in moral practice, both as primary objects of moral theorizing and as oft-used tools for moral decision-making. The issue is not how best to characterize actual moral practice, however, but how best to engage in moral practice. As a prescriptive thesis about the form moral practice should take, particularism is consistent with the existence of sound moral principles so long as principles are conceived as *standards* (see Chapter 1). If our defense of generalism is to be comprehensive, we must turn to the value of principles in moral practice; we must defend principles conceived as *guides* as well. In this chapter and the next, we defend the view that principles should play an important role in moral practice.

Intuitively, moral practice gives two prominent roles to moral principles. First, the articulation of moral principles is taken to be at least one important aspect of moral thought and discourse. Whether we consider the sophisticated methods of professional moral philosophers or the thoughtful discussions of citizens, the identification of a sound moral principle is often taken to be a primary goal.[1] Viewed in this light, the identification of a moral principle is a product of successful moral thinking. It is this role for principles that shall primarily concern us in the present chapter. A second role for principles, to which we turn in Chapter 9, is that of guiding virtuous agents. Obviously these two roles are intertwined. If moral principles can provide guidance to virtuous agents, then one reason to devote moral thought to articulating them will be to acquire valuable tools for guiding action. Consequently, the argument of the present chapter will be strengthened and supplemented by the further argument of Chapter 9. In the present chapter, however, we wish to explore reasons for articulating principles which do not depend on their potential role in guiding the virtuous agent.

## 8.1. Where Lies the Difference?

David McNaughton claims that moral principles are "at best useless and at worst a hindrance" (McNaughton 1988: 191). Jonathan Dancy echoes the sentiment when he claims that "generalism is the cause of many bad moral decisions, made in the ill-judged and unnecessary attempt to fit what we are to say here to what we have said on another occasion" (Dancy 1993: 64). Margaret Little suggests that our moral practice overemphasizes the effort to subsume particular cases under general principles. As a result, our theories

start valorizing deployment of inference as the height of moral maturity rather than the crutch of the blind. This tradition, moreover, is dangerously self-reinforcing, for in overemphasizing the skills involved in subsuming under generality, skills of discernment and interpretation atrophy. (Little, 2000: 304)

The supposed problem here is not simply (or even largely) that whatever moral principles we may articulate will be false. It is that placing moral principles at or near the center of moral practice is supposed to result in a pernicious form of moral thinking. It might then seem easy to say what divides particularists and generalists on the question of articulating moral principles. Generalists stand in favor of it, particularists opposed.

---

[1] See e.g. Scheffler 1992: 47, 51 and Hooker 2000a: 19–23.

While not false, this way of framing the debate conceals more than it reveals. This is because it does not yet tell us where particularists and generalists stand when it comes to actual moral practice. Do particularists think that we have a basically sound moral practice, but one that has been mischaracterized by generalists and is liable to corruption as a result? Or do they believe that our existing moral practice is deeply flawed and in need of thoroughgoing particularist reform? Rather than settling this question on behalf of particularists, we can clarify the dialectic by noting that we have been largely content to accept the particularists' characterization of certain aspects of moral practice. In describing moral practice in previous chapters, we have freely appropriated many of the concepts and distinctions deployed by particularists. Indeed, part of the motivation for our project is to illustrate how some of the insights developed by particularists can be advantageously appropriated by generalists. We have treated reasons as considerations that favor particular responses in particular circumstances and distinguished between reasons, defeaters, enablers, intensifiers, and diminishers. We have been careful always to make room for holism about reasons even though our arguments do not depend on its truth, and generalism as a regulative ideal is officially neutral about holism in the theory of reasons. In actual moral practice, we strive to articulate reasons and their defeating/enabling conditions as well as the relative force of different reasons in different contexts. Call this a practice of *discriminating* our reasons. This much should be common ground between particularists and generalists.

If our previous arguments have been successful, though, then our actual practice of discriminating our reasons works towards the articulation of moral principles. To identify a consideration as a moral reason is implicitly to identify a corresponding default principle. To spell out the specific defeating and enabling conditions relevant to that reason and to assess its comparative weight relative to other potential reasons in various circumstances is to articulate unhedged principles. Moreover, practical wisdom consists in large part in the internalization of such unhedged principles. Of course, we do not suppose that our moral practice has yet hit upon a fully adequate system of unhedged moral principles. Generalism as a regulative ideal embraces the idea that moral theorizing remains a work in progress, just as scientific theorizing remains a work in progress. We claim only that our practice of discriminating our reasons is rightly viewed as a practice of articulating the very principles we have independently argued must be available to us. So our argument is a defense of existing practice.

We believe that our actual moral practice, at least those features of it that serve the articulation of principles, is well supported by good reasons. Particularists who think the articulation of moral principles ought not to be central to moral practice may then take issue with generalism in one of two ways. First, particularists may endorse the practice of discriminating our reasons, but deny that this practice serves to articulate moral principles. Secondly, particularists may reject as unnecessary or pernicious the practice of discriminating our reasons.

We shall have little to say in the present chapter about the first sort of disagreement. Though we expect this is where most actual particularists will disagree, settling this disagreement turns entirely upon the arguments of previous chapters. Of course, even particularists who take issue with our position in this first way are advancing a kind of reformist agenda, but this agenda is largely directed at philosophy, and only indirectly at ordinary moral practice. It is philosophers, according to these particularists, who introduce the idea that moral thought requires principles. According to particularists, this idea is both false and potentially pernicious. To the extent that a belief in generalism has infected ordinary moral practice for the worse, particularists may hope that a (philosophical) refutation of generalism will have a salutary effect. To the extent that this is an agenda for the reform of moral practice, though, it is reform as *restoration*, restoration of moral practice to the form it would naturally take if uncorrupted by a misplaced belief in generalism. Since we have argued that a commitment to moral principles follows from deep features of our moral practice, we reject the possibility of such a restoration project.

This leaves open a different and more radical reform project, though, one that rejects as unnecessary or pernicious our very practice of discriminating reasons. Insofar as we are asked to exchange our current moral practice for something new, this is reform as *revolution*. To be fair, we do not think any actual particularist has advocated such a position; we discuss it only because it is a fallback position to which particularists could retreat if our arguments against the restorative version of particularism are compelling. Revolutionary particularism is difficult to assess in its own right without knowing just what would replace our actual moral practice. It is difficult, however, to take pleasure in the prospect of a world in which people are less concerned to articulate their reasons than they now are. This is because understanding each others' reasons is something we typically care about very deeply. A failure to care about what other people take to be good reasons for acting in ways we find inappropriate seems like a very dangerous form of dogmatic conservatism. Few experiences are so distinctively infuriating as confronting someone who refuses outright to explain the basis for their decisions. "That's just the way it is," someone says to us, and we quietly (or not so quietly) pull out our hair.

The concern that people have to reach a shared understanding of their reasons has been given powerful expression by those who think that the basis of important moral distinctions is a concern to justify our choices and actions to each other (Scanlon 1998). However, one need not accept this view of the basis of (some) moral distinctions to agree that we are deeply concerned with each others' reasons and that this concern is reflected in our expectation of each other that we be willing to articulate and defend our reasons. Still we can ask whether we are right to care. In this chapter we will present the evidence for retaining the central features of moral practice that serve the articulation of moral principles.

It is important to see that the generalist can afford to be ecumenical. It is not our intention to claim that we should always and tirelessly attempt to discriminate our reasons and hence to articulate moral principles. There will be times when this would be unwise and the generalist can and should agree that under those circumstances we should not try to articulate principles. This concession, however, does nothing to undermine the idea that there is good reason for all of us to accept a standing commitment to articulate our reasons. It is the revolutionary particularist who must contend that the search for principles is always a misuse of our intellectual resources. Nor do we intend to defend every aspect of current moral practice. Like virtually everyone who reflects on morality, we can see room for improvement. However, it will come as no surprise that we think many of the needed improvements will help us better articulate moral principles.

## 8.2. Moral Progress

There is an obvious and compelling defense of discriminating reasons. Our practice of identifying our reasons, spelling out their relative weights across contexts, and articulating their defeating or enabling conditions contributes to moral progress. Discriminating helps us to shed untenable commitments, and replace them with ones that are closer to the mark.[2] Even if our moral commitments remain imperfect (as they surely do), they have undergone progressive improvement. This is not a trivial achievement. The untenability of a moral commitment is something that often must be uncovered, especially when that commitment is ensconced in the prevailing culture. Nevertheless, human beings have improved their moral commitments over time. Just as our

---

[2] We do not assume that improving our moral commitments is the only form of moral progress. Even when it comes to sound moral commitments we may seek to improve the degree to which we are motivated to act on those commitments, and even when we are well motivated we may seek to make our action more effectively serve our commitments.

scientific theories are closer to the mark now than they were a century or two ago, our moral commitments are better too. The improvement of moral commitments is not the only dimension along which we can measure moral progress. We can also ask whether the moral conditions of the world have improved, whether, in Dale Jamieson's apt phrase, there has been progress "on the ground."[3] In view of the widespread atrocities characteristic of recent human history, this is, sadly, very doubtful.[4] Our argument in the present chapter does not depend upon the assumption that there has been this sort of progress. We assume here that improving our moral commitments is itself a worthy goal and that along that front substantial progress has been made.

When we turn to the improvement of our moral commitments, any specific historical example is liable to dispute. Furthermore, it is easy to lament the fact that moral progress has not come more quickly or been more thoroughgoing. Still, progress there has been, and this is at least partially attributable to our attempts to discriminate reasons. In our view, this is a powerful reason to engage in moral theorizing. It is worth considering a few examples.

In the United States, the moral commitments that supported racial segregation and inequality have been substantially dismantled. Even if the social institutions created under segregation remain in need of reform, the moral justifications once offered for racist institutions have been largely discredited. To the extent that they survive, their survival depends largely upon their remaining hidden from public view. There is no need to dispute the obvious fact that more work remains to be done in order to recognize that great progress has been made. Such progress is at least partially attributable to the moral scrutiny that was brought to bear upon purported reasons for maintaining racist institutions. Of course, change did not arrive by the drawing of better moral distinctions alone. It was also necessary to make white people vividly aware of the real human costs of racist institutions, and to spell out how social institutions might better be structured. As people came to have a better appreciation of the cruelty and deprivation of opportunity inherent in racist institutions, they also came to see that the reasons used to defend such institutions were untenable.

The indefensibility of racist institutions could not be discovered overnight. Opponents of reform were resourceful in their attempts to justify racist institutions. Even when their arguments were unsound, they were often persuasive. Ultimately, however, the arguments used to defend racist institutions were discredited. This happened, however, only because those who defended racist

---

[3]  See Jamieson 2002b.

[4]  For a more thorough discussion of recent moral history, see Glover 2000.

institutions felt obligated to identify and defend the reasons they saw in favor of them. Put another way, even those who took up radically different sides in the debates over segregation shared a commitment to identify and defend their reasons.

Consider a contemporary example. Popular debates over the morality of homosexual conduct often turn on whether homosexuality is natural. Both sides of the debate often seem to allow that homosexual sex is morally acceptable if and only if it is natural. This seems to reflect an implicit agreement that the unnaturalness of some sexual practice would be a decisive reason against it. Social conservatives contend that homosexual sex must be unnatural because it cannot lead to procreation while liberals counter that homosexuality can be found in other species and has a genetic basis.

The liberal has another more promising strategy, though, namely questioning the moral relevance of naturalness itself. In order to meet this challenge the social conservative should try to articulate a moral principle which adequately expresses what they take the moral relevance of naturalness to be. It is not too hard to see how the attempt to articulate such a principle might lead to the realization that this commitment is untenable. In most circumstances unnaturalness is morally irrelevant and obviously so, and the attempt to find plausible ways of distinguishing unnaturalness in the context of homosexuality from other forms of unnaturalness in a way that would vindicate the social conservative is likely to emerge as a hopeless cause. It then becomes plausible to suggest that it is really a prior and independent conviction that homosexuality is wrong that drives the effort to find defeaters in the endless array of other cases in which unnaturalness is morally innocent. This might lead the social conservative to realize that the appeal to unnaturalness is really an attempt to rationalize a prejudice which is in fact based on some combination of primitive reactions of disgust, nonrational social or religious indoctrination, and the like, and not a plausible moral norm after all. That articulating our principles and testing them in other cases can lead to moral progress in this way is an important reason to articulate the principles underlying our judgments.

Even in cases where the direction of moral progress remains in doubt, we can be confident that any progress we do make will be partially attributable to our practice of discriminating our reasons. Over the last few decades there has been renewed energy in the debate over the character of our obligations (if any) to nonhuman animals and their similarity or dissimilarity to our obligations to other human beings.[5] This debate has occupied the attention not only

---

[5] See Jamieson (2002a) for an interesting discussion of the moral status of nonhuman animals and moral progress.

of professional philosophers and determined activists. It has also engaged the attention of large segments the general population. Those who think that our practices with regard to nonhuman animals are morally indefensible have pressed hard on the distinctions used to defend the status quo. It may not yet be clear what the outcome of this exchange of views will be. However, whatever progress we make will be partially attributable to our practice of discriminating reasons.

It is important to note that our argument here does not depend upon any specific view of the general kinds of adjustments in moral attitude that constitute progress. Those who hold specific normative theories are often led to specific metanarratives about the character of moral progress. For example, according to one influential view, moral progress occurs as we 'expand the circle' of moral concern. This view of moral progress, however, is closely wedded to a utilitarian account of morality more generally. Those who do not share this view of morality will want to find some other way to characterize the kinds of shifts in attitude that constitute progress. For example, Kantians may think that progress consists in our adopting attitudes that better reflect the dignity of persons. Sentimentalists, by contrast, may think that moral progress consists in restricting moral virtue to those character traits that are useful or agreeable to ourselves or others. In each case, a particular view of morality gives rise to a view of what constitutes moral progress. Just as we have remained neutral about the specific content of moral norms, we can also remain neutral between such metanarratives about the character of moral progress. If a particular normative theory such as utilitarianism or Kantianism is vindicated, then its associated metanarrative may be vindicated as well. This does nothing to falsify our claims here, however, since it will be precisely our attempts to articulate our reasons that led to the vindication of a particular normative theory.

Our aim in the foregoing discussion has not been to suggest that particularists are enemies of moral progress. To the contrary, we suspect that most particularists share our view that the attempt to identify our reasons together with their relevant defeating and enabling conditions is a salutary practice. Here, for example, is Jonathan Dancy:

The coherence of an overall outlook can be questioned in the following way without generalist motivation. 'Here you think that the fact that she was unhappy functions as a reason in one way, and there you took it to function in quite another. To me they seem to be functioning in much the same way both times, so that I can't really see how you can distinguish in the way you do. What is the relevant difference between the two cases?' This challenge can always be made within the constraints of particularism, and there must be an answer to it if one's position across the two cases is to emerge as coherent. (Its consistency was not at issue.) (Dancy 1993: 63–4)

As should be clear, our disagreement with Dancy arises over whether what we call discriminating can comfortably fit within the constraints of particularism, not over whether we have good reason to articulate our reasons carefully.

## 8.3. Generalism as a Regulative Ideal and Moral Philosophy

The arguments developed in Chapters 6 and 7 were couched in terms of the articulation of moral principles underlying our particular judgments. In the present chapter we have so far argued that articulating the reasons behind our particular judgments is a valuable tool for making moral progress. Traditionally, though, moral theorizing has also aimed to find deeper underlying principles which can unify the seemingly disparate principles more immediately recognized by common sense. Generalism as a regulative ideal agrees that we should look for such deeper unifying principles, and for much the same reason. For more systematic moral philosophy can also help ensure our actions really are justifiable and promote moral progress.

Of course, to say that we have reason to engage in systematic moral theorizing had better not be to say that to be a virtuous person one must be a full-time moral philosopher. We advocate a division of labor, with some people devoting far more of their time to systematic moral philosophy than others. Neither, though, should we overstate this point; the distance between ordinary moral practice and systematic moral theorizing is easily exaggerated. Granted, ordinary people do not frequently discuss the doctrine of double effect or the distinction between killing and letting die, but sometimes they do (albeit not always in these terms). These issues arise from time to time in ordinary discussions of abortion and the morality of warfare, for example. Whether a given individual will have any reason to consider these kinds of questions will depend in large part on what sorts of situations she is likely to face. Someone considering a career in medical research, for example, might have more reason to consider some of the distinctions relevant to the debate over stem cell research than someone for whom those issues are more distant (though not entirely removed; in a democracy such issues may still be relevant when deliberating about how to vote). In any event, these kinds of questions do arise in the ordinary course of human reasoning. For example, the question of whether 'the end can justify the means' shows how ordinary people are sensitive to some of the issues dividing Kantians from consequentialists. Moral philosophy is to this extent continuous with ordinary practice.

Still, moral theorizing is best understood and practiced as a collective enterprise, and like most collective enterprises it benefits from a division of labor. Consequently, even if moral philosophy is continuous with ordinary moral practice, it should not be surprising if some individuals rightly devote more resources to systematic moral theorizing than others. When morally decent people find themselves living together in a community, they have a shared interest in helping each other live well. Insofar as each of us makes it our end to act morally well, we have reason to cooperate if doing so would enhance our chances of acting well. We think it is clear that such cooperation can be fruitful, not least of all because it allows for the benefits of a division of labor. Moral philosophers can then devote considerable time and intellectual resources to becoming specialists in moral theorizing. The hope would be that whatever progress moral philosophers might make with those questions would be available to anyone who takes an interest in such questions and that this might help others act well. Often the moral philosopher may help only by uncovering important distinctions which had previously been neglected or by providing a useful structure for the debate. In addition to people seeking out what moral philosophers have had to say which might be of relevance to a particular moral issue, moral philosophy can and often does 'trickle down' into the culture at large.

Such trickle-down can happen in numerous ways and unfortunately often involves a good deal of distortion. However, the distortion is not always so great as to remove the benefits of such a trickle-down. Peter Singer's work on our duties to nonhuman animals clearly has had an impact on millions of people, for example, and the basic logic of his argument may well not have been too badly distorted in the process. Since the nineteenth century utilitarianism has been absorbed into the culture to a great extent. We have heard it remarked that undergraduates now come to university 'front-loaded with utilitarianism,' and this has a ring of truth about it. Even those who do not themselves accept utilitarianism are often implicitly aware of the distinctions and arguments used in its development. We do not here mean to endorse Singer's account or utilitarianism. Instead, we just want to call attention to the fact that the division of labor characteristic of our moral practice facilitates the introduction of novel and important moral ideas to the culture at large. Just as it facilitates the introduction of such ideas, it can also facilitate criticism of them.

How might moral philosophy help bring about moral progress? Moral philosophers can help by doing the same sorts of things as non-philosophers, but to a greater extent, with more persistence and depth of inquiry, and with the advantages of the familiar tools of philosophical inquiry. The continuity of moral philosophy with ordinary practice is again relevant. Moral philosophers should articulate moral principles just like non-philosophers. However, philosophers have special reasons to focus on more esoteric kinds of situations which others might reasonably ignore. Nonetheless, we as a society should often consider these situations before we confront them under real-time pressure. New moral problems that might arise in virtue of new scientific or social developments provide a nice illustration. For example, human cloning may soon be a reality. Having philosophers think carefully about the issues raised by such new technologies before they are developed could help us deal with them if and when they become a reality.

Moral philosophers should not just consider esoteric cases at the fringes of modern science, though. Moral philosophers also have a role in helping us deal with hard cases where there is moral perplexity and widespread moral disagreement. Here many familiar topics come to mind—abortion, our duties to nonhuman animals, environmental ethics, the moral constraints appropriate during wartime, euthanasia, and our duties to help those in great need in faraway lands. Moral philosophers might use familiar techniques of thought experiments and arguments by analogy to help us get some leverage on these cases. Part of the idea here is to find cases about which we have more confidence but which seem identical in all morally relevant respects to the hard case (hence our disagreement in Chapter 7 with Dancy about our capacity to learn from fictional cases). A vivid imagination and ability to discern less obvious analogies are important virtues. Just as important, however, is the ability to see less obvious disanalogies. As we strive to subsume cases under ever better generalities, we need to be just as prepared to find the differences between cases as to find what they share, and only a foolish form of generalism would insist otherwise.

Moral philosophers should also tease out the implications of commonly accepted moral principles, always vigilant for apparent inconsistencies between those principles and people's actual judgments. The history of moral thought and a general sense of our own fallibility provide reason to think such inconsistencies are there to be found. Precisely because inconsistencies are frequently the result of bias and self-interest, they are often deeply masked.[6] Uncovering these inconsistencies often requires a great deal of careful thought, open-mindedness, and imaginative comparisons in light of background principles. It therefore seems unrealistic and inefficient to have people in general try to

---

[6] We return to these issues in Ch. 9.

discern inconsistencies in common moral thinking. Once again, a division of labor is sensible.

The subtlety of discovering inconsistencies does mean that more than logic and a stock of moral principles will be necessary to distinguish real inconsistency from a nuanced appreciation of subtle differences between cases. Moral philosophers, like everyone else, should do their best to be sensitive and open-minded as to the possible relevance of features they had not previously considered or given sufficient weight. Nonetheless, there will be cases in which it is plausible to suppose that no further relevant distinctions are to be found but where many people nonetheless disagree. By calling our attention to such inconsistencies, moral philosophers can sometimes provide the impetus for finding plausible ways of resolving them.

Moral philosophers should also carefully consider the merits of various kinds of critiques of ordinary moral ideas and distinctions. Moral anthropology and moral psychology can be relevant here. For example, a careful examination of the social forces that led us to give weight to the distinction between killing and letting someone die may serve to debunk the moral significance of that distinction. Perhaps the distinction seems to carry the weight it does only because the powerful and the weak both share an interest in rules against killing but only the weak have an interest in rules against letting die. If this is the case we might have reason to doubt the moral significance of our own intuitions in these matters.[7] This example is of course a localized one but much more wholesale critiques of morality should also not be dismissed out of hand.

The rigorous application of principles to cases in order to tease out possible inconsistencies in common moral thinking might well lead philosophers to catalogue different kinds of defeaters. When we suspect inconsistency, we must look to be sure that there is no defeater of an apparently crucial reason which is present in one case but not in the other case. It might be helpful in this regard, as well as interesting and important in its own right, to have a checklist of features which commonly function as defeaters of various candidate reasons. Once again, it would be unwise ever to assume with certainty that any checklist is complete. Nor should we assume in advance that what has been a defeater in some cases will necessarily be a defeater in new cases. We should always be open-minded about defeaters we have not yet even considered, and approach moral philosophy in full recognition of our own fallibility.

We should also be sensitive to possible 'metadefeaters'—features which cancel the status of another feature as a defeater. For example, the fact that it would be sadistic might be a defeater of the fact that it would be pleasant. However, the

---

[7] Cf. Harman 1977.

fact that the pain in which the agent would take pleasure is deserved might make it permissible to take pleasure in the victim's pain, thereby canceling the sadism's status as a defeater. This, of course, is controversial and a purely illustrative example. Moral philosophers presumably should catalogue what metadefeaters if any there are while again bearing in mind their own fallibility. A provisional checklist of reasons, defeaters, and metadefeaters could be instructive and useful since looking over the checklist could alert us to interesting patterns amongst the items on the list, which might in turn lead us to a deeper account of the relevant reasons or defeaters. Such lists could help us to avoid overlooking important reasons and defeaters in other cases. This could be helpful to ordinary people who try to learn by critically engaging with philosophy and could also be helpful to philosophers themselves in their further inquiries. The fact that such lists are nothing like a logical guarantee against overlooking still further reasons or defeaters does nothing to suggest that such lists might not still be helpful. In particular, such lists could be particularly helpful for a given person if there are certain features she is especially prone to overlook. They might also help call attention to possible defeaters which some people had not yet really even considered.

## 8.4. Pluralism and Explanatory Depth

In addition to cataloguing the apparently diverse reasons, defeaters, and meta-defeaters of morality, moral philosophers should look for deeper principles which could plausibly serve to unify those apparently varied features. That is to say, moral philosophers should look for deeper moral principles which could plausibly serve to unify the seemingly heterogeneous principles culled from common sense. Finding deeper unities in a seemingly diverse set of reasons and defeaters can help us notice other reasons and defeaters to which we might otherwise have been blind. After all, once we see a pattern emerge amongst defeaters A, B, and C, this may lead us to notice defeaters D and E which are also subsumed by this pattern but which we could have otherwise easily missed.

Such deeper principles can be more or less wide in their scope. They might unify and explain all of the principles culled from common sense or only some narrow subclass thereof. Utilitarianism is a clear example of a moral principle intended to have very wide scope and explanatory power, but we think it is important to emphasize the possibility of deeper principles of more localized significance. For example, suppose we began with two principles, one of which is couched in terms of lying and the other of which is couched in terms of implying (but not asserting) something the speaker knows to be false. These two principles might plausibly be understood as being theorems derived from some more basic principle couched in terms of deception. A principle couched in terms of deception might be in an obvious sense a deeper principle from which the original two principles could be derived. These sorts of localized deeper principles will fall well short of the grandiose ambitions of utilitarianism, but provide illumination of important tracts of moral territory all the same.

In fact we believe that generalism as a regulative ideal suggests an appropriate attitude towards both the possibility of pluralistic normative theories and the demand that normative theories achieve a measure of explanatory depth. In Chapters 6 and 7 we have argued that there are only a limited number of morally relevant kinds of considerations and that these interact in predictable ways. We have not, however, tried to argue against pluralism, the view that there is a plurality of morally relevant considerations none of which is reducible to some master reason or value. Normative theories that countenance a plurality of ultimately relevant moral considerations have long been criticized for lacking explanatory depth.[8] Since it is widely (and in our view rightly) claimed that normative moral theories should have explanatory depth, pluralistic theories are often thought to fall short of a basic desiderata for normative theories. As Sidgwick famously put the point:

It is difficult to accept as scientific first principles the moral generalities that we obtain by reflection on the ordinary thought of mankind, even though we share this thought. Even granting that these rules can be so defined as perfectly to fit together and cover the whole field of human conduct, without coming into conflict and without leaving any practical question unanswered, - still the resulting code seems an accidental aggregate of precepts which stands in need of some rational synthesis. In short, without being disposed to deny that conduct commonly judged to be right is so, we may yet require some deeper explanation *why* it is so.[9]

The form of generalism we have been defending does not presuppose a plurality of ultimate moral considerations, but it is compatible with such a plurality.

Some generalists might take this to be an insufficient defense of tradition. Moreover, our account starts from ordinary claims to moral knowledge and generates default principles from these. We have argued that we have good reason to articulate the reasons that would vindicate our particular moral judgments and so to articulate principles. In this respect, our methodology recalls the approach of intuitionists who believe moral theorizing should start from what is often called 'common-sense morality.' Consequently, it may seem

---

[8] For discussion, see McNaughton 1996.    [9] Sidgwick 1967: 102 [1907].

that by starting with default principles we will *inevitably* be left with a pluralistic theory, even if we trim the hedges and generate nondefault principles. The worry then is that our methodology is likely to lead to little more than an unconnected heap of principles.

We do not wish here to enter into the long-standing debate about the content of standards for good explanation. Instead we argue that, whatever view one has about explanation, there is no reason to think that the view we are defending should lead to normative theories that lack explanatory depth. Of course, if simple pluralistic theories are explanatorily adequate as they stand, then there is little reason to be suspicious of our approach. In the present context, however, we assume for the sake of argument that this is not the case.

Defenders of pluralistic theories have long felt it important to distinguish primary from secondary reasons. As we have urged, however, there are good philosophical reasons for thinking that in the cases that supposedly illustrate the distinction, at most one of the considerations can really be a reason for action; that is, can really stand in the favoring relationship to the action. In the case of promising we have argued that the real reason for action is the primary reason—the fact that an action would fulfill a promise is what favors the action. The distinction is a poor one because the so-called secondary reason is not really a reason at all.[10]

Why does generalism as a regulative ideal provide all of the explanatory depth it is reasonable to demand? To answer this question, let us begin by supposing that we have mischaracterized the distinction between primary and secondary reasons. Suppose that there is such a distinction but that the real reason—what actually favors the action—is not the primary reason but the secondary one. If I have promised to buy a red sweater, my reason to buy a particular red sweater is *that the sweater is red* not *that buying the sweater would fulfill a promise*. Now imagine a pluralistic theory that simply listed genuine reasons together with their defeating conditions. Perhaps we would have default principles such as: For all agents A, if x is a red sweater then A has a reason to buy x, unless A has not promised to buy a red sweater, in virtue of the fact that x is a red sweater. We could even imagine an infinitely long list of such principles, one corresponding to each possible content of a promise. The key point is that such a list would be explanatorily deficient. For everything it tells us, it fails to point out the obvious, namely that promising to do something typically generates a reason.

Now return to pluralism as we maintain it should be formulated. The only real reasons are the so-called primary reasons, but there is an irreducibly

---

[10] This characterization follows Urmson 1975.

heterogeneous set of such reasons. Why might such a pluralist theory be explanatorily inadequate? It would be if there were some further explanation (omitted by the theory) for why these considerations and not others are reasons. If there simply is no explanation for why some considerations and not others are reasons, then it is difficult to see any objection to a normative theory that simply spells out the reasons and how they function. All the same, we have every reason to try to articulate the factors that explain why some considerations and not others are (primary) reasons. Doing so would give us a greater understanding of our reasons and would also serve as a helpful guide to whether we have in fact identified all the reasons that there are. At their best, pluralistic theories do aspire to such explanatory depth.[11] For example, Ross at points suggests that each prima facie duty is a duty because of some morally salient relationship between persons.

A second worry about explanatory depth arises not from pluralism but from the fact that our account starts from ordinary claims to moral knowledge. It may be urged that such claims are themselves far from perfect and that the method of generating default principles provides no resources for improving such knowledge. Suppose, for example, that as I am searching for a parking place I find a lone spot near the store entrance at the same time as another elderly driver arrives at the same spot. Suppose that I judge that I have a reason to defer to the other driver because he is an old man. If this amounts to a case of moral knowledge, then we might formulate a default principle about deferring to the elderly. Here though, it seems we really are just replicating a very superficial aspect of moral experience in our default principles. It is hard to know what to say about such ordinary cases of moral judgment. Only a very restrictive account would deny that such judgments represent knowledge. The person is right that there is reason to defer, and the reason identified (age) is typically and nonaccidentally related to the actual reason giving consideration. Still, we might say, the view of the moral landscape might be sharper than the view displayed in their common-sense judgment. How critical we should be about such roughly sound moral judgments in ordinary practice is a question we set aside for now. There is good reason for us to make some effort to identify more accurately the genuine reason providing consideration, and this is an effort that sound moral philosophy should undertake.

Principles as we understand them make explanatory claims, and it is important how sound such claims are. When it comes to deferring to others over parking spots, age may be some explanation, but it is not a very good one. Better, we'd say, to explain such reasons in terms of vulnerability and need. The practice of

---

[11] For a nice discussion of some of these issues, see McNaughton 1996.

discriminating our reasons which we have here defended is a practice of finding the 'real' or so-called primary reason for action, and this is a matter of finding ever-better explanations of the suitability of a range of morally salient responses. If, as we have claimed, normative moral philosophy is an extension of ordinary moral practice, it should be no surprise if much of moral philosophy is devoted to arguing about which of several possible considerations provides the best explanation of why we should act in certain ways. For example, attempts to give an account of moral standing may be thought of as attempts to identify the best explanation of why we should act in certain ways. Is it because another individual is human? Is it because the individual has higher-order desires or has a self-concept? There is overlap between these categories, and it would not be surprising if we found all of them playing a role in common-sense morality. However, moral philosophy will rightly concern itself with which features actually provide the best explanations. We do not assume that the best explanations must mirror common-sense morality.

Common-sense morality may be pluralistic, but this does not mean that moral philosophy should be equally pluralistic—or even pluralistic at all. Whether our best moral theory is pluralistic—and if so how pluralistic it will be—depends upon how many sorts of reasons the theory must recognize if it is to identify the considerations that best explain what favors moral action. Indeed it is possible on our approach even to reject holism. Those who reject holism think that a consideration that is ever a reason will be one in any context. We have tailored generalism as a regulative ideal to be compatible with holism. However, at the end of the day moral philosophy should give greater allegiance to sound explanation than holism if the two conflict. If it turned out that the best explanations always involved considerations that are reasons regardless of context, then that would provide some evidence against holism. We do not pretend to have settled that debate here. What we have shown is that the debate over holism should take place within a generalist framework instead of being wrongly understood as the key point of contention between particularists and generalists.

Finally, moral philosophers have good reason to give special attention to existing normative theories. We have argued that there is a route from principles underlying our common-sense judgments to more systematic moral theories if such systematic theories have greater explanatory power. And we have argued that we have reason to engage in the activities that would produce such systematic theories. Such reasons are unlikely to be special to our particular moment in history. To the contrary, they would be equally strong two hundred or two thousand years ago. If that is right, then there has long been reason to engage in the activities that would reveal more systematic moral patterns. In engaging in serious moral reflection of the kind we have described, people have been doing what they have good reason to do. One product of such reflection is the normative theories we now have, and these theories warrant further investigation.

## 8.5. Summary and Preview

The arguments of this chapter and the preceding ones establish that generalism is a regulative ideal in the following sense. Moral thought and judgment presuppose the availability of moral principles and we have good moral reason to articulate them. The analogy with science is perhaps illuminating. For scientific thought and judgment arguably presuppose the availability of scientific principles (laws of nature) and we have good scientific reasons to articulate them as well. The analogy is of course imperfect; the methodology of science and the methodology of moral philosophy are very different, for a start. However, the points of analogy are striking and important too. In both cases, we have a work in progress and grounds for cautious optimism that we can continue to make closer and closer approximations of the ideal at which we aim. In this respect, our position is a sort of compromise between constitutive generalism and particularism. On the one hand, we insist that moral theory really is a work in progress. We reject the constitutive generalist's assumption that morality is a finished work at least in the sense that competence with moral concepts is sufficient for commitment to the ultimate principle(s) of morality. If this were right, then reflection on our own concepts should in principle be sufficient for a full descriptive codification of the moral landscape, but for reasons discussed in Chapter 5 we find this thesis indefensible. On the other hand, we reject the particularist's claim that moral thought and judgment do not presuppose the availability of a suitable stock of moral principles. For although moral theory is a work in progress, it is a work in progress the legitimacy of which is presupposed by moral thought and judgment themselves.

Moreover, like the development of scientific theory, moral theory is a collective work in progress which we have excellent reasons to pursue with confidence. This emphasis on the collective nature of moral theorizing inevitably puts a certain spin on our claim that moral thought and judgment presuppose the availability of a suitable stock of moral principles. For the thesis itself must be understood from a collective point of view. In other words, our claim is that *our* moral thought and judgment presuppose that a suitable stock of moral principles is available to *us*. We do not claim to have these principles at our fingertips here and now. However, they are available to us in the sense that we have very good reason to think that if we continue moral theorizing in earnest then we are likely eventually to articulate them.

Some may complain that our moral theorizing to date does not inspire confidence, as the history of moral theory is littered with falsehoods. Note, however, that this is also true of the history of science. For example, in spite of its enormous predictive power Newtonian physics was eventually replaced by physical theories based on relativity and quantum phenomena. The history of science also gives us reason to think that today's best scientific theories are likely eventually to be shown to be false. Nonetheless, most people do not hesitate to agree that we have made (and continue to make) scientific progress. This is in part because old scientific theories are discarded as false precisely because we have found better theories—theories that could explain what seemed like anomalous phenomena on the old theory, for example. We have argued that progress has been made in the development of our moral commitments as well. So there is some degree of parallel here in spite of the obvious and important difference between moral and scientific theorizing. Moreover, it is early days for moral philosophy that is not heavily constrained by religion. Here we think Derek Parfit's closing comments in his famous *Reasons and Persons* are very much to the point:

[T]here could be higher achievements in all of the Arts and Sciences. But the progress could be greatest in what is now the least advanced of these Arts and Sciences. This, I have claimed, is Non-Religious Ethics. Belief in God, or in many gods, prevented the free development of moral reasoning. Disbelief in God, openly admitted by a majority, is a recent event, not yet completed. Because this event is so recent, Non-Religious Ethics is at a very early stage. We cannot yet predict whether, as in Mathematics, we will all reach agreement. Since we cannot know how Ethics will develop, it is not irrational to have high hopes. (Parfit 1984: 454)

Our defense of generalism as a regulative ideal is not, however, complete. For we have not yet explained how moral principles can and should guide action. In Chapter 9 we turn our attention to this question at some length. Here, more than in other chapters, we think some of the most interesting questions arise out of the empirical literature and our discussion in Chapter 9 is itself more empirical than it has been in previous chapters. We address worries about an action-guiding role for principles which emerge out of certain models of moral thought developed in cognitive science which give pride of place to moral exemplars or moral prototypes. We argue that these interesting empirical models do not ultimately undermine the idea that moral principles can and should play an important role in guiding action.

# 9

# Principled Guidance

I can resist everything except temptation.

(Oscar Wilde)

So far we have seen that morality is principled and that we should engage in moral theorizing. However, morality is a practical matter. It concerns choice and action, and a sound moral outlook should be capable of motivating someone to act virtuously. Hence it is reasonable to expect that moral principles might play an important role in guiding action. Those who believe that morality is principled are apt to think that a virtuous moral agent will be principled.

The only form of particularism we have not yet argued directly against is Principle Abstinence Particularism, according to which principles are morally pernicious and should be avoided. In this chapter we meet the challenge posed by Principle Abstinence Particularism by explaining why moral principles can and should play an important role in guiding action. We begin by exploring some different models of principled guidance. We then develop a positive case in favor of principled guidance. Finally, we conclude by exploring how our account fits with some relevant empirical evidence.

## 9.1. Models of Principled Guidance

Though seemingly familiar, the idea of a principle guiding an agent's choices and actions can be extraordinarily elusive. One challenge that both deserves and receives much attention is to account for moral motivation and moral psychology more generally. It is natural to assume that if the acceptance of moral principles is to guide behavior, then such acceptance must be appropriately linked to motivational states of mind. Just how an agent's acceptance of a moral principle could be so linked is hotly debated. In the present discussion, we put many of these more general issues to one side since they are equally challenges for particularists. In this section we spell out some of the important senses in which a moral principle can function as a guide, and how guides may be related to principles conceived as ultimate standards.

Perhaps the most significant obstacle to a proper understanding of principled guidance stems from the seemingly vast distance between the kinds of thoughts or rules that might claim to figure explicitly in moral reasoning and anything that could count as an ultimate standard. If we reflect on our own experience, we may suspect that the rules we apply in reaching moral decisions do not even appear to be viable candidates for standards. Imagine, for example, a corporate whistleblower who, at considerable personal cost, makes public his employer's attempts to conceal product safety problems. If we assume that the whistleblower's decision is made with ample forethought and is understood by him as a moral decision, then this would seem to be a favorable case in which to find guidance by moral principle. It is striking that someone making such a decision might cite a principle no more complex than 'Deceiving people for profit is wrong.' Yet no one is likely to look upon this principle as providing an airtight sufficient condition (much less necessary and sufficient conditions) for the application of 'wrong.'

It may be replied that the whistleblower is unconsciously aware of and acts in light of further considerations beyond those contained in the foregoing expression of the rule. Indeed, the principle at work here might be best understood as a default principle in our sense. However, it seems ad hoc to assume that this must be what is happening in every case. Moreover, even if we suppose that someone like the whistleblower is nonetheless relying unconsciously upon a more nuanced principle, this does not do away with the fact that he is also and at the same time consciously relying upon a very crude rule. The striking fact remains. Moral agents seem regularly to be guided by shockingly crude rules, rules that even by our own lights could never function as genuine standards.

Two points stand out in cases like the case of the whistleblower. First, the guidance is understood by the agent as moral. The whistleblower sees her decision as one made for moral reasons. Secondly, the guidance seemingly provided by such crude rules is often highly successful. Agents who have internalized an assembly of even very simple rules quite regularly and indeed systematically seem to succeed in acting well by following them. The connection is systematic in the sense that the rules pick up on features which are in some sense morally relevant. The whistleblower's rule against deception for profit picks up on the morally relevant feature of deception. Such rules contrast with other sorts of rules or heuristics which actually refer to features which are not really relevant at all.

To take a fanciful example, someone who had a morally infallible guru might adopt the maxim 'do what the guru says' and this maxim would indeed lead the agent to do the right thing. However, on no plausible account are actions right or wrong because of the guru's advice. By contrast, deception is plausibly part of what can make an action wrong. Even a utilitarian can reasonably invoke facts about deception when explaining the wrongness of an action so long as those facts are invoked alongside facts about the consequences of deception. So we seem to have a reliable and systematic connection between crude moral rules and right action. What, then, could be going on here if the appearances are not misleading? We explore two rather different generalist accounts of how ordinary agents might reasonably be guided by rules which fall short of ultimate standards—deliberative simplification and local specification. We shall not argue for one model in favor of the other. For which of these two models is most plausible will depend on what the ultimate moral standards are like and our defense of generalism is neutral on the content of morality.

### 9.1.1. Deliberative simplification

Deliberative simplification is widely associated with consequentialism. According to this model, the principles we typically employ in deliberation are not standards of right conduct. However, an agent who employs them in deliberation will regularly and systematically act rightly. An especially well-known version of this model is defended by Hare, who calls reliance on such principles "intuitive moral thinking." By contrast, "critical moral thinking" proceeds in terms of the actual standards of moral conduct, in Hare's case a utilitarian standard (Hare 1981). This model raises two related questions. First, why should we not be guided directly by the ultimate moral standards? Secondly, what justifies our use of principles that fall short of ultimate standards, like Hare's principles of intuitive moral thinking?

In answer to the first question, there may be many reasons agents cannot or should not attempt to use moral standards to guide their action directly. The ultimate moral standards may be too complex to remember. Ordinary agents may lack the computational capacities to access the facts necessary for successful application of the standards. This second difficulty is famously acute when the standard in question is some version of the principle of utility. Emotional deficits may also disable people from properly appreciating the force of acknowledged facts. For example, applying an impartial moral standard directly might require a degree of emotional identification that is not always possible. Even if agents could guide themselves by standards, the costs of doing so might be great.[1]

---

[1] See e.g. Mill's discussion in *Utilitarianism*, ch. 2.

Finally, as we shall see in Section 9.2, moral principles are especially import-ant as a check on the all too familiar tendency to engage in special pleading and rationalization. However, the ultimate moral standards may not play this role very effectively. Any plausible candidate for an ultimate moral standard presumably will be sensitive to the consequences (either actual or expected) of an agent's actions; one does not have to be a consequentialist to think the consequences can matter. This sensitivity to consequences may in turn make it all too easy for someone guided directly by the correct moral standard to convince themselves to perform an action when tempted which is actually wrong. The basic point is that any moral principle sufficiently sensitive to the consequences of our actions to be a plausible candidate standard may thereby be too flexible to constrain those who are prone to special pleading and self-deception. In this sense, moral rules that are at least somewhat crude may be indispensable for creatures like us precisely because they are crude. For crude rules do not invite deliberation about possible exceptions and special circumstances. This may help keep flawed moral agents on the straight and narrow more effectively than a principle which stands a much better chance of being immune to counter-example.

Whether this is true will of course vary from person to person and indeed from a person at one time to that same person at another time. Even so, we still have good reason to try to identify the correct moral standard. Those especially prone to special pleading may have less to contribute on this front. This should be no surprise given our emphasis on the need for a division of labor when it comes to society's efforts to determine the correct ultimate moral standards. We have already seen (in Chapter 8) how such moral theorizing can be an essential catalyst for moral progress. One way in which this moral progress might help guide action is by 'trickling down' in helping us to gauge the utility of the various crude moral rules upon which some people may need to rely. We explore the possibility of such a trickle-down effect in more detail in Section 9.3 but we hasten to add that we do not mean to deny that we must be careful when modifying existing moral rules. As John Stuart Mill has eloquently argued, many of the crude moral rules upon which ordinary people generally rely are themselves the result of our collective experience of what works and what is problematic, and hence should not be revised lightly (see Mill 1979 [1861]). Moreover, the force of Mill's point survives extraction from its utilitarian setting. If we are right to think that crude and familiar moral rules are the output of long moral experience and reflection, then there is likely to be some truth in them, even if it is not a utilitarian truth.

Against this background, what justifies our relying on other principles to guide our behavior is that doing so will systematically lead us to act well—where what counts as acting well is determined by the standards. As Hare puts the point, "The best set [of principles for intuitive moral thinking] is that whose acceptance yields actions, dispositions, etc. most nearly approximating to those which would be chosen if we were able to use critical thinking all the time" (Hare 1981: 50). In Mill's terms, "All action is for some end, and rules of action, it seems natural to suppose, must take their whole character and color from the end to which they are subservient" (Mill 1979: 2). Naturally, adherence to crude rules will also have costs and sometimes lead people astray, but the basic idea is that these benefits will very often outweigh the costs. Actually, putting the point in terms of benefits and costs helps sharpen the idea. For a crude rule would not really be very useful if it led us reliably to act rightly only when the stakes were low while leading us to act wrongly when the stakes were high. So we need something along the lines of the utilitarian idea of expected utility to gauge the usefulness of a given crude moral rule, though the idea of expected utility itself should be understood very broadly.

Thus far, the model of deliberative simplification embodies two elements necessary to any account of moral guidance by principle. First, an agent's acceptance of certain general principles plays a role in the explanation of how the agent acts (though we have not undertaken to explain just how an agent's acceptance of such a principle moves her to act.) Secondly, the acceptance of those principles will reliably lead agents to act well (in light of the real moral standards). In saying that a principle will reliably lead an agent to act well, we should not assume that someone who accepts the principle will reliably do the right thing. Rather, we should assume only that someone who accepts the principle will reliably do the right thing if their acceptance of the principle is sufficiently motivating. This qualification is necessary in the present context to maintain a measure of neutrality about the motivational powers of moral principles and the motivational demands of morality. If morality is very demanding in the sense that it regularly requires normal people in the actual world to make large sacrifices of personal goods, then even someone who sincerely accepted a reliable moral principle might not reliably muster sufficient motivation to act on it. Here, though, the problem is not with the principle's reliability but with its motivational power.[2] So deliberative simplification provides one account of how ordinary agents like our hypothetical whistleblower might sensibly follow seemingly crude moral

---

[2] We do not mean to suggest that in such cases that the agent is to be faulted. If morality is highly demanding, then it might be unreasonable to expect an agent to be sufficiently motivated by her acceptance of moral principles.

rules. We now turn our attention to a second model which might explain the sensibility of such rules.

### 9.1.2. Local specification

Historically this model is associated with the natural law tradition. On this model, the moral standard is apt to be a highly abstract principle that does not apply straightforwardly and invariably to our actual circumstances. Guiding principles, on this model, are ways of applying an abstract principle to our local circumstances. They both specify what, under local circumstances, would count as compliance with the moral standard and provide usable guidance to agents who are in those circumstances. Consider, for example, a principle such as 'All persons must be treated as moral equals.' Famously, such principles do not have straightforward applications. For it must be settled just who are persons and what it is to treat persons as moral equals. It is the business of guiding principles to specify these further particulars and make guidance possible. On this model the obstacle to using the standard as a direct guide to conduct is not that we lack the cognitive resources, but that the standard is itself not sufficiently concrete. In contrast to the model of deliberative simplification, it is not clear that such a principle could be (even in theory) applied directly to a case at hand simply given the relevant facts. Independent of decisions about whom to count as persons and what to count as equal treatment, the content of the principle may be too indeterminate to yield answers. More specific principles are needed to apply the standard, and once adopted these more specific moral principles may function as guides without themselves being ultimate moral standards.

What then justifies the adoption of specific guiding principles? If the moral standards do not have determinate content independently of such guiding principles, then we cannot say that guiding principles are justified if they reliably lead us to do what we would do if we directly applied the standard correctly. Somehow, the adoption of specific guiding principles must be justified on grounds that the guiding principles provide a morally defensible interpretation of the standard.[3] It might be tempting to think that the guiding principles are, on this model, themselves moral standards. Importantly, however, this is not the case. On the model of local specification, the guiding principles provide a way of complying with the standard in our local circumstances, and it is only

---

[3] Just what distinguishes morally defensible interpretations from morally spurious interpretations is a question we here leave aside. On some accounts, the morally defensible interpretations are the ones that reveal the content of the moral principle. On other accounts, however, the choice of interpretations is deeply pragmatic, and it is less clear what makes one interpretation better than another.

as an interpretation of the standard that the principles explain why particular acts have the moral status they do.

With these two models in hand, we are ready to turn to a defense of principled guidance. Because we are here neutral about the ultimate content of morality, we do not take a position as to which of the preceding two models is most helpful. The point of our discussion of these two models is simply to provide some idea of how a more specific moral theory might develop the idea of principled guidance in more detail. Our arguments in favor of principled guidance should work on either of the two models we have laid out in this section.

## 9.2. Special Pleading

In our view, principled guidance is a good solution to some otherwise pressing problems. The first of these problems is that people are often easily tempted to evade moral requirements when their own interests are at stake. The problem is especially insidious in that those who have an eye on their self-interest—that is, virtually everyone—are thereby prone to interpret their moral requirements in ways that are favorable to those interests. Call this special pleading. The agent who engages in special pleading does not explicitly choose to violate moral requirements, or claim that she is excused from them. Rather, someone who engages in special pleading tailors her sense of what morality requires in ways that are favorable to her own welfare.

We do not mean to deny that our moral duties should be sensitive to self-interest.[4] Someone who engages in special pleading, however, lets her own interests distort her sense of duty beyond what the proper accommodation of self-interest would allow. If morality is to succeed as a system of practical guidance, there must be some provision to counteract our all too human tendency to engage in special pleading. This is challenging for at least two reasons. First, people who engage in special pleading do not even realize that they are doing so. Methods of coercive enforcement that presuppose that agents know what they are doing are therefore unlikely to work, at least by themselves. Secondly, we cannot respond to the problem of special pleading simply by adding further moral duties. It is not enough just to say that, in

---

[4] In the present discussion we assume that morality does not entirely coincide with enlightened self-interest. Those who reject this assumption can recast the present argument, though. Instead of being put in terms of the dangers of special pleading, it can be put in terms of the dangers of being 'tempted' by an over-narrow or unenlightened view of one's interests. For one very clear defense of the first assumption, see Scheffler 1992.

addition to all our other duties, we also have a duty not to engage in special pleading. Because special pleading arises from how we understand our duties, we cannot respond to it simply by adding more duties.

How might the adoption of principles help address this problem? One advantage of moral principles is that they can be adopted and internalized well in advance of situations in which duty and self-interest conflict. All else being equal, someone who has adopted a moral principle forbidding a certain sort of action is less likely to rationalize such an action when faced with temptation than someone who is unprincipled.

To see this, let us compare two agents. The first agent has adopted a principle according to which it is wrong to cause someone else to suffer significant pain without consent unless doing so is the only way to avoid even more suffering. The second agent has adopted no principle about causing pain, but has noticed in the past that the fact that an action would cause someone to suffer significant pain very often (though not always) makes the action wrong. The second agent has at most adopted a rule of thumb according to which instances of causing someone else to suffer significant pain are typically wrong. The second agent will have much greater latitude for special pleading. Precisely because she has not adopted a firm and clear principle in advance of temptation it will be easier for her sense of duty to be distorted by temptation when it arises. "Sure, it is usually wrong to cause someone else to suffer significant pain, but this case is different in some way I can't quite articulate," the agent might tell herself. If the agent is slightly more reflective, then she might identify some specific feature of the situation in a spurious attempt to justify causing pain here—that the victim should not have put herself in harm's way in the first place, for example. The second agent, by contrast, should know perfectly well that, if she causes pain in the case at hand, then she is violating a moral principle which she adopted in a cool and reflective moment. Of course, even the prior adoption of a suitable moral principle is no panacea; there is no realistic fail-safe cure for special pleading. Our suggestion is only that the adoption of a suitable principle makes special pleading less likely than the particularist alternative.

It might seem that we are suggesting here a caricature of the moral agent earnestly cobbling together moral principles on his own. However, if articulating moral principles is a virtue because it provides a safeguard against special pleading, then, as we have already emphasized, there is also good reason to think that articulating moral principles is best accomplished collectively. What makes the problem of special pleading so difficult is precisely that those who engage in it do not realize they are doing so. They genuinely think that their own case is special. If articulating moral principles is to address the problem of special pleading, then agents cannot be left to themselves to discover that they are privileging their own interests. (Of course it does sometimes happen that an agent, on her own, discovers that she has been engaging in special pleading, but to treat this as a solution is to treat hope as a strategy.) The virtue of articulating moral principles does not require merely trying to articulate a principled basis for our own actions, but also challenging others to find a principled basis for theirs. We should therefore not expect that the activity of articulating moral principles will be a cold and earnest one. Given the problem of special pleading, articulating moral principles will require confronting individuals whose interests hang in the balance. And getting other individuals to face up to the question of whether they are arbitrarily favoring their own interests may require a healthy dose of rhetoric. In short, the activity of articulating moral principles can be understood as continuous with ordinary everyday moral discourse and discussion.

The particularist might at this point raise the following dilemma. Either principled guidance is just the inflexible application of previously adopted principles to the case at hand or principled guidance is compatible with revising one's principles in light of new information. On the first horn of the dilemma, the particularist can argue that unless we are sure our prior principles admit of no exceptions, we risk going badly astray. All too familiar are agents who follow a basically sound policy in ruthless and inhumane ways precisely because, having seen that the policy 'applies' to the case at hand, they refuse to countenance any further facts as relevant. Often, the proper reaction to a novel case is to leverage it to revise previously held principles. As Dancy puts the point, "We all know the sort of person who refuses to make the decision here that the facts are obviously calling for, because he cannot see how to make that decision consistent with one he made on a different occasion" (Dancy 1993: 64). On the other horn of the dilemma, we understand principled guidance in a more flexible way, so that the principled agent can reexamine her principles at the moment of choice. The problem then is that it is no longer clear how principles can effectively battle special pleading any better than an unprincipled sensibility. For if we can always reexamine our principles, then it seems that the door to special pleading is opened as wide as ever.

Generalism as a regulative ideal insists that we can evade both horns of this dilemma. The *ex ante* adoption of a moral principle in effect 'raises the stakes' so that the costs for the agent of abandoning that principle are increased. Here we build on some of Robert Nozick's work, which itself builds on work in decision theory by George Ainslie. Ainslie's work concerned rational pursuit of self-interest in spite of immediate temptation rather than acting morally in spite of temptation. Leaving aside the details of Ainslie's account (see Ainslie 1975 and 1986), the crucial point here is that by adopting a principle we in effect lump together all of the possible actions which are subsumed under the principle. Then each instance of adhering to the principle symbolizes all that the principle stands for. Nozick expands this idea to the ethical case:

Holding and following ethical principles, in addition to the particular purposes this serves, also has a symbolic meaning for us ... Kant felt that in acting morally a person acts as a member of the kingdom of ends, a free and rational legislator. The moral action does not *cause* us to become a (permanent) member of that kingdom. It is what we would do as a member ... The moral acts get grouped with other possible events and actions and come to stand for and mean them. Thereby, being ethical acquires a symbolic utility commensurate with the utility these other things it stands for have. (Nozick 1993: 29)

When Nozick speaks of utility he has in mind utility in the sense in which decision theorists use that term, not in the sense in which utilitarians use it. We take the general idea here to be a plausible one, and indeed one which does not really depend on the truth of decision theory. By adopting, for example, a principle which forbids lying I come to see my lying in a new light. For in that case, in addition to the particular wrong of lying to someone my lying will now constitute my abandonment of an ideal of honesty which I presumably value (why else did I adopt the principle?). This in itself can provide a further motivation to adhere to the principle and retain one's status as a person who is genuinely and robustly committed to honesty. In this way, the adoption of a principle raises the stakes in situations in which we might be tempted to violate the principle knowingly, and can provide further motivation to act in accordance with the principle.

We hasten to add that we are not here taking a position in the vexed debate between causal decision theorists and evidential decision theorists. For even if the causal decision theorists are right that the mechanisms Ainslie identifies are in some sense irrational, it still might be rational to inculcate such irrationality. A smoker who can abandon smoking only by being irrationally motivated by the fact that he has adopted a rule against ever smoking again might well be perfectly rational in making himself into the sort of person who is irrational in just this way.[5]

So far, so good. However, we still have no answer to the dilemma posed by the particularist. Nozick's point concerned knowingly violating a principle you continue to endorse in some sense even as you knowingly violate it. This is not special pleading. Special pleading would instead be to abandon one's old principles altogether in favor of some new principle for what is in fact a bogus

---

[5] Thanks to Roy Sorensen for useful discussion here.

reason though it does not seem bogus to the agent at the time of decision. However, we want to suggest that the Nozick/Ainslie point can be extended to apply to special pleading as well. For just as the adoption of a principle raises the stakes when it comes to deliberate violation of the principle, it also functions to raise the stakes when it comes to abandoning the principle in favor of another one.

Here it is relevant that anyone who adopts a principle in the first place should also know that people, herself included, are prone to temptation and special pleading. For after all, this is not only common knowledge, it is one of the primary motives for adopting a principle in the first place. Someone who adopts a principle for this reason will attach disvalue to being the sort of person who engages in special pleading. This, in turn, will make the agent reluctant to abandon her principle in favor of another one when faced with a concrete situation which calls for decision. For such shifts in a person's principles can be associated with special pleading, and *this* symbolic value can increase the stakes and make it less likely that the agent will shift principles. The agent can say to himself, "If I shift my principle in this way in a situation where this is in my interest, then there is a very good chance that I will thereby have shown myself to be the kind of person who tailors his principles to fit his interests, and I do not want to be that sort of person." Of course, the case is not exactly like the one Nozick discusses, since here there is only a risk of the symbolic disvalue in question, whereas in Nozick's case the agent could be certain about the relevant symbolic disvalue. This uncertainty may reduce the strength of motivation somewhat, but it should not eliminate it altogether.

We are now finally in a position to see how to meet the particularist's dilemma, according to which principled guidance is either hopelessly inflexible or no antidote to special pleading. Adopting a principle *does* produce new symbolic values and thereby makes it less likely that the agent will shift her principle in light of the specific features of the case. In this way, adopting a principle is an effective antidote against special pleading. So the second horn of the dilemma is easily avoided. Why, though, does this not impale generalism as a regulative ideal on the first horn? Here it is important to realize that, while adopting a principle does increase the stakes for the agent, it does not raise them so high that the agent could never revise her principle. This is part of the reason that principles can only help to some extent with special pleading but are no panacea. Whether an agent will be motivated to revise her principle in the case at hand will be a function of both her certainty that the new principle is correct and the costs associated with switching principles if she is mistaken. So the principled agent need not be too inflexible. If it is dead obvious that her original principle has been shown to be mistaken, then the risk of showing oneself to be a mere special pleader will also appear very low. If, however, it is not so clear that the original principle has been shown to be false, then the agent may well not switch principles out of a concern to not show herself to have been a mere special pleader. This, however, is just what we are after—an extra motivation not to switch principles at the moment of choice the strength of which is commensurate with the agent's certainty that the shift in principle is correct. Again, this is still no panacea, as the rot can sometimes go even deeper, and the agent's certainty that revising her principles is correct can also be unconsciously skewed by a desire to promote her self-interest. This, however, is just to call attention to the limits of *any* strategy for preventing special pleading.

Finally, the particularist is subject to a *tu quoque* reply when it comes to the first horn of this dilemma according to which principled guidance is hopelessly inflexible. The point is that the particularist does not actually have any sort of clear advantage when it comes to the avoidance of inflexibility. According to particularists, the alternative to guidance by principle is guidance by a kind of unprincipled sensibility. However, there appears to be nothing inherently progressive about sensibilities. Just as familiar as the person who stubbornly insists on (mis)applying an old principle to a new case is the person who 'just sees' situations in the same old way even when things have changed. Think, for example, of parents who fail to see their grown children as independent adults. Such parents need not be in the grip of a principle to fall prey to this vice; a faulty unprincipled sensibility seems equally likely to stand behind their perspective. If someone fails to see the obvious, then their sensibility is deficient. In thinking about the efficacy of guidance by sensibility, however, we can no more assume a perfect sensibility than in assessing guidance by principle we can assume a perfect set of principles. No one is born with a perfect set of moral principles and no one is born with a perfect moral sensibility. Any sane conception of either must allow that they develop over time, that some individuals achieve more development than others, and that even the best among us remain fallible. The question, then, is whether the development of a moral sensibility will better enable agents to take a proper view of new circumstances as they present themselves.[6]

Although we do not wish here to take a stand on how best to understand the idea of a moral sensibility, it is often held that a moral sensibility is something that can be improved with exercise. Thus if we can get people off to a start with

---

[6] This way of putting the question is meant to allow that the internalization of rules might be a necessary step in the development of a moral sensibility. For example, they may be important for the moral education of children. Once a sensibility is developed, the thought goes, these rules can be done away with. For purposes of guidance, they are *replaced* by a sensibility. See McNaughton 1988.

some degree of moral sensibility, they can, through their own exercise of that sensibility, refine it. The virtuous person is thus often portrayed as someone who has achieved a fine sensibility in large part through experience. This portrait of the virtuous sensibility is also consonant with our understanding of other sensibilities. If a person has some sense for jazz music, then it is reasonable to expect that if he continues to listen to jazz music attentively his sense for it will become more developed and refined. Yet this provides little grounds for optimism about inflexibility. The dictum that practice makes perfect is sound only when what we practice is sufficiently similar to what we must perform.

It is just here, surprisingly, that one of particularism's key insights might loosen our confidence in the progressive tendencies of sensibilities. If the particularist is right then there is no way of knowing 'in advance' whether some novel feature or combination of features might have some very novel practical import. In that case, though, there is little ground for confidence that our sensibility will be prepared for it. If our sensibility has been practicing on old cases, why think it will be prepared for new ones? If it is not adequately prepared for new cases, then is it not likely to keep seeing new cases in the 'same old way?' This is not to say that a sensibility could not serve well in an entirely novel case. Some people who have a sense for jazz, when exposed to opera, find that they have a sense for that too. Then we might say, "They have a sense for music." But it is entirely possible that someone with a sense for jazz music—even one that has been refined and developed—'just doesn't get' opera. So too, someone who has a sensibility for familiar moral features might well be blind to novel kinds of moral features.

It is difficult to escape the thought that, given our limited capacities, a certain amount of conservatism will be endemic to any mode of practical decision-making. Whether an agent who is guided by a somewhat crude principle is deftly responding to those limitations or ham-handedly ignoring moral distinctions she should take account of depends in part upon how limited and prone to special pleading we are (questions we have not tried to settle). Nevertheless, we are limited animals, and when we must decide what to do it is often not feasible or unwise to use even our limited capacities to the full. In these cases (which are to be sure most cases) we will be apt to assimilate our actions to old patterns, whether these patterns are understood in terms of principles or in terms of sensibilities. We can expect that there will be mistakes, and the mistakes will have costs, but these are costs we must face regardless of whether we opt for principled guidance or guidance by sensibility. The advantage of principled guidance is that it provides an extra incentive to avoid special pleading.

The fact that guidance by sensibility is prone to some of the same problems as principled guidance might lead to a new objection. For strategies with similar costs often have similar resources for dealing with those costs. Perhaps the particularist could try to co-opt our account by insisting that an agent could attach symbolic value to not shifting sensibilities for the wrong reason in much the way that we have argued they can attach symbolic value to not shifting principles. However, on reflection it is hard to see how guidance by something as vague and open-ended as an unprincipled sensibility could provide an equally effective antidote in this way. Within the framework of principled guidance it should often be clear enough to the agent when she is switching principles or failing to live up to them and when she is sticking to her guns. This is not to say that there will not be penumbral cases in which it is unclear whether the agent has shifted principles as opposed to specifying a previously vague principle in a more determinate way. Nonetheless, there will also be cases in which acting in a certain way would very clearly amount to a shift in principle or a failure to live up to a principle still embraced. For example, suppose someone accepts the maxim, 'Do unto others as you would have others do unto you' but always fails to stop at crosswalks even though he always complains bitterly when he is a pedestrian and drivers fail to stop at a crosswalk for him. In this case it will be clear enough that the person is either failing in a pretty spectacular way to live up to his maxim or has implicitly rejected it.

By contrast, if an agent is guided by an unprincipled sensibility, then it will often be very unclear to the agent whether choosing a given course of action in light of a feature not previously encountered or consciously considered constitutes a shift in sensibility or is instead simply a new deployment of a preexisting (albeit previously entirely dispositional) aspect of the agent's existing sensibility. The very fact that the sensibility is unprincipled will make it harder to tell when someone's sensibility has evolved as opposed to when a new dispositional aspect of the preexisting sensibility has been triggered for the first time. This, in turn, will increase the risk of special pleading. For the agent guided by an unprincipled sensibility may well end up tailoring her sensibility to her self-interest without even realizing that she has shifted her sensibility at all.

On the other hand, it will often be extremely clear what one's initial principles require in the case at hand. This, in turn, will make it painfully clear to the agent whether a given course of action would involve a shift in her principled sensibility. Because principles are discursive and can be relatively easy to apply, the internalization of a principle can make it very clear to the agent when a proposed course of action would violate her existing standards.

Actions which violate clearly stated principles should 'jump out' at the agent as raising a moral problem, and this should reduce the risk of special pleading.[7]

What have particularists actually had to say about the problem of special pleading? As far as we know, very little. Here is Jonathan Dancy's way of dealing with the problem in his article on particularism in the *Stanford Encyclopedia of Philosophy*:

> But really the remedy for poor moral judgement is not a different style of moral judgement, principle-based judgement, but just better moral judgement. There is only one real way to stop oneself distorting things in one's own favour, and that is to look again, as hard as one can, at the reasons present in the case, and see if really one is so different from others that what would be required of them is not required of oneself. This method is not infallible, I know; but then nor was the appeal to principle. (Dancy 2001; http://plato.stanford.edu/entries/moral-particularism/)

Dancy's reply is utopian. Admittedly, the ideal solution to special pleading is for the agent simply to stop being prone to distortions due to self-interest. Perhaps for a few moral saints this is possible, but for most mere mortals the danger of special pleading is likely to remain with us. Nor is it to the point to observe that no solution will be infallible. For the question is not whether any available approach is infallible, but which approach is better. Moreover, the suggestion that we should avoid the problem of special pleading not with principles but instead simply by making better moral judgments is in tension with one of the particularist's own important points. For particularists have often followed Aristotle in insisting that, if agents do not acquire the sensibilities necessary for good moral judgment early in life, then it will quickly become too late for them to improve their judgment substantially. This, however, amounts to a recognition that the strategy of 'just making better moral judgments' probably is not available to most of those of us who need it. Dancy himself endorses this Aristotelean idea:

> To have the relevant sensitivities just is to be able to get things right case by case. The only remaining question is how we might get into this enviable state. And the answer

---

[7] Here our account has much in common with Barbara Herman's discussion of what she calls "rules of moral salience." See Herman 1993: 73–93. An interesting point of comparison and contrast is Brad Hooker's discussion in Hooker 2000b. Hooker argues roughly that, *ceteris paribus*, a particularist would be less predictable and that the spread of particularism would therefore make cooperation less feasible. Our point is the rather different one that particularists would (in virtue of special pleading) quite predictably be more likely to break promises when it is in their interest to do so (and would predictably be more likely to engage in other forms of moral wrongdoing as well). This too undermines the prospects for cooperation, but we do not think the point is well put in terms of predictability since we can after all have pretty good inductive evidence about how any specific particularist will act, and we can also appeal to background theories about human nature and the person's culture or subculture to make such predictions even if she is a particularist. We do agree, however, with Hooker that the widespread adoption of particularism would reduce the prospects for mutually beneficial cooperation.

is that for us it is probably too late. As Aristotle held, moral education is the key; for those who are past educating, there is no real remedy. (Dancy 1993: 64)

Of course, we reject the claim that there is no real remedy if that is meant to imply that moral principles can provide no substantial help for those who were given a poor moral education in their youth (though admittedly some hard cases will be beyond reform). The crucial point, though, is that this contention does not fit well with Dancy's suggestion that the best available solution to special pleading is just to make better moral judgments. For by his own lights, for many if not most of us, substantial improvement in our moral sensibilities is simply impossible. For someone with a flawed sensibility, looking harder at the reasons will often be of little help. This is not to deny that people should not look harder at the reasons at hand. But we must also look to further strategies, including principled ones, for dealing with special pleading. We should not abandon a good strategy for the sake of a strategy which may be better in the abstract but is typically unavailable or only minimally helpful in the real world.

## 9.3. Framing Effects

Special pleading is not the only distortion of our moral thinking that the internalization of moral principles could counter. Common sense is, after all, prone to a number of errors (e.g. affirming the consequent, the gambler's fallacy) which are not due in any obvious or direct way to self-interest. It would be very surprising if morality were an exception to this general rule. Many of these distortions may well be even more insidious than special pleading in that their presence may be even harder to detect. In these cases too, principled guidance can help. Here we shall discuss just one example to illustrate the basic idea. The example emerges from some interesting work in empirical psychology.

Daniel Kahneman and Amos Tversky have defended a theory of decision-making which they insist explains the way people actually make decisions much better than classical expected-utility theory. They call their theory "prospect theory." Tamara Horowitz has argued that prospect theory can also explain why people give more weight to the distinction between doing and allowing than they otherwise would (Horowitz 1998). Prospect theory divides decision-making into two stages. In the first stage, the agent reformulates the options to simplify decision-making at the second stage. The crucial aspect of reformulation for present purposes is that agents frame options by classifying one outcome as the 'neutral' outcome and other outcomes as either gains or losses relative to the baseline of the outcome classified as neutral (Horowitz 1998: 371, summarizing findings from Kahneman and Tversky 1979). Crucially, different descriptions of options which are identical in all relevant respects can lead to the selection of different 'neutral' baselines. These 'framing' effects can lead agents irrationally to form opposite preferences over outcomes which are identical in all relevant respects but differently described. For example, when subjects are asked to imagine themselves $300 richer and then choose between (a) a sure gain of $100 or (b) a 50 percent chance of gaining $200 and a 50 percent chance of gaining nothing most people choose (a)—the sure gain. However, when subjects are told to imagine themselves $500 richer than they now are and then choose between (c) a sure loss of $100 or (d) a 50 percent chance of losing nothing and a 50 percent chance of losing $200, most people choose (d)—the risky option. The crucial point is that in all relevant respects (a) is identical to (c) and (b) is identical to (d). Both (a) and (c) amount to a sure gain of $400, while both (b) and (d) represent a 50 percent chance of gaining $500 and a 50 percent chance of gaining $300.

This pattern of choices would make sense only if someone thought that it matters whether gaining $n$ dollars by first gaining $n + m$ dollars and then immediately losing $m$ dollars is worse than gaining $n$ dollars by gaining a $n - p$ dollars and then immediately gaining $p$ more dollars. On reflection, it is hard to see why this distinction should matter. Kahneman and Tversky argue that the descriptions of the options in the first case leads people to classify a gain of $300 as the neutral baseline while the descriptions of the options in the second case leads people to classify a gain of $500 as the neutral baseline. This alone would not explain the pattern of choices, but prospect theory insists that departures from the neutral baseline are not ranked on the basis of a multiplication of probability times payoff as in classical expected utility theory. Instead, probabilities of losses relative to the baseline seem to be factored in at more than their face value, while probabilities of gains relative to the baseline are factored in at less than their face value (Kahneman and Tversky 1979).

Some studies of such choices include moral decisions. Kahneman and Tversky presented subjects with a choice between two programs to combat a disease which is expected to kill six hundred people if nothing is done. The first set of subjects was presented with the following choice:

> If program A is adopted, two hundred people will be saved. If program B is adopted, there is a one-third probability that six hundred people will be saved, and a two-thirds probability that no people will be saved.

The second set of subjects was presented with this choice:

> If program C is adopted, four hundred people will die. If program D is adopted, there is a one-third probability that nobody will die and a two-thirds probability that six hundred will die.

Programs A and C are identical in terms of expected survival rates, as are programs B and D. Yet the majority of subjects in the first group chose A over B while a majority in the second set chose D over C. The upshot seems to be that when outcomes are characterized positively in terms of 'lives saved' subjects are risk-averse, but when outcomes were stated in negative terms like 'lives lost' subjects are more tolerant of risk.

How might these findings, if sound, bolster the case for the utility of moral principles as guides? Any particular application of these findings will rely on philosophically controversial assumptions, so the following application is primarily intended to indicate the sorts of applications we think are available to generalists, though we do also think the particular application is a plausible one. A number of philosophical arguments and thought experiments support the conclusion that the distinction between killing and letting die either has no moral weight in itself or at best has far less moral weight than is often assumed. This is not the place to review those arguments, but they do in our view make a powerful case for this conclusion. Horowitz's application of Kahneman and Tversky's work can be seen as bolstering those philosophical arguments by providing a debunking explanation of our pretheoretical moral intuitions to the contrary (for an opposed perspective, see Kamm 1998).

Suppose we ultimately decide that most people tend not to care nearly enough about letting people die as opposed to killing. Perhaps we could offset this tendency with principles couched in terms that prospect theory predicts would lead people to attach greater weight to lives lost due to decisions to let people die. Suppose ordinary people typically accept the following moral principle:

(SL)  If an action would save a life then that is a moral reason to perform the action.

Presumably the acceptance of such a principle would motivate a morally virtuous agent to at least some extent to perform actions which would save a person's life. The problem seems to be that the motivation is weaker than it should be, and not nearly as strong as the motivation to avoid killing others. However, we could instead encourage people to accept the following principle:

(CL)  If not performing an action would lead to someone's death then that is a moral reason to perform the action.

Prospect theory presumably would predict that the internalization of (CL) would provide greater motivation to perform actions which save lives than (SL). For (SL) is couched in terms of saving lives, and we have seen from the disease case that couching choices in terms of saving lives seems to lead people to frame their choices in ways which give less weight to those lives than they would if they instead characterized the choice in terms of the lives to be lost. Characterizing the choice in terms of lives lost sets the baseline as the outcome in which the person is alive while characterizing the choice in terms of lives saved sets the baseline as the outcome in which the person is dead. We have already seen how prospect theory can then explain why (SL) would lead agents to give less weight to those lives than (CL).

The details of this particular example will of course be controversial. However, our general point is that how we frame our choices can have profound influences on the decisions we reach, and those influences may often be both invisible to the agent at the time and pernicious. If we uncover such pernicious tendencies, then one way to overcome them would be to get agents to frame issues differently. We have already seen that the acceptance of a suitable principle can lead people to see a situation differently. For example, someone who has accepted the maxim 'avoid doubled pawns' will see the prospect of doubled pawns rather differently from someone who has not internalized such a principle. The point here is more subtle, in that principles which entail exactly the same conclusions in all possible cases can have very different motivational consequences for typical human beings. Nonetheless, the basic mechanism is the same. By internalizing principles couched in terms of 'lives lost' rather than in terms of 'lives saved' people will come to see life and death situations rather differently, and this will have important motivational consequences. Of course, this particular hypothesis is an empirical one, and would benefit from further empirical confirmation. The main philosophical point is that, if that hypothesis is sound and if we have good reason to think people typically do not give enough weight to saving lives, then we could address that problem effectively by encouraging people to internalize principles couched in terms of lives lost rather than in terms of lives saved. Moral principles can in this way have an important role to play in offsetting biases built into ordinary human reasoning.

Perhaps particularists could try to deploy similar strategies without invoking moral principles. However, it is not obvious what such a strategy would look like and we doubt very much that it could be as effective at combating deeply entrenched biases in reasoning. One worry would be that the promulgation of particularism might itself lead agents to reject any general advice to frame issues in one way rather than another on the grounds that this might blind them to the context-sensitivity of correct framing. After all, someone sympathetic to particularism might well insist that while framing the issue in terms of 'deaths avoided' is often the right way to see a situation, in some cases we should instead see the issue in terms of 'lives saved.' However, people thinking in these more flexible particularist terms will in practice probably mean that they will often frame issues the wrong way and remain insufficiently motivated to save lives.

The particularist might instead go further and hold that people should *always* frame issues in one way rather than another. Just as particularists can allow for some invariable reasons without abandoning holism, they also can allow for some invariable norms for framing issues without abandoning their view. This is fine as far as it goes, but the question becomes what methods we could realistically use to get people to frame issues in the right way. One option would be to get people to read the relevant philosophical and empirical literature to see why they should frame issues in one way rather than another to avoid distortion, but this seems highly unrealistic. A much simpler and more realistic strategy would be to begin promulgating and arguing for moral principles framed one way rather than the other. There need be nothing deceptive or elitist about this practice; for those who are interested enough to wonder why a given principle is framed in a particular way it can be made clear that the motivation for this shift in framing is to offset apparently irrational and pernicious tendencies in human thought.

Perhaps there are alternative and unprincipled ways the particularist could try to help offset pernicious framing effects. We shall not here second-guess how a particularist might best do this, but instead leave it to the particularist to tell us how they would address these problems. Our suspicion, though, is that the promulgation of particularism itself will make people temperamentally averse to the suggestion that an issue should *always* be framed in one way rather than another. In the meantime, we take it that we have made a good case for thinking that the articulation and internalization of suitably framed moral principles can have an important and legitimate role to play in dealing with these all too common psychological distortions and biases.

## 9.4. Prototypes and Exemplars

So far we have explored two different models for how we might understand principled guidance and offered two reasons for thinking such guidance is superior to an unprincipled approach to moral decision-making. How closely do these recommendations fit with actual practice, though? Perhaps the idea that ordinary moral agents actually are regularly guided by moral principles is no more than a subtle illusion.

Instead, a moral sensibility might be understood in terms of what cognitive scientists would call the 'prototypes' of moral rightness and wrongness. Cognitive science has provided substantial evidence for prototype theory and exemplar theory, and some argue that these theories imply that principles play little or no role in guiding the actions of ordinary agents. Moreover, the empirical challenge from cognitive science can be buttressed by what Jonathan Haidt has called the "social intuitionist" account of moral decision-making. The social intuitionist emphasizes some very interesting empirical data which seems to suggest that people articulate principles *post hoc* in an attempt to justify their actions to others and that these *post hoc* principles serve only to rationalize actions already performed or decisions originally made in a nonprincipled way. In this section we review the details of this empirical challenge from cognitive science and argue that it can be met.

Prototype theory is inspired by Wittgenstein's famous account of concepts in terms of what he called a "family resemblance" rather than in terms of necessary and sufficient conditions for the application of the concept. Wittgenstein argued that it should come as no surprise that we have great trouble articulating individually necessary and jointly sufficient conditions for the application of ordinary concepts. For on his account grasping a concept is not in any interesting sense a matter of grasping necessary and sufficient conditions for its application. Rather, competence with a concept should be understood in terms of an ability reliably to classify particulars as falling under that concept in virtue of one's recognition that a given particular has enough of a range of prototypical features associated with the concept. No one of these prototypical features may be strictly speaking necessary for the application of the concept, though some features may be more important than others. For example, most chairs have four legs but some (like many office chairs) have only one. Having four legs might be a prototypical feature of a chair but is not necessary for something to count as a chair.

Prototype theory maintains that people's neural networks are trained up on a range of examples. This yields a knowledge base of the most typical features associated with the concept. In effect, by generalizing across a range of examples we construct a prototype corresponding to the concept in question. A prototype is sometimes characterized as a "point or region in a space which has one dimension for each possible feature" (Clark 2000: 270). Future cases are then judged to fall under the concept in virtue of where they fall in this multidimensional space. A prototype itself need not correspond to any actual instance of the concept, since it is a kind of abstraction from all of the various particulars to which the agent has been exposed. For example, a given agent's prototypical dog could in principle have some features typical of poodles and yet have some features typical of Great Danes and may well be nothing like any actual dog.

One example of the explanatory power of prototype theory is its ability to explain why some instantiations of a concept seem more difficult for people to recognize than others. Apples, peaches, figs, raisins, pumpkins, and olives are all fruits. Yet people are quicker to classify apples and peaches as fruits than they are to classify figs and raisins as fruits, and they are quicker to classify figs and raisins as fruits than they are to classify pumpkins and olives as fruits (Goldman 1993: 339). If asked to retrieve examples of fruit from memory, most people would list apples and peaches long before pumpkins or olives. Prototype theory can explain these asymmetries. For most people's prototype, apples and peaches exhibit far more of the core features typically associated with the category of fruits than pumpkins and olives. Moreover, the features subjects list as relevant to the concept of fruit are not strictly necessary (e.g. olives aren't sweet) for something to fall under that concept. These findings fit better with a prototype model than with a classical model. For on a classical model, falling under a concept is simply a matter of satisfying the individually necessary and jointly sufficient conditions which define that concept. We have reason to doubt that there are such features, and the implicit suggestion that falling under a concept is always all or nothing (either something meets the necessary and sufficient conditions or it does not) also fits poorly with the typicality findings emphasized by cognitive science.[8]

In addition to prototype theory, cognitive science provides another account of how people classify particulars. Exemplar theory maintains that people represent concepts by internalizing specific exemplars with which they are familiar. For example, a given person's concept of bird may be represented by the set of birds the person has encountered or perhaps by some specific birds the person encountered when first learning the meaning of 'bird.' According to exemplar theory, a person categorizes a new case not by reference to some abstract prototype, but simply by comparing the given particular with the representations derived from the agent's stock of exemplars. In effect, exemplar theory 'cuts out the middle man' of prototypes and maintains that we go more directly from the exemplars which inform our sensibility to a judgment in a particular case. Of course, these two theories do not need to be understood as rivals. Perhaps sometimes people classify particulars directly via comparison to salient exemplars and sometimes rely on a prototype. It is

---

[8] Actually, there is some empirical evidence which suggests that the defenders of prototype theory have read too much into typicality findings. Sharon Armstrong, Lila Gleitman, and Henry Gleitman have found similar typicality results for such predicates as 'is an even number,' 'is a female,' and 'is a plane geometry figure' (see Armstrong, Gleitman, and Gleitman 1983). Since the subjects were themselves well aware that being an even number, being female, and being a plane geometry figure do not come in degrees and that something either does or does not instantiate those properties, the standard prototype interpretation of these findings seems threatened by these results. However, this is admittedly a very complex empirical issue and we shall not pursue it further here. Thanks to Roy Sorensen for useful discussion here.

only if exemplar theory insists that we never rely on prototypes or if prototype theory insists that we never rely directly on exemplars that the two theories must conflict.

The plausibility of prototype theory and exemplar theory has led some to conclude that we do not need to take the phenomenology of moral principles as action-guiding very seriously (Churchland 1998). After all, the moral principles which people avow are far too crude and simplistic to capture the fine distinctions actually reflected in their practice. On this account, it is much more plausible to suppose that ordinary people are actually guided in their decision-making and judgment by the prototypes of moral rightness and wrongness stored in their neural network than it is to suppose they are guided by the simplistic moral rules they avow. Admittedly, moral rules play a role in teaching morality to young children, but the suggestion is that these rules are somewhat like training wheels. In effect, to reach moral maturity is for one's prototypes to have been sufficiently well trained that one can make reliable moral judgments without reliance on the oversimplified moral rules of youth.

If our moral judgments are driven by prototypes and exemplars rather than moral principles, then why do so many ordinary moral agents think they are guided by moral principles? Dreyfus and Dreyfus go some way to answering this question by arguing that moral rules and principles do not figure prominently (if at all) in the phenomenology of the moral expert (Dreyfus and Dreyfus 1990). However, their model does imply that for the moral novice or even the merely competent (most of us?) moral principles play an important role in guiding the agent's decisions. The challenge from cognitive science, as developed by Churchland and Goldman, suggests that even the merely morally competent are not really guided by moral principles. While we may think our decisions are guided by moral principles, the challenge from cognitive science suggests that this is some kind of illusion. On this account, once we move beyond our moral infancy and begin to appreciate some of the complexity of the moral terrain, our decisions are guided directly by either prototypes or exemplars. What, though, is the source of the illusion that our moral decisions nonetheless are at least sometimes guided by moral principles?

Here the challenge from cognitive science seems to get support from what Jonathan Haidt has dubbed the "social intuitionist approach to moral judgment" (Haidt 2001). Haidt argues that most people's moral judgments and decisions are immediate and driven by stereotypes, emotional reactions, desires to agree with one's friends, and other nonrational psychological tendencies. Haidt surveys an impressive range of empirical evidence which suggests that people very often form snap judgments on the basis of very thin evidence and stick with these judgments as contrary evidence emerges. However, a person's moral judgments and decisions typically have important implications for others, so people are often challenged to defend their moral judgments and decisions. Haidt contends that it is at this stage, after the agent's decision has already been made, that moral reasoning and moral principles come into play. On Haidt's account, agents invoke moral principles *ex post facto* to defend decisions which were made in an unprincipled way. Haidt also argues that these *ex post* appeals to principles are often rather strained, which is what one might expect given the nonrational etiology of the initial moral judgment or decision. Nonetheless, having articulated a principled defense of their decision or judgment, agents may become convinced that the principles they invoked actually motivated their original judgment. Hence, the social intuitionist approach can help explain why we might be under the illusion that our actions are driven by moral principles when they are in fact driven by prototypes or exemplars.

The challenge from cognitive science is formidable, but we must not rush to judgment. Haidt's social intuitionist account should serve to remind us that moral principles could be important and worth articulating even if they were not directly action-guiding. As we have argued in Chapter 8, the articulation of moral principles can play an important role in making sure one's actions are justifiable to others. Haidt points out that people in fact often only construct such justifications when pressed interpersonally to do so. Sadly, these attempts at justification often turn out to be desperate rationalizations. Common sense tells us that some people are more reflective and open-minded than others, following an argument where it leads even if it conflicts with some of their gut feelings or intuitions. Generalism as a regulative ideal emphasizes the importance of moral reflection even when one is not pressed by others for such a justification. Moreover, generalism as a regulative ideal articulates an important role for moral principles in the attempt to ensure that one's decisions are justifiable to others.

To be clear, Haidt himself certainly does not imply that a tendency only to reflect when pressed and to reflect in a biased and rationalizing way are necessary or inevitable, much less that they are desirable. The fact that people very often are unreflective or dogmatic in their moral judgments, which is what Haidt's data seem to suggest, in no way implies that we should acquiesce in this state of affairs. Haidt himself emphasizes that he does not mean to draw any normative conclusions. Indeed, he even implies that because reliance on immediate intuition is so unreliable people would do well to engage in moral reasoning to a greater extent. Moreover, Haidt himself allows that there is interpersonal variation here, with some people engaging in moral reasoning to a greater or lesser extent. He also notes in passing that some evidence suggests that philosophers tend to fit much better into what he calls the rationalist account of moral judgment than most ordinary people. Admittedly, the social intuitionist account does imply that fostering the habits of mind emphasized by generalism as a regulative ideal will be difficult, but nobody ever said moral virtue would be easy. Moreover, this is equally a problem for particularists, who should agree that people ought not form snap judgments and invent rationalizations to support them.

In our view, the inference from prototype theory or exemplar theory to the conclusion that moral principles have no important role to play in guiding our actions rests on a false dichotomy, according to which our actions are either guided by prototypes/exemplars or moral principles, but not both. There is no obvious reason to endorse this false dichotomy and indeed good reason to reject it. Our suggestion is not that agents sometimes are motivated by moral principles and sometimes by their prototypes and exemplars, although there may be some truth in that as well. Rather, our suggestion is that an agent's deployment of moral prototypes and exemplars can itself be shaped and guided by moral principles.

Consider again the nonmoral example of fruit classification understood in terms of prototype theory. Suppose someone has just internalized the principle 'If something is the reproductive body of a seed plant then it is a fruit.' The question is an empirical one. However, probably someone who has just internalized this principle and appreciates its generality (having considered some unorthodox examples of fruits) would be quicker to see an olive or a pumpkin as a fruit than someone who had not. The basic idea is that the internalization of a principle can make the inputs to our deliberation appear to us in a rather different light. Someone who accepts this principle about fruits and bears it in mind will, we suggest, be more likely to 'see' a pumpkin or an olive as a fruit than someone who has not internalized such a principle.

Andy Clark makes a similar point about how moral principles might shape our perception. Clark's example is taken from yet another form of expertise—expertise at the video game Tetris. In Tetris, one aims to place geometric objects of different shapes which 'fall' from the top of the screen into a compact formation at the bottom of the screen. When one row is completely filled at the bottom of the screen the row disappears, for which the player gets points. If the stack of shapes reaches to the top of the screen, the game is over. As the game proceeds the objects come at increasingly rapid rates, and Tetris experts must react very quickly. This seems like a very clear case of decision-making via pattern-recognition, in which something as cumbersome as a principle or maxim would play no role whatsoever. Interestingly, even here principles or maxims seem to play a background role in influencing how the expert plays the game; indeed, a principled approach to the game seems to be the distinctive mark of the expert player:

Instead, expert play looks to depend on a delicate and nonobvious interaction between a fast, pattern-completing module and a set of explicit, higher-level concerns or normative policies. The results are preliminary, and it would be inappropriate to report them in detail here. But the key observation is that true Tetris experts report that they rely not solely on a set of fast, adaptive responses produced by, as it were, a trained-up network but also on a series of high-level concerns or policies that they use to monitor the output of the skilled network so as to "discover trends or deviations from normative policy" (Kirsh and Maglio 1992, 10). Examples of such policies include "don't cluster in the center, but try to keep the contour flat" and "avoid piece dependencies" (Kirsh and Maglio 1992, 8–9). On the face of it, these are just the kind of rough and ready maxims we might (following Dreyfus and Dreyfus) associate with novice players only. Yet attention to these normative policies seems to mark especially the play of real experts. Still, we must wonder how such policies can help at the level of expert play, given the time constraints on responses ... Here Kirsh and Maglio (1992) make a suggestive conjecture. The role of high-level policies, they suggest, is probably indirect. Instead of using the policy to override the output of a trained-up network, the effect is to alter the focus of attention for subsequent inputs. (Clark 1998: 118–19)

The idea seems to be that principles can serve to make certain features of one's immediate situation more salient, and that this alteration in the input can influence the assessment made by the relevant pattern-recognition network. More generally, Clark argues that a more basic pattern-recognition part of our brains is influenced by the brain's more distinctively human linguistic abilities and in particular by the brain's ability to formulate generalizations.

The basic idea that principles can helpfully shape our perception of concrete situations applies at least equally well in moral contexts. Perhaps Haidt is right that we often articulate moral rules only when pressed by others to defend our actions. However, this is compatible with those principles then having a life of their own. For if the agent is being sincere then she really does endorse the principle she has articulated, and she may well internalize that principle. That principle, in turn, may color the agent's perception of other novel cases in unanticipated ways. For example, suppose someone defends her support for a particular political candidate on the grounds that the candidate opposes racial quotas aimed at offsetting racial discrimination. When pressed for a justification of her opposition to quotas the person invokes a meritocratic principle of some kind. Suppose it then emerges that this same candidate also has no inclination to challenge so-called 'legacy' programs used at many universities. Legacy programs basically count the fact that someone's parents were students at the university as a reason to accept the student ahead of someone who might be more qualified. The explicit articulation and internalization of a meritocratic principle might well lead the person to see the candidate's unwillingness to challenge legacy programs in a different light.

This does not mean the agent's judgment will not be driven by prototypes. The point is rather that prototypes work because an agent recognizes various features which are taken to be typical (to various degrees) of instances of the concept. The articulation and internalization of a moral principle might well serve to extend one's prototype to include further features (promotion of meritocracy, say). Alternatively, the articulation of a moral principle might simply serve to make certain typical features which were already part of an agent's prototype more salient when they appear in novel situations. No doubt further empirical work should be done to explore these hypotheses. Nonetheless, the plausibility of the model of principles as shaping perceptions seems not to be undermined at all by prototype theory, exemplar theory, or social intuitionism. So the challenge from cognitive science as it currently stands does not prove that ordinary moral agents are not guided by moral principles after all. Therefore generalism as a regulative ideal need not be understood as any kind of revisionist doctrine, but instead fits comfortably with ordinary practice.

## 9.5. Conclusion

In previous chapters we have seen that moral knowledge presupposes a suitable and manageable stock of moral principles and that we have good moral reasons to articulate these principles. This, in effect, was enough to refute Principle Eliminativism, Principle Skepticism, Anti-Transcendental Particularism, and Principled Particularism (in Holton's sense). The only remaining form of particularism we had not argued against was Principle Abstinence Particularism, which insists that, even if moral principles are fine in theory, they are useless or downright pernicious in practice. So far from being useless or pernicious, moral principles have an important role to play in guiding action.

This completes our defense of generalism as a regulative ideal. Although we reject particularism in all of its important forms, our conception of generalism has, we hope, been substantially enhanced by its engagement with the particularist challenge. In our view, the defense of particularism has generated many important insights. Many of those insights can without distortion be extracted from their original particularist environment and deployed to good effect in a robustly generalist context. For example, generalists should not be too quick to dismiss holism about reasons, as that doctrine can be accommodated within a generalist framework to good effect. In this sense, the theoretical utility of holism itself seems, ironically enough, not to be context-sensitive. To take another example, particularists are right to argue that competence with moral concepts is not sufficient for the implicit grasp of the ultimate standards of morality. We should therefore reject constitutive generalism. Our aim throughout has been to incorporate what is important and right in the particularist challenge within a robustly generalist framework. Generalism as a regulative ideal aims for the best of both worlds.

# Appendix: 'That's It'

In this Appendix we contrast the default principles defended in Chapter 6 with Richard Holton's interesting '*That's It*' principles (Holton 2002). Default principles bear important similarities to Richard Holton's '*That's It*' principles and our thinking about default principles has indeed benefited from Holton's work. Nevertheless, there are important differences that lead us to favor our own approach. Holton's principles take the following form:

(K) For all actions (x): If x is a killing and *That's It*, then x is forbidden.

In effect, *That's It* serves the same function as the 'no other feature of the situation explains why…' clause of a default principle; hence the similarity between our views. When (K) appears as a premiss in a moral argument, we need another premiss that *That's It* as well as the premiss that a given action is a killing. If we do have a case of killing, however, and *That's It*, then there is a principled argument that the action would be wrong. Despite the similarities between our approaches, Holton's approach differs from ours in a number of ways which tell in favor of default principles.

First, Holton's *That's It* clause refers not simply to further features of the situation but also to further moral principles, and this has an implausible consequence. Holton's characterization of *That's It* invokes the idea of 'supersession:'

Suppose we have a set of non-moral predicates {F1, F2 … Fm} and suppose that these occur in a moral principle of the form $\forall x((F1x \& F2x … \& Fmx) \rightarrow Fcx)$ and in a corresponding set of non-moral sentences {F1a, F2a, … Fma}. Then we say that that principle and those non-moral sentences are *superseded* by another moral principle $\forall x((G1x \& G2x … \& Gnx) \rightarrow Gcx)$ and a corresponding set of non-moral sentences {G1a, G2a, … Gma} just in case (i) (G1x \& G2x … \& Gnx) entails (F1x \& F2x … \& Fmx), but not *vice versa*, and (ii) Fcx is incompatible with Gcx. (Holton 2002: 198–9)

A *That's It* clause claims that "there is no true moral principle and set of *true* non-moral sentences which supersede those that appear in this argument."[1] This entails that any principle which is superseded is true for the simple reason that the *That's It* clause of its antecedent is false. Of course, since *That's It* is false, arguments relying on the principle will be unsound, but the mere fact that such principles are true at all looks implausible enough. Secondly, because *That's It* makes reference to the very principle in which it appears, a moral principle takes a truth value at all only in the context of a particular argument. These features together create problems for Holton's account. For it appears that what we might call a perverse principle will be trivially true in virtue of

[1] Holton 2002: 199.

being superseded by what we might call a goofy principle.[2] Consider, for example, the following argument.

(1) For all actions (x): If x is the torturing of a small child and *That's It*, then x is required.

(2) X is the torturing of a small child.

(3) *That's It*.

(4) X is required.

The first premiss is intuitively perverse; it is not merely false but inverts the moral significance of the fact it is about. On Holton's account, though, (1) and the corresponding nonmoral sentences seem to be superseded by the following goofy principle and the corresponding set of nonmoral sentences:

(G) For all actions (x): If x is the torturing of a small child and bees make honey and *That's It*, then x is forbidden.

On Holton's definition, (G) and the corresponding nonmoral sentences ('x is the torturing of a small child' and 'bees make honey') supersede (1) and its corresponding nonmoral sentences ('x is the torturing of a small child'). This, however, implausibly entails that (1) is true.

Holton tries to avoid this problem by claiming that propositions like (G) are not moral principles at all, on the grounds that moral principles must be 'minimally contentful'—they must not contain anything unnecessary in the antecedent. This is meant to capture the idea that moral principles must *explain* moral verdicts. Since principles can only be superseded by other principles, (G) does not supersede (1). This solution faces serious problems. First, the proposal has the implausible consequence that any false principle is not really a principle at all, since the features listed in the antecedent will then certainly not explain the truth of the consequent. This problem may not be so serious, though, since Holton could insist that 'principle' as used in his account is simply a term of art and not meant to capture (all of) what we might mean in ordinary language by 'principle.'

A second problem is more serious. The problem arises in cases of overdetermination. Consider the following principle:

(O) For all actions (x): If x is a lie, x would hurt someone's feelings, and *That's It*, then x is wrong.

(O) is plausibly both true and a moral principle even on Holton's account of what it takes to be a moral principle. The features in the antecedent are all morally relevant and indeed explanatory; being a lie and hurting someone's feelings can serve to explain why an action is wrong. Moreover, each of these moral reasons when taken alone might be insufficient in some contexts to make an action wrong (depending on what

---

[2] The problem apparently was first highlighted by Timothy Williamson.

reasons there are on the other side of the equation), in which case the principle also has a fair claim to being minimally contentful. It is worth noting in passing that this case illustrates how being minimally contentful and citing only explanatory features can easily come apart, since the motivation for Holton's 'minimally contentful' constraint is supposed to be that it captures the idea that moral principles should be explanatory. Put this complaint to one side, though. The problem is that (O) seems to pose a problem just like the problem posed by the 'bees make honey' principle. For it is also plausible to suppose that lying and hurting someone's feelings are each enough to make an action wrong all by themselves in at least some contexts—so long as *That's It*. If this is right, then Holton's account faces the following problem. (O) plus the corresponding true nonmoral sentences supersede and hence make trivially true the following perverse principle (and corresponding nonmoral sentences) by falsifying its *That's It* clause:

(P)  For all actions (x): If x is a lie and *That's It*, then x is required.

The same line of reasoning also shows that on Holton's account the following principle comes out as true as deployed in any context in which x is an instance of hurting someone's feelings:

(P★)  For all actions (x): If x is an instance of hurting someone's feelings and *That's It*, then x is required.

These results are highly implausible. (P) and (P★) should never come out as true. Holton can reply that these principles will come out as true only in the context of an unsound argument. For it will never be the case that *That's It* in these cases, owing to the fact that (O) supersedes the principles in question. However, this hardly seems a sufficient reply. Philosophically, we should give weight to our intuitions about which principles are actually true as well as our intuitions about which arguments are sound, at least when those intuitions are widely and firmly held.

Although these problems with Holton's account may not be insuperable, our approach has comparative advantages. First, we concur with Holton that the proper diagnosis of the problem he faces involves noting that moral principles must be explanatory.[3] Rather than claiming that for a generality to count as a principle it must be explanatory, our account imports explanatory elements into the content of default principles while at the same time our equivalent of *That's It* ranges only over further features of the circumstances and not over further moral principles. Being explanatory is then part of the truth-conditions of a moral principle, and not a condition on something counting as a moral principle. So on our account, even if what are intuitively 'goofy principles' turn out to be true moral principles, this will not entail the more damaging result that what we have called perverse principles are ever true. For on our account

---

[3] We are not confident, however, that restricting principles to generalities that are explanatory shows that perverse principles are not trivially true. Even if goofy principles are not principles (and so cannot supersede genuine principle), perverse principles like (1) may be superseded by non-goofy principles such as: For all x, if x is an instance of torturing a small child and somebody minds it, and *That's It*, then x is forbidden.

the truth of a perverse principle simply has nothing to do with the truth of a goofy principle. That connection in Holton's account is simply an artefact of the way in which *That's It* is defined in terms of other principles and nonmoral sentences.

Secondly, default principles have truth values outside the contexts of specific arguments. As a result, they are better suited to playing an investigative role in determining whether a particular act is right.[4] On Holton's account it seems that we can determine whether a principle is true as deployed in an argument only after we have worked out whether the principle is superseded in that context. Determining whether the principle is superseded, in turn, looks like it will require determining whether the action in question really is right or wrong. For the assessment of a putatively superseding principle and corresponding set of true nonmoral sentences requires that we know whether that principle and set of sentences really is true, but knowing that a superseding principle and corresponding set of nonmoral sentences is true is tantamount to knowing the moral verdict in the case. For that superseding principle and set of true nonmoral sentences will themselves *entail* a moral verdict in the case at hand. So it is hard to see how *That's It* principles could help us determine whether an action is right or wrong; we can determine the truth of the principle in a context only if we already know the verdict. By contrast, on our account an agent can bring a provisionally settled stock of default principles to a moral situation and be relatively confident that those principles are true. The application of those principles will still require judgment and sensitivity to other features of the situation, but at least there will be a way of knowing whether the principle is true without already having determined the verdict in the case at hand. In fairness to Holton, he explicitly indicates that *That's It* principles are supposed to play a justificatory role but not an investigative role. We are simply appealing to the plausible idea that principles which can effectively play both roles would be better, all else being equal.

---

[4] Holton makes another point which we do not address here. He draws a very useful distinction between two ways of interpreting particularism. On the first interpretation, particularism holds that there is no finite set of principles which can be combined with the descriptive facts in a given case and be sure to entail the correct moral verdict. On the second interpretation, particularism holds that for each moral truth there is no finite set of moral principles which, when combined with the descriptive facts in a given case will be sure to entail the correct moral verdict. The distinction between these forms of particularism can be seen by way of analogy with first-order arithmetic, which Godel proved cannot be captured by any single finite set of axioms. Nonetheless, for any truth of first-order arithmetic there is a finite set of axioms which entails it. So first-order arithmetic seems to illustrate the possibility of the second form of particularism being false while the first form of particularism is true in a given domain. Holton rightly points out that the first form of particularism is much stronger than the second and that his account of *That's It* principles is compatible with the second but not the first. Given the affinity of default principles with *That's It* principles, it will perhaps come as no surprise that our account of default principles is logically consistent with the second form of particularism, which Holton calls "principled particularism." As we argue in Ch. 7, however, there are good reasons to look for the kinds of principles which principled particularism rejects.

# Bibliography

ABBOTT, E. A. 1952 (originally published in 1884). *Flatland: A Romance of Many Dimensions.* New York: Dover.

AINSLIE, G. 1975. "Specious Reward: A Behavioral Theory of Impulsiveness and Impulse Control." *Psychological Bulletin,* 82: 463–96.

—— 1986. "Beyond Microeconomics." In Elster 1986: 133–75.

ARMSTRONG, S., GLEITMAN, L., and GLEITMAN, H. 1983. "What Some Concepts Might Not Be." *Cognition,* 13: 263–308.

BAIER, A. 1985. "Doing Without Moral Theory?" in *Postures of the Mind: Essays on Mind and Morals.* London: Methuen. Reprinted in Clarke and Simpson 1989: 29–48.

BALDWIN, T. 2002. "The Three Phases of Intuitionism." In Stratton-Lake 2002: 92–112.

BALL, S. 1991. "Linguistic Intuitions and Varieties of Ethical Naturalism." *Philosophy and Phenomenological Research,* 51: 1–30.

BAUMEISTER, R., et al. 1998. "Ego Depletion: Is the Active Self a Limited Resource?" *Journal of Personality and Social Psychology,* 74: 1252–65.

BLACKBURN, S. 1981. "Rule-Following and Moral Realism." In Holtzman and Leich 1981: 163–87.

—— 1984. *Spreading the Word.* Oxford: Oxford University Press.

—— 1993. *Essays in Quasi-Realism.* Oxford: Oxford University Press.

BONJOUR, L. 1998. *In Defence of Pure Reason: A Rationalist Account of A Priori Justification.* Cambridge: Cambridge University Press.

BRINKMAN, K. 1999. *The Proceedings of the Twentieth World Congress of Philosophy,* i. *Ethics.* Bowling Green, OH: Philosophy Documentation Center.

BURGE, T. 1993. "Content Preservation." *Philosophical Review,* 102: 457–88.

CAMPBELL, R., and HUNTER, B. 2000. *Moral Epistemology Naturalized: Canadian Journal of Philosophy,* suppl. vol. 26 (2000) (Calgary: University of Calgary Press), 307–12.

CHURCHLAND, P. 1998. "The Neural Representation of the Social World." In May, Friedman, and Clark 1998: 91–108.

—— 2000. "Rules, Know-How and the Future of Moral Cognition." In Campbell and Hunter 2000: 291–306.

CLARK, A. (1998). "Connectionism, Moral Cognition, and Collaborative Problem Solving." In May, Friedman, and Clark 1998: 109–28.

—— 2000a. "Word and Action: Reconciling Rules and Know-How in Moral Cognition." In Campbell and Hunter 2000: 267–89.

—— 2000b. "Making Moral Sense: A Reply to Churchland." In Campbell and Hunter 2000: 307–12.

CLARKE, S. (1987) "Anti-Theory in Ethics." *American Philosophical Quarterly*, 24/3: 237–44.

\_\_\_\_\_ and SIMPSON, E. (eds.) 1989. *Anti-Theory in Ethics and Moral Conservatism*. Albany, NY: SUNY Press.

CRISP, R. 2000. "Particularizing Particularism." In Hooker and Little 2000: 23–47.

CULLITY, G. 2002. "Particularism and Presumptive Reasons." *Proceedings of the Aristotelian Society*, suppl.: 169–90.

DANCY, J. 1981. "On Moral Properties." *Mind*, 90: 367–85.

\_\_\_\_\_ 1982. "Intuitionism in Meta-Epistemology." *Philosophical Studies*, 42: 395–466.

\_\_\_\_\_ 1983. "Ethical Particularism and Morally Relevant Properties." *Mind*, 92: 530–47.

\_\_\_\_\_ 1985. "The Role of Imaginary Cases in Ethics." *Pacific Philosophical Quarterly*, 66: 141–53.

\_\_\_\_\_ 1991a. "Intuitionism." In Singer 1991: 411–20.

\_\_\_\_\_ 1991b. "An Ethic of Prima Facie Duties." In Singer 1991: 219–29.

\_\_\_\_\_ 1993. *Moral Reasons*. Oxford: Blackwell.

\_\_\_\_\_ 1997. *Reading Parfit*. Oxford: Blackwell.

\_\_\_\_\_ 1999a. "Can the Particularist Learn the Difference between Right and Wrong?" In Brinkman 1999: 59–72.

\_\_\_\_\_ 1999b. "Defending Particularism." *Metaphilosophy*, 30: 25–32.

\_\_\_\_\_ 2000. "The Particularist's Progress." In Hooker and Little 2000: 130–56.

\_\_\_\_\_ 2001. "Moral Particularism." *Stanford Encyclopedia of Philosophy*. Online at http://plato.stanford.edu/entries/moral-particularism/.

\_\_\_\_\_ 2003. "Are There Organic Unities?" *Ethics*, 113: 629–50.

\_\_\_\_\_ 2004. *Ethics without Principles*. Oxford: Oxford University Press.

\_\_\_\_\_ forthcoming. "Defending the Right." *Journal of Moral Philosophy*.

DANIELS, N. 1996. *Justice and Justification: Reflective Equilibrium in Theory and Practice*. New York: Cambridge University Press.

DARWALL, S., GIBBARD, A., and RAILTON, P. 1992. "Toward *Fin de Siècle* Ethics: Some Trends." *Philosophical Review*, 101: 115–89.

DEGROOT, A. 1978. *Thought and Choice in Chess*. The Hague: Mouton.

DENNETT, D. 1995. *Darwin's Dangerous Idea*. New York: Simon and Schuster.

DREFYUS, H. I., and DREYFUS, S. E. 1986. *Mind over Machine: The Power of Human Intuitive Expertise in the Era of the Computer*. New York: Free Press.

\_\_\_\_\_ 1990. "What is Morality? A Phenomenological Account of the Development of Ethical Expertise." In Rasmussen 1990: 237–64.

DRIVER, J. forthcoming. "Autonomy and the Asymmetry Problem for Moral Expertise." *Philosophical Studies*.

ELSTER, J. (ed.) 1986. *The Multiple Self*. Cambridge: Cambridge University Press.

EVANS, G. 1985. "Reference and Contingency." in *Collected Papers*. Oxford: Oxford University Press.

FIRTH, R. 1952. "Ethical Absolutism and the Ideal Observer." *Philosophy and Phenomenological Research*, 12: 317–45.

FRANKENA, W. 1939. "The Naturalistic Fallacy." *Mind*, 48: 464–77.

FRIED, C. 1981. *Contract as Promise*. Cambridge, MA: Harvard University Press.

GERT, B. 1966. *The Moral Rules*. New York: Harper and Row.

—— 1998. *Morality: Its Nature and Justification*. New York: Oxford University Press.

—— 2004. *Common Morality: Deciding What to Do*. Oxford: Oxford University Press.

GIAQUINTO, M. 1998. "Epistemology of the Obvious: A Geometrical Case." *Philosophical Studies*, 92: 181–204.

GIBBARD, A. 2003. *Thinking How to Live*. Cambridge, MA: Harvard University Press.

GLIGORIC, S. 2002. *I Play against Pieces*. London: Batsford.

GLOVER, J. 2000. *Humanity: A Moral History of the Twentieth Century*. New Haven, CT: Yale University Press.

GOLDMAN, A. 1993. "Ethics and Cognitive Science." *Ethics*, 103: 337–60.

HAIDT, J. 2001. "The Emotional Dog and its Rational Tail: A Social Intuitionist Approach to Moral Judgment." *Psychological Review*, 108: 814–34.

HARE, R. M. 1981. *Moral Thinking*. Oxford: Clarendon Press.

HARMAN, G. 1977. *The Nature of Morality*. New York: Oxford University Press.

—— 1989. *Change in View*. Cambridge, MA: MIT Press.

HART, H. L. A. 1961. *The Concept of Law*. Oxford: Clarendon Press.

HAWTHORNE, J. 2002. "Deeply Contingent A Priori Knowledge." *Philosophy and Phenomenological Research*, 65/2: 247–69.

HERMAN, B. 1993. *The Practice of Moral Judgment*. Cambridge, MA: Harvard University Press.

HOLTON, R. 2002. "Principles and Particularisms." *Proceedings of the Aristotelian Society*, suppl.: 169–20.

HOLTZMAN, S., and LEICH, C. (eds.) 1981. *Wittgenstein: To Follow a Rule*. London: Routledge and Kegan Paul.

HOOKER, B. 2000a. *Ideal Code, Real World*. Oxford: Oxford University Press.

—— 2000b. "Moral Particularism: Wrong and Bad." In Hooker and Little 2000: 1–22.

—— 2002. "Ross-style General Principles." In Stratton-Lake 2002: 161–83.

—— and LITTLE, M. 2000. *Moral Particularism*. Oxford: Oxford University Press.

HOROWITZ, T. 1998. "Philosophical Intuitions and Psychological Theory." *Ethics*, 108: 367–8.

HUME, D. 1985. *Essays: Moral, Political and Literary*. Indianapolis: Liberty Fund.

HURSTHOUSE, R. 1995. *Virtues and Reasons: Philippa Foot and Moral Theory*. New York: Clarendon Press.

IRWIN, T. 2000. "Ethics as Inexact Science: Aristotle's Ambitions for Moral Theory." In Hooker and Little 2000: 100–29.

JACKSON, F. 1998. *From Metaphysics to Ethics*. Oxford: Oxford University Press.

—— and PETTIT, P. 1995. "Moral Functionalism and Moral Motivation." *Philosophical Quarterly*, 45: 20–39.

—— —— and SMITH, M. 2000. "Ethical Particularism and Patterns." In Hooker and Little 2000: 79–99.

JAMES, R. 1989. *The Complete Chess Addict*. London: Faber and Faber.

JAMIESON, D. 2002a. *Morality's Progress*. Oxford: Oxford University Press.

—— 2002b. "Is There Progress in Morality?" *Utilitas*, 14: 318–38.

JONES, K. 1999. "Second-Hand Moral Knowledge." *Journal of Philosophy*, 96/2: 55–78.

KAHNEMAN, D., and TVERSKY, A. 1979. "Prospect Theory: An Analysis of Decision under Risk." *Econometrica*, 47: 263–91.

KAMM, F. 1998. "Moral Intuitions, Cognitive Psychology and the Harming vs. Not-Aiding Distinction." *Ethics*, 108: 463–88.

KANT, I. 2002 (originally published in 1784). *Groundwork for the Metaphysics of Morals*, ed. and trans. T. E. Hill, Jr. and A. Zweig. New York: Oxford University Press.

KIRSH, D., and MAGLIO, P. 1992. "Reaction and Reflection in Tetris." In J. Handler (ed.), *Artificial Intelligence Planning Systems: Proceedings of the First Annual International Conference, AIPS 92*. San Mateo, CA: Morgan Kauffman.

KRIPKE, S. 1972. *Naming and Necessity*. Cambridge, MA: Harvard University Press.

LANCE, M., and LITTLE, M. 2004. "Defeasibility and the Normative Grasp of Context." *Erkenntnis*, 61: 435–55.

—— and —— 2005. "Particularism and Anti-Theory." In D. Copp (ed.), *Essays in Ethics*. Oxford: Oxford University Press.

—— and O'LEARY-HAWTHORNE, J. 1997. *The Grammar of Meaning: The Normativity of Semantic Discourse*. Cambridge: Cambridge University Press.

LANGE, M. 2002. "Who's Afraid of Ceteris Paribus Laws? Or: How I Learned to Stop Worrying and Love Them." *Erkenntnis*, 57: 407–23.

LITTLE, M. 1994. "Moral Realism II: Non-Naturalism." *Philosophical Books*, 35/4: 225–32.

—— 1995. "Seeing and Caring: The Role of Affect in Feminist Moral Epistemology." *Hypatia*, 10/3: 117–37.

—— 1997. "Virtue as Knowledge: Objections from the Philosophy of Mind." *Nous*, 31: 59–79.

—— 2000. "Moral Generalities Revisited." In Hooker and Little 2000: 276–304.

—— 2001. "On Knowing the 'Why:' Particularism and Moral Theory." *Hastings Center Report*, 32–40.

McDOWELL, J. 1979. "Virtue and Reason." *The Monist*, 62: 331–50.

—— 1981. "Non-Cognitivism and Rule-Following." In Holtzman and Leich 1981: 141–62.

—— 1985. "Values and Secondary Qualities." In T. Honderich, *Morality and Objectivity*. London: Routledge and Kegan Paul, 110–20. Reprinted in Sayre-McCord 1988: 166–80.

—— 1998. *Mind, Value and Reality*. Cambridge, MA: Harvard University Press.

MACKIE, J. 1977. *Ethics: Inventing Right and Wrong*. London: Penguin.

McGRATH, S. forthcoming. "Moral Knowledge." *Philosophical Perspectives*.

McKEEVER, S., and RIDGE, M. 2005. "What Does Holism Have to Do with Particularism?" *Ratio*, 18: 93–103.

McNAUGHTON, D. 1988. *Moral Vision*. Oxford: Blackwell.

McNaughton, D. 1996. "An Unconnected Heap of Duties?" *Philosophical Quarterly*, 46: 443–7.

——and Rawlings, P. 2000. "Unprincipled Ethics." In Hooker and Little 2000: 256–75.

May, L., Friedman, M., and Clark, A. (eds.) 1998. *Mind and Morals*. Cambridge, MA: MIT Press.

Mill, J. 1979 (originally published in 1861). *Utilitarianism*. Indianapolis: Hackett.

Moore, G. E. 1903. *Principia Ethica*. New York: Cambridge University Press.

Nagel, T. 1970. *The Possibility of Altruism*. Oxford: Oxford University Press.

——1979. *Mortal Questions*. Cambridge: Cambridge University Press.

Nozick, R. 1993. *The Nature of Rationality*. Princeton, NJ: Princeton University Press.

Ogilvy, J. (ed.) 1986. *Revisioning Philosophy*. Albany, NY: SUNY Press.

Parfit, D. 1984. *Reasons and Persons*. Oxford: Oxford University Press.

Penrose, R. 1989. *The Emperor's New Mind: Concerning Computers, Minds, and the Laws of Physics*. Oxford: Oxford University Press.

Pietroski, P., and Rey, G. 1995. "When Other Things Are Not Equal: Saving Ceteris Paribus Laws from Vacuity." *British Journal for the Philosophy of Science*, 46: 84–110.

Railton, P. 1984. "Alienation, Consequentialism, and the Demands of Morality." *Philosophy and Public Affairs*, 13/2: 134–71.

Rasmussen, D. (ed.) 1990. *Universalism vs. Communitarianism*. Cambridge, MA: MIT Press.

Reti, R. 1960 (originally published in 1943). *Modern Ideas in Chess*. New York: Dover.

Ridge, M. 2003a. "Review of Judith Thomson's *Goodness and Advice*." *Ethics*, 113/2: 447–50.

——2003b. "Non-Naturalism in Meta-Ethics." *Stanford Encyclopedia of Philosophy*. Online at http://plato.stanford.edu/entries/moral-non-naturalism/.

Ross, W. D. 1930. *The Right and the Good*. Oxford: Oxford University Press.

——1939. *The Foundations of Ethics*. Oxford: Oxford University Press.

Rowson, J. 2000. *The Seven Deadly Chess Sins*. London: Gambit.

Salmon, W. 1967. *The Foundations of Scientific Inference*. Pittsburgh, PA: University of Pittsburgh Press.

Sayre-McCord, G. 1988. *Essays in Moral Realism*. Ithaca, NY: Cornell University Press.

Scanlon, T. 1998. *What We Owe to Each Other*. Cambridge, MA: Harvard University Press.

Scheffler, S. 1992. *Human Morality*. Oxford: Oxford University Press.

Sidgwick, H. 1967 (originally published in 1907). *The Methods of Ethics*, 7th edn. Chicago: University of Chicago Press.

Sinnott-Armstrong, W. 1999. "Some Varieties of Particularism." *Metaphilosophy*, 30: 1–12.

Smith, M. 1994. *The Moral Problem*. Oxford: Blackwell.

Sommerfield, D. 1991. "Modest A Priori Knowledge." *Philosophy and Phenomenological Research*, 51: 39–66.

SORENSEN, R. 1995. "Unknowable Obligations." *Utilitas*, 7/2: 247–71.

STEWART, I. 2001. *Flatterland: Like Flatland, Only More So*. London: Pan.

STRATTON-LAKE, P. 2000. *Kant, Duty, and Moral Worth*. New York: Routledge.

——— (ed.) 2002. *Ethical Intuitionism: Re-Evaluations*. Oxford: Oxford University Press.

THOMSON, J. 1971. "A Defense of Abortion." *Philosophy and Public Affairs*, 1: 47–66.

——— 2001. *Goodness and Advice* (ed. A. Gutman). Princeton, NJ: Princeton University Press.

URMSON, J. 1975. "A Defence of Intuitionism." *Proceedings of the Aristotelian Society*, 75: 111–19.

VÄYRYNEN, P. 2004. "Particularism and Default Reasons." *Ethical Theory and Moral Practice*, 7: 53–79.

WATSON, J. 1998. *Secrets of Modern Chess Strategy*. London: Gambit.

WILSON, T., and SCHOOLER, J. 1991. "Thinking Too Much: Introspection Can Reduce the Quality of Preferences and Decisions." *Journal of Personality and Social Psychology*, 60: 181–92.

WOLFF, J. P. 1970. *In Defense of Anarchism*. New York: Harper.

# Index